RUSSIA'S HAWAIIAN ADVENTURE, 1815–1817

The HAWAIIAN ISLANDS

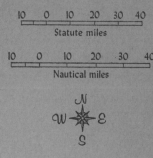

Statute miles

Nautical miles

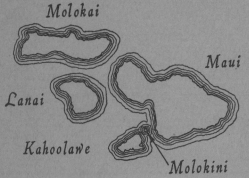

Molokai

Maui

Lanai

Kahoolawe

Molokini

Hawaii

Kawaihae

Waimea

Mauna Kea

Hilo

Kailua

Kilauea

Kealakekua

Mauna Loa

Russia's Hawaiian Adventure,

1815-1817

by Richard A. Pierce

UNIVERSITY OF CALIFORNIA PRESS · 1965
BERKELEY AND LOS ANGELES

University of California Press
Berkeley and Los Angeles, California

Cambridge University Press
London, England

Preface

THESE ANTIQUE LETTERS, journals, and agreements hold many a tale. In them sturdy New England trading vessels sail on long-forgotten business, each voyage an epic in itself. Therein are preserved, amid the timeless setting of tropic romance, the temples and taboos, internecine strife, and benevolent despotism of the Old Hawaii of Kamehameha the Great. There are glimpses of Russian America (Alaska), of the scattering of sleepy coastal settlements which then was California, the teeming waterfronts of Macao and Canton, and the chancellories of faraway St. Petersburg. Interwoven is the story of a man whose ambition exceeded his talents, but who for a few short months felt the thrill of power in an exotic land.

The attempt by the German surgeon and adventurer, Georg Anton Schäffer (or Egor Nikolaevich Sheffer, as he was known in Russia), to engineer Russian annexation of the Hawaiian Islands has been described before.[1] However, there are gaps and errors in accounts of the affair, and very little has been known of Schäffer himself.

Lack of materials has been the main cause of these deficiencies. The documents in this volume will answer many questions about Schäffer and the events he took part in, and should add to knowledge of the international relations, trade, and way of life in the Pacific Basin in that period.

Most of these documents were copied in St. Petersburg in 1874 by a young French ethnologist, Alphonse Pinart,[2] for the historian of the American West, Hubert Howe Bancroft, then preparing his histories of Alaska, the Northwest coast, and California. The copies, in Pinart's hasty, often exasperatingly difficult Cyrillic script, are bound in a folio now in the Bancroft Library of the University of California. In 1939 about two-thirds of this material was translated, in preliminary form, by the late Professor G. V. Lantzeff, then a graduate student, and S. G. Stewart, under the direction of Professor R. J. Kerner. It was slated to become a volume in a documentary series covering Russian expansion in the North Pacific, but the war caused the project to be shelved.

After Kerner's death in 1956 the translation was deposited in the Bancroft Library. I have checked this and made various corrections, rearranged the selections, translated the remaining portion, added several pertinent items (Nos. 40, 41, 44, 48, 60) from the Russian-American Company *Journals of Correspondence,* and drawn additional text for another (No. 46) from the original source.

Pinart did not indicate the location of the documents which he copied, but it is possible to make some fair guesses at where most of them might be found today. F. A. Golder, in his search in Russian archives just prior to World War I for materials on American history, found that in 1870 the Russian-American Company, seeking to dispose of "forty wagonloads" of its records, in the end transferred a mere thirty-four items to the archives of the Ministry of Finance, Section of Commerce and Industry, and that these were consulted by Pinart in the spring of 1874. But, says Golder: "This is the last record of the papers. The archivists of the Section of Commerce and Industry made a special search for these documents in the summer of 1914 without finding a single one of them. The documents have disappeared without leaving even a trail behind them."[3]

Pinart, writing Bancroft from Russia on February 6, 1875, had stated: "I must tell you that the archives of Russia are very poor in documents relating to Russian America, they having been in some way destroyed. I was able to put my hand only on very few of them. Most of the notices relating to the colonies are printed in papers or reviews, some of them exceedingly hard to find."[4]

Pinart may have used documents dealing with the Russians in Hawaii which are listed by Golder as being in the Archives of the Ministry of Trade and Manufactures, Department of Manufactures and Internal Trade.[5] Others—or possibly the same—were cited in 1936 by the Soviet historian S. B. Okun' as being in "two voluminous tomes" (*dva ob'emistykh toma*) in the Leningrad Section of the Central Historical Archive.[6]

It would have been desirable, of course, to have worked from the documents used originally by Pinart. Unfortunately, my attempts to obtain microfilms of the documents cited by Golder and Okun' from the U.S.S.R. have been unsuccessful.

There would seem to be little doubt, however, of the reliability of the Pinart materials. Two of the documents—the long memorandum by Berkh (No. 45), and Schäffer's report on leaving the Islands (No. 39)—are actually (and rather unaccountably) contemporary official copies. The texts of two versions of Kaumualii's act of allegiance (No. 12, No. 45) are close to, though not identical with, that published by Okun' in the journal *Krasnyi Arkhiv*.[7] Pinart gives the text of Schäffer's memorandum to the Emperor Alexander I in French, whereas Okun' gives a contemporary Russian translation with a commentary by Company officials appended.[8] This translation is also found in the Russian-American Company *Journals of Correspondence,* a copy having been sent by St. Petersburg to Sitka. Pinart provides the French version of Schäffer's supplement to his memo, whereas Okun' gives a Russian translation. Pinart gives a lengthy though condensed version of Schäffer's diary, probably worked over by Schäffer himself in support of his projects and then recopied by the Company, whereas Okun' gives only an abstract of the diary, also made by the Company.

Two of Pinart's documents, otherwise identical with versions in the *Journals of Correspondence,* have brief parts missing. Hagemeister's report to the Main Office of April 6, 1818 (No. 61) lacks a final paragraph, inconsequential except for one sentence, which I have added to the translation. Another, from the Main Office to Schäffer (No. 43), lacks the signatures found in the *Journals of Correspondence* version, also added here.

Such omissions were probably not the fault of Pinart. It must be kept in mind that not even the documents he or Okun' used were necessarily the originals. When the latter were composed, there was no way of reproducing materials—short of printing—except copying and recopying by hand. Thus one or more contemporary copies of a document, variously abstracted or extracted, may exist, whereas the original may long since have perished, perhaps as part of the presumably lost "forty wagonloads" of Company archives. Such comparisons as can be made, and cross-checking of the mass of details concerned in the story, indicate that Pinart's copies were painstakingly executed and are highly reliable.

The documents here are grouped with relation first of all to the origins of the Schäffer mission, including instructions which Baranov sent before he knew of the developments that had taken place, then to the mission itself, next to reactions in St. Petersburg, and finally to action taken in Company headquarters in Alaska. I have omitted the several items in the Pinart folio identical with those already published by Okun', as well as several shorter items which are repetitious or of little consequence, merely indicating the content of these in the Introduction or Notes.

I have used a modified version of the Library of Congress system for transliteration of names from Russian to Latin script. Hawaiian names have been changed to fit modern usage. Thus, Kamehameha instead of Tomi-Omi, Kaumualii instead of Tomari, Kauai instead of Atuvai. The original forms are indicated in parentheses in the index. On the other hand, the vintage designations of Hawaiians as "Indians," and of northern California as "New Albion," are retained. Western forms are used for European names of non-Russian origin, for example, Alexander, Krusenstern, Hagemeister, Gyzelaar, and Wilcocks; the names of foreign ships; and Russian names similar to European forms, for example, the vessels *Maria* and *Finlandia,* rather than the cumbersome though exact transliterations of *Mariia* and *Finliandiia.* Schäffer's name is given in whatever form it appears in the documents, usually in the Russian form— Sheffer. The wayward spelling in the several documents originally written in English has been preserved.

Dates are as given in the original text. In general, Russian sources at this time used the Old Style (Julian) calendar, then twelve days behind the New Style (Gregorian) calendar. In Russian America there was the added complication that as the international date line had not yet been conceived, eastbound ships failed to drop a day, and the Russian colonies remained only eleven days behind the Gregorian calendar. In addition, ships' logs began each 24-hour period—as they still do—at noon, which must be remembered in dating a morning arrival. In

general, Company correspondence and government documents may be considered as dated in Old Style, while
documents signed or witnessed by foreigners, as well as
Schäffer's journal, are in New Style. Human error is also
present. The entries in Schäffer's journal frequently sum-
marize happenings of some days past. Tarakanov's and
Osipov's reports were made by men at best only semi-
literate, whose recollections of dates may have been
faulty. As it is impossible to resolve these variables, I
have left all dates in their original state, only adding
occasionally, in brackets, the Old or New Style date if it
could be ascertained with reasonable likelihood.

Illegible passages—rarely more than a word or two,
and each conceded only after long travail—are marked as
follows: [——]. Ellipsis marks (. . .), unless otherwise indicated, are as they appeared in Pinart's transcrip-
tions.

The Introduction is intended both as a reconstruction
of the story and as a guide to the documents. Inevitably,
certain aspects may seem to merit fuller explanation.
Some of this information may be found in specialized
works, but many questions must await further study.

The shifting locations of vessels and personnel involved in the story has posed a peculiar problem. Rather
than encumber the book with a mass of notes on minute
points I have summarized shipping and biographical
details in the Index. Most of this data is derived from the
documents themselves and from the works cited in the
Bibliography, especially F. W. Howay's extremely useful
list of trading vessels.

The aid given by staff members of several libraries is
gratefully acknowledged. Much of my research has been
carried on at the University of California Library in
Berkeley, unexcelled for its convenient working conditions, and particularly in the extensive collections of its

affiliate, the Bancroft Library. I have also benefited from the resources of the Library of Congress, the New York Public Library, the Widener and Baker libraries of Harvard University, the Peabody Museum and the Essex Institute of Salem, Massachusetts, and the Douglas Library of Queen's University. I am grateful to Mr. Paul Doobnitsky, of Oakland, California, for his aid in deciphering and transcribing portions of the manuscript, and to Mr. J. F. Isaak, of Kingston, Ontario, for advice on various points of translation. Mr. Gavan Daws, of the University of Hawaii gave advice on a number of Hawaiian names and terms in the manuscript. Mr. Hector Chevigny, of New York City, shared freely his extensive knowledge of the history of the Russian-American Company and made many helpful suggestions. Professor Enrico Schaeffer, of São Paulo, Brazil, gave me valuable information on the life of his collateral forebear, G. A. Schäffer, the central figure in the story. I should also like to thank Miss Beppie Anne Duker for her work in the final editing of the manuscript. Finally, I am indebted to Professor George V. Lantzeff, from whose lectures on the history of Russian eastward expansion I first heard of this Hawaiian adventure, and upon whose translation much of this volume is based.

RICHARD A. PIERCE

April, 1964
Queen's University
Canada

Contents

Introduction

THE PACIFIC OCEAN, all but empty of sail until Cook's epoch-making voyages in the 1770's, became in little more than a generation the scene of a thriving and far-flung commerce. While Europe was preoccupied with war, new patterns of power took shape on the shores of Asia and the Americas. Foreign shipmasters began to touch with impunity on the forbidden Spanish coasts. In the north, a handful of Russian *promyshlenniks* (traders) extended the imperial domain of Catherine II to the shores of Alaska. On the Northwest coast, Yankee skippers swapped cloth, cutlery, and trinkets with the Indians for furs, then exchanged the furs in Canton for porcelain, tea, and fine fabrics, which in turn sold at premium prices in New England. All around the Pacific Basin, towns and hamlets destined to become great ports were already well-known trading centers.

The Sandwich (Hawaiian) Islands formed the hub of this traffic. Their convenient location made them a favorite stopping place to pick up supplies, refresh scorbutic crews, and perhaps augment cargoes of furs with sandalwood.

The conquest of most of the Hawaiian Islands by Kamehameha I coincided with the rise of the Russian-American Company holdings in Alaska under the able

Chief Manager, Alexander Baranov. Kamehameha, noble savage and "Napoleon of the Pacific," and Baranov, hard-drinking, shrewd, and resourceful builder of a commercial empire on beggarly means, were already legends in their own time. The two never met, but heard of one another from American and British shipmasters.

The first Russian visit to the islands occurred in June, 1804, during the first of a notable series of round-the-world voyages aimed at providing supplies and naval support to the Pacific colonies. The sloops *Nadezhda* (Hope) and *Neva,* under Lieutenant-Captain Ivan Fedorovich Krusenstern and Lieutenant Iurii Fedorovich Lisianskii, stopped first at the island of Hawaii, Kamehameha's residence, but the monarch was then with his army on the island of Oahu, preparing an invasion of the realm of a lesser rival, Kaumualii. Hearing that a disastrous epidemic had beset Kamehameha's army, the Russians by-passed Oahu and visited Kaumualii's capital on the island of Kauai. Kaumualii, who spoke English, described his fears of aggression by Kamehameha, and begged for protection. Although unable to grant his plea, the Russians sailed away impressed by the King's character and the justice of his claim to the rest of the islands.[1] In 1806, Kamehameha made known to Baranov through a foreign shipmaster "that he understood from persons trading to that coast how much the Russian establishment had sometimes suffered in winter from the scarcity of provisions; that he would therefore gladly send a ship every year with swine, salt, batatas [sweet potatoes] and other articles of food if they would in exchange let him have sea otter skins at a fair price." [2] In the following year, 1807, a small vessel, the *Nikolai,* under a Russian promyshlennik, Pavel Slobodchikov, detoured to the islands while en route from California to Sitka. Slobodchikov was well treated by Kamehameha, who furnished a cargo of foodstuffs in exchange for furs.[3]

In 1808, following the return of the *Neva,* now under Lieutenant L. A. Hagemeister, to Russian America, Baranov sent her to the islands for a cargo of salt.[4] There is some question as to whether a Russian colony was to be established during this visit. The voyage coincided with dispatch by Baranov of the schooner *Sv. Nikolai* (later wrecked) and the ship *Kad'iak* to reconnoiter the coast southward and to establish a colony in California, so could have been part of a larger design. Archibald Campbell, a sailor given passage on the *Neva* from Novo-Arkhangel'sk (Sitka) to Hawaii, claims rather ambiguously that a settlement was intended:

It would appear that the Russians had determined to form a settlement upon these islands; at least, preparations were made for the purpose; and I was informed by the commandant, that if I chose, I might get a situation as interpreter. The ship had a house in frame on board, and intimation was given that volunteers would be received; none, however, offered; and I never observed that any other steps were taken in the affair.[5]

While the *Neva* was at Hawaii, Campbell talked to a fellow Scot, residing on the island, and told him

that I understood the Russians had some intention of forming a settlement on the Sandwich Islands. This reached the Captain's ears, and he gave me a severe reprimand for having, as he expressed it, betrayed their secrets. He desired me to say no more on the subject in future, otherwise I should not be permitted to quit the ship. I know not what obstacle prevented this plan from being carried into effect, but although the *Neva* remained several months in the country, I never heard any more of the settlement.[6]

Hubert Howe Bancroft asserts: "Baranov certainly instructed Hagemeister to found a settlement, and a copy of his instructions has been preserved in the *Sitka Ar-*

chives . . ."[7] However, the surviving *Archives,* or more properly the *Journals of Correspondence* of the Russian-American Company, turned over to the United States upon its purchase of Alaska in 1867 and now housed in the National Archives, begin (except for a lone document dated 1802) in 1817, and contain no such instruction. Document No. 1 of the series presented here, giving the substance of two letters from Hagemeister himself, written in 1809 after leaving Hawaii and paraphrased for Company use a decade later, contains only a discussion of ways and means of securing territory, indicating that the venture was primarily a reconnaissance.[8] This is further supported by Hagemeister's comment in a dispatch of 1818 on the possibilities of obtaining sandalwood from the island of Kauai: "After my first voyage was the right time, but no one then paid any heed" (No. 61).

Visiting Kauai, the *Neva* was once again welcomed by Kaumualii, who again sought Russian aid, but without success.

During the war of 1812–1814 between the United States and Great Britain, several American captains, fearing British warships or privateers, sold their vessels to Baranov. Thus, early in 1814 Baranov bought from Captain James Bennett the ship *Atahualpa,* renamed the *Bering,* and later in the year the brig *Lydia,* renamed the *Il'mena.*

In April, 1814, Baranov sent the *Bering,* still under her erstwhile owner, Captain Bennett, to the Pribylov Islands for seal skins, to be used as part of the payment for the ship. From there she sailed to Okhotsk, and thence to Hawaii to obtain foodstuffs for Sitka. The ship touched at Waimea Bay, Kauai, early in October, 1814, then traded among the islands. A letter from Kaumualii to Baranov via Captain Bennett, written at this time, pledges friendship but makes exaggerated demands for foodstuffs, arms, and a ship (No. 2).

After undergoing repairs at Honolulu, the *Bering* sailed for Alaska on January 25, 1815, but on January 29 stopped at Kauai once more for supplies. Two days later she was thrown on the beach at Waimea Bay by a gale. Kaumualii thereupon appropriated the vessel and cargo on grounds that anything thrown on the coast belonged to him.[9] Captain Bennett and his men had an uncomfortable sojourn on Kauai but were finally rescued, on April 11, 1815, by the American ship *Albatross* (Captain William Smith)[10] and taken to Sitka.

Bennett's arrival at Sitka with this bad news was soon followed by other troubles. Wilson Price Hunt, leader of the overland expedition sent out by John Jacob Astor in 1810 in support of the short-lived Astoria trading post, was given sanctuary by Baranov until the end of the war with Great Britain. For alleged illegal trade with the Indians around Sitka, on July 19/31, 1815, Baranov seized Hunt's ship, the *Pedler*. Lieutenant M. P. Lazarev, commander of the *Suvorov*, another Russian round-the-world vessel then at Sitka, took Hunt's part. Threatened with removal from his command by the choleric old Chief Manager, Lazarev took unauthorized leave rather than submit.

Lazarev left behind his supercargo and the ship's doctor. The latter, Georg Anton Schäffer, had not gotten along well with Lazarev, which probably helped gain him Baranov's favor. Shorthanded as always, needing someone for the delicate task of recovering the cargo of the *Bering,* Baranov put aside initial doubts (indicated in No. 40) and chose the well-traveled, educated newcomer.

Schäffer, the fast-working interloper who for a short time was to disturb the torpor of premissionary Hawaii, was born in Münnerstadt, Bavaria, on January 27, 1779, a miller's son. He was baptized in the Catholic Church, received a good education, and was set up as an apothecary. Something in his makeup even then drew him to distant places, for he pursued his profession as far afield as Hungary and Galicia. In 1805, despite earlier expulsion for unspecified disciplinary difficulties, he passed the "surgeon's examination" at St. Julius Hospital in Würzburg, and became eligible to practice medicine. At about the same time he married the daughter of the hospital miller. In 1808 he was invited to Russia, possibly to take part in the Franco-Russian expedition against India which was then under discussion. He served in the army as a staff physician, and in 1812 took part in an abortive project, under a German charlatan named Leppich, for construction of balloons to combat Napoleon's invading army. In 1813 he signed on with the Russian-American Company in St. Petersburg as surgeon on the Company vessel *Suvorov,* for the voyage which left him in Alaska.[11]

No Company vessels were at hand, so Baranov arranged for Schäffer to go to the islands on the American ship *Isabella* (Captain Tyler). In careful instructions (No. 3) Baranov directed Schäffer to appear only as a naturalist until he had won King Kamehameha's confidence. When two Company ships, the *Otkrytie* (*Discovery*) and the *Kad'iak* (or *Mirt-Kad'iak,* recalling its earlier name, the *Myrtle*), arrived, he was to gain Kamehameha's help in retrieving the cargo of the *Bering* or obtaining compensation for it in sandalwood. He was to try to obtain trading privileges and a monopoly on sandalwood within Kamehameha's domains similar to a concession granted earlier to two Americans, Captains William Heath Davis and Nathan Winship.[12] In a letter to be given Kamehameha when the time was ripe, Baranov reviewed the story of the *Bering* and revealed Schäffer's authority to act for the Company (No. 4).

On October 5/17, 1815, accompanied by two "creole" (half-Russian, half-Indian) boys, one of them Baranov's son Antipatr, Schäffer sailed for the islands on the *Isabella*.

Several months passed before Baranov could send reinforcements to his envoy. The *Otkrytie* had come in from a trading expedition only four days after Schäffer's departure, but needed extensive repairs and new equipment. In instructions of February 15, 1816, to Lieutenant I. A. Podushkin, commander of the *Otkrytie*, Baranov reviewed his instructions to Schäffer. Podushkin was to meet Schäffer at Kamehameha's residence on the island of Hawaii, from whence they were to go to Kauai. They were to obtain the *Bering*'s cargo by peaceful means if possible, but if force proved necessary they were to conquer the island for Russia. The *Kad'iak,* carrying a cargo of timber, was to follow later, and be sent to Macao with sandalwood or the cargo of the *Bering*. On the way back to Alaska it was to poach for furs on the California coast or trade for furs "in the Straits" along the Northwest coast. If permission could be obtained, the *Otkrytie* was to leave a party on Oahu to establish a trading post (No. 5, No. 6).

In further instructions to Schäffer, sent with the *Otkrytie*, Baranov mentioned the likely arrival of another round-the-world ship from St. Petersburg, from which Schäffer could ask help if necessary. Schäffer was to get payment for the *Bering* cargo, salvage what he could from the wreck, and return immediately on the *Otkrytie*. If the situation required force, Schäffer was to wait until arrival of the *Kad'iak,* and then take both ships to Kauai (No. 7, No. 8).

Schäffer, meanwhile, had arrived on the island of Hawaii early in November, 1815. There he ran into unexpected opposition. The elderly British seaman, John

Young, Kamehameha's chief advisor, suspected at once that the visitor was more than a naturalist, and warned the King against him. According to Schäffer, several Americans on the *Isabella* did the same. So did John Ebbets, veteran master of Astor's ship *Enterprise,* arriving in December en route from New York to the Northwest Coast, and W. P. Hunt, on the *Pedler,* en route from Sitka to Canton and Boston. Fearing encroachment on their privileges, the American skippers intensified Kamehameha's fears of Russian designs.

By medical aid and personal assurances Schäffer finally managed to mollify the King so that the latter ordered a house built for him and agreed to grant land to the Company and to permit establishment of a factory on the island of Oahu. Kamehameha's chief consort, Queen Kaahumanu, gave Schäffer "Veikarua" (Kailua?) in the province of "Kollau" (Koolaupoku?) on the southeast side of Oahu, "fishing grounds seven versts along the seashore," and ten sheep and forty goats. The Queen's brother, Kuakini, known to foreigners as "John Adams," gave him the tract of "Koaiai" (Hoaeae?) on the Eva, or Pearl, River, near Honolulu.

Early in January, 1816, an American acquaintance described Schäffer's situation thus:

"I found that Dr. Shafford [Schäffer] had succeeded in removing the prejudices of the King, had acquired his favour, and stood high in his good graces; he was at this time attending one of the queens, who was indisposed, as her physician. The King had caused a house to be built for him in the center of a breadfruit grove, where the doctor could pursue his botanical researches without interruption. I visited him there and passed some hours with him.[13]

This was only an interlude, however, and before long, conditions again grew difficult. Provisions were supplied irregularly; Schäffer's movements were circumscribed, and some of the King's advisors, he claims in his journal, urged that he be killed. He asked permission to move to Oahu, and the King finally consented, though in adherance to his usual policy of prohibiting foreigners from building permanent structures, he assigned the Company one of his own warehouses at Honolulu for a factory.

About May 3, the *Otkrytie* arrived at Honolulu, and Schäffer could finally prepare for the expedition to Kauai. Then, on May 11, another Russian ship, the *Il'mena,* hove in unexpectedly from California.[14]

The *Il'mena* (former *Lydia*), if we piece her story together from several sources, had had her share of misadventure. After being purchased by Baranov late in 1813, she was sent in January, 1814, under an American, Captain William Wadsworth, to the Russian outpost at Fort Ross, California, with supplies. On board was a party of Aleut hunters led by a veteran Company employee, Timofei Tarakanov,[15] and John Elliot de Castro,[16] a former physician to Kamehameha, who had gone to Alaska for some reason and there had been engaged by Baranov because of his knowledge of Spanish and claimed acquaintance with the Spanish missionaries of California.

The *Il'mena* had engaged in the usual poaching for sea otter on the California coast, and in the summer of 1814 Tarakanov and eleven Aleuts were seized by the Spanish near San Pedro.[17] The vessel then seems to have wintered at Bodega, the Russian port a few miles south of Fort Ross, and in 1815 went south for more poaching.

On September 18, 1815, another Russian and twenty-four hunters were seized, and on the twenty-first Elliot and five others were taken.[18] The *Il'mena* then went to Bodega for repairs.[19] Somehow Tarakanov and presumably some of the Aleuts were released by the Spaniards, and there rejoined the ship. Sailing from Bodega in November for Sitka, the *Il'mena* was damaged at the harbor entrance, remained through another winter for more repairs, and finally set sail once more in April, 1816. She soon sprang a leak, however, and her captain, Wadsworth, detoured to the islands for repairs, arriving early in May, 1816.[20]

Ordering Wadsworth to remain at Honolulu with the *Il'mena,* and leaving the factory in the hands of the promyshlennik Petr Kicherev, Schäffer sailed first for Hawaii. He wanted to pick up cargo and to get an order from Kamehameha for Kaumualii.[21]

Having little success with Kamehameha, Schäffer sailed for Kauai, and on May 16/28, according to his journal, the *Otkrytie* anchored in Waimea Bay.

After dispelling Kaumualii's initial suspicions and apprehensions, Schäffer found conditions far more agreeable than in Kamehameha's nominally friendly domains. Kaumualii, probably at the prompting of John Ebbets, master of the *Enterprise,* which stopped at the islands en route to the Northwest coast, had already had second thoughts about the advisability of appropriating the *Bering* cargo. On February 5, 1816, he had written Baranov that he was sending the furs with Ebbets, and would deliver other Russian property if a ship was sent (No. 11). Kaumualii now told Schäffer the same story he had told earlier visitors, complaining of Kamehameha's usurpation, and stating his desire for alliance with Russia. However, he apparently failed to mention one fundamental change in his status since his earlier requests: In 1810 he had made his peace with Kamehameha and acknowledged the latter's suzerainty. Schäffer's appearance on the scene evidently rekindled Kaumualii's hopes of regaining what he saw as his lawful patrimony and tempted him to overlook his pledge.[22]

Schäffer, on the other hand, was eager to grasp what seemed a great opportunity for the Company and himself alike. Vancouver had laid claim to the island of Hawaii in 1794, but England had never taken the matter farther. With the islands open to claim, and a personal invitation from their rightful ruler, a dazzling prospect presented itself. So far he had followed orders, but this unexpected development appears to have left no doubt in his mind about the justification of his taking the initiative.

All in one glorious day, May 21/ June 2, 1816, Schäffer achieved his original objectives and a great deal more. Kaumualii not only agreed to restore what remained of the *Bering*'s cargo, but in addition pledged allegiance to the Emperor Alexander I (No. 12), promised to trade exclusively with the Russian-American Company, to supply cargoes of sandalwood to it alone, to allow it to establish factories anywhere in his domains, to supply men to aid in the erection of Company buildings and in the development of plantations, and to furnish provisions for Russian ships.

In return Schäffer promised Kaumualii the protection of the Russian Empire and a fully armed ship when the first cargo of sandalwood was ready (No. 14). He bestowed on the King a silver medal and made him a line staff officer in the Russian navy (No. 13).

During the weeks that followed, Schäffer began building a house at Waimea, and established a trading post in a stone building given the Company by Kaumualii. On May 31/June 11, leaving two Russians and a number of Aleuts behind, he sailed for Oahu on the *Otkrytie*.

According to his journal Schäffer intended to settle trade affairs on Oahu and to await the Company ship *Kad'iak*. Instead the *Otkrytie* ran into a severe storm, lost two masts, and had to take shelter at the island of Niihau. After emergency repairs Lieutenant Podushkin then took the ship directly to Alaska.

Schäffer made his way back to Waimea in a *baidarka*

(an Aleutian boat) with one Aleut. There he settled down, planting an extensive garden and preparing his houses. On July 1, 1816, he and the King exchanged still wider commitments in a secret treaty. Kaumualii agreed to send an army of five hundred men, under Schäffer's command, to reconquer the islands held by Kamehameha, and to help build a Russian fort on each of the islands. The King promised to give the Company one half of the island of Oahu, strips of land on each of the other islands, and all of the sandalwood on Oahu, and to "refuse to trade with citizens of the United States." Schäffer agreed to supply ammunition and ships for the prospective conquest, to supply the King with fish and timber from Russian America (the timber to be cut by islanders sent to Sitka), and "to introduce a better economy, which will make the natives educated and prosperous" (No. 17). As a token of esteem, Kaumualii placed his mark on a paper making Baranov a chief of the Sandwich Islands (No. 18).

On August 15, the American schooner *Lydia,* under Captain Henry Gyzelaar, arrived from Oahu with messages for Schäffer from the Russians there. The *Il'mena* was still at Honolulu, and the *Kad'iak,* under her American captain, George Young, had arrived at the end of June. The *Kad'iak,* leaking badly, was a dubious asset, but the men aboard swelled the complement at Schäffer's disposal.

Gyzelaar bore a proposal from Captain John Ebbets to Kaumualii that the King buy the *Lydia.* Kaumualii was eager to acquire the vessel, and to keep his word Schäffer felt bound to buy it for him. He sailed to Oahu on the *Lydia* to complete arrangements.

In the Company factory at Honolulu, on August 24 (September 4, New Style?), in the presence of Captains John and Richard Ebbets, Nathan Winship, Betts [?],

Gyzelaar, George Young, and Wadsworth, along with
John Young and a Doctor Daniel W. Frost, Schäffer
purchased the *Lydia* from Gyzelaar, giving a promise of
payment by the Company.

Schäffer invited all participants in the transaction to a
dinner at the Russian factory, but the affair broke up in a
quarrel with John Young, who was incensed over the
presence of two Russian armed guards at the factory,
which he regarded as a breach of Hawaiian sovereignty.
Further unpleasantness occurred with Captain Alexander
Adams, master of Kamehameha's newly purchased brig,
the *Forester* (renamed *Kaahumanu*), over the Russian
flag being flown over the factory and at Kauai.

Schäffer now decided on yet another ship purchase.
While the *Il'mena,* and presumably the *Lydia* and the
Kad'iak, sailed for Waimea, Schäffer sailed on the American ship *Avon* (Captain Isaac Whittemore) for the bay
of Hanalei, on the north side of Kauai. He liked what he
saw, and on return to Waimea gave the *Lydia* to Kaumualii in return for the valley and port of Hanalei, in a
convention witnessed by Captains Whittemore, William
Smith, and Gyzelaar (No. 21). He next arranged for
Company purchase of the *Avon* from Whittemore for
200,000 piastres, payable in Sitka. Kaumualii, in exchange
for the protection and added assurance the *Avon* would
afford his expansionist projects, agreed to compensate the
Company with three cargoes of sandalwood (No. 20).
On September 6, Captain Whittemore sailed for Sitka
with the *Avon,* to conclude the purchase. Baranov's son
Antipatr accompanied him as a passenger.

On September 12, on land donated by Kaumualii,
Schäffer began construction of a stronghold, built of lava
blocks, to be called Fort Elizabeth, after the consort of
the Emperor Alexander I.

On the same day, Schäffer sent Captain Gyzelaar to

Honolulu with the *Lydia* to see how the Company post there was faring. Ten days later the vessel returned, bearing the men from the factory with news that the natives, allegedly egged on by John Young and "the American hot heads," had burned it. Another writer, much later, probably on the basis of native tradition, states that the men of the *Il'mena* and *Kad'iak* built a blockhouse at Honolulu, mounted guns and hoisted the Russian flag. This alarmed the natives, who informed Kamehameha on Hawaii. Kamehameha sent a large force, which caused the men on the *Il'mena* and *Kad'iak* to leave for Kauai. Chief Kalanimoku (otherwise known as "Billy Pitt"), in consultation with John Young, then built a more substantial fort to forestall any future Russian incursion.[23]

Two days after the return of the *Lydia,* on September 24, the American ship *O'Cain* (Captain Robert McNeil) arrived at Waimea en route to Canton and Boston. It bore as passengers Captains Nathan Winship, William Smith, Richard Ebbets, and Henry Gyzelaar, and Doctor Frost. Winship, Smith, and Gyzelaar came ashore and tried to haul down the Russian flag, but were prevented by a guard placed by Kaumualii.

This threat foiled, Schäffer went to Hanalei, and on September 24/October 6, at a formal ceremony, raised the Russian flag over the valley. He writes that Kaumualii had asked him to attach his name to the valley and to give Russian names to several of the chiefs there. Thus, the valley becomes "Schäfferthal" in his journal; the main chief, Kallavatti, takes the old name of the valley, becoming "Hanalei"; Chief Taera becomes "Vorontsov," after the Russian statesman; and Kaumualii's deputy, Obana Tupigea, becomes "Platov," probably after a Russian hero of the Napoleonic wars. Two forts of earthworks, which he ordered placed on heights overlooking the river mouth, received the names "Alexander" and "Barclay," the one after the Emperor, the other presumably after the Russian general, Barclay de Tolly.

Returning to Waimea on October 8, Schäffer received a seven-gun salute, the Russian flag was run up, and Kaumualii signed over Hanalei province and harbor to the Company. Other notables of the island then proclaimed their devotion by deeding land in exchange for gifts.

The references to the land grants are scattered and conflicting, and cannot be linked to present-day place names with certainty. Chief Kamahalolani gave the Company a strip of land called "Guramaia," on the right bank of the Waimea River, for a building and vegetable gardens, and another strip, called "Vaikari," inhabited by twenty families, on the left bank of the river. The King's (or Queen's, in another version) sister Taininoa (or Naoa) gave the Company a village on the left bank of the Waimea River with fourteen (or eleven) families, a tract called "Hamalea" on the Mattaveri (Makaweli?) River with thirteen families, and the uninhabited valley of "Mainauri" (perhaps Makaweli Gulch?), "eight versts" from Waimea. Chief Obana Platov gave the Company a village called "Tuiloa" (Koloa?), with eleven families, in the province of Hanapepe, four miles inland from Hanapepe Bay, "on the right bank of the river Don" (the latter is evidently the Hanapepe River, renamed by Schäffer). Kaumualii gave the Company the uninhabited islet of Lehua, which Schäffer stocked with sheep and goats. A little later, Kaumualii gave Tarakanov a village with eleven families on the left bank of "the River Don." At the same time. Queen Monalau gave Schäffer land in the "Khainakhil'" (perhaps Kuunakaiole?) valley, renamed the Georg valley, presumably after Schäffer, in Hanapepe province. The latter is further described as being on the coast southwest of Hanapepe Bay, "a large piece of land nine versts long and fifteen wide between the port of Waimea and Hanapepe, along the seashore where one could gather a great deal of salt."

Early in December word came of the arrival at Honolulu of the Russian brig *Rurik*, under Lieutenant Otto von Kotzebue. Schäffer received a letter from John Elliot de Castro, former commissioner of the *Il'mena*, released from arrest in California by Kotzebue's intercession with the Spanish authorities, and brought to Hawaii on the *Rurik* (No. 28).

Schäffer had been expecting the *Rurik*, sent out from Kronstadt in July, 1815, and could now look forward to supplies and reinforcement, but the anticipated arrival was delayed. Instead, troubles began to mount. Captain Wadsworth of the *Il'mena* told Kaumualii that Schäffer intended to arrest the King and his chiefs.[24] Schäffer thereupon ordered Wadsworth's arrest and confinement on the ship. In Wadsworth's place he appointed the pilot, Voroll Madson, though reluctantly, "for he, too, is an American. But where am I to get anyone else?"

Soon afterward came news of trouble with the natives at Hanalei, who had killed one Aleut there and burned the Russian distillery (No. 27).

In January, 1817, word finally came from Baranov, borne by the *Cossack* (Captain Brown). Whittemore had arrived in Sitka with the *Avon* at the end of September, expecting payment for the ship. Instead, Baranov had promptly repudiated the transaction arranged by Schäffer. Whittemore's reactions to this wild-goose chase are not indicated; he went on to the California coast early in 1817, and thence back to Hawaii. Nor do we have Baranov's letter, but he is quoted as having forbidden further speculation and demanding return of the *Kad'iak* and the *Il'mena,* their crews, and the capital which had been entrusted to Schäffer.[25]

Schäffer probably felt that his main hope of saving the situation lay in support from Kotzebue. Weeks passed, however, without word from the *Rurik,* so he finally sent the *Il'mena* to Honolulu to find out about it. On February 6, 1817, the *Il'mena* at last returned, bearing news that Kotzebue had departed before its arrival. It also bore a second letter from Elliot, declining Schäffer's invitation to come to Kauai because it might offend Kamehameha (No. 29).

What had happened? Kotzebue's *Travels,* describing the voyage, tell the story. Following orders, the *Rurik* had been supposed to go from Unalaska to Hawaii, but had detoured to California to avoid unfavorable winds. At San Francisco it had liberated Elliot. During the voyage to Hawaii (November 1–24, 1816), Kotzebue had found that the diminutive Elliot "possessed much natural understanding" and that "his society was very agreeable." They arrived at Hawaii, and there were struck by the "reserved and suspicious manner" of the first native they met. "Elliot was of the opinion that some disagreeable circumstance had occurred on the island, which required the greatest precaution." [26]

Elliot went ashore and was told that five months before, two Russian ships had stopped there, and that there had been disputes. When the ships left the islands their officers had threatened to return soon with a strong force and a ship of war. King Kamehameha told Elliot that Schäffer had come to botanize, but had gone to Oahu, profaned the sanctuary so that it had to be destroyed and a new one built, and had incited King Kaumualii to rebel.

Elliot reassured the King of the *Rurik's* peaceful intentions, and the rest of the party was allowed to come ashore. Kotzebue was grateful to Elliot, without whose help "we should probably have fallen victims to the faults of others." He made it clear to Kamehameha that he wanted no part of Schäffer's enterprise.

They went on to Honolulu, where there were more complaints. "Pitt" told them, through John Young, "We never did the Russians any injustice, and yet they rendered us evil for good!" "I assured him," wrote Kotzebue, "that everything done by Schäffer had been contrary to the will of our Emperor, and tried to make him easy respecting the future." [27]

Kotzebue ordered his men to survey the harbor, only to find the islanders incensed by his men putting up flags as markers. Schäffer, they told him, had put up a flag saying "I take possession of this island." [28] Kotzebue mollified the natives by having brooms substituted for the flags, but when he tried to inspect the new fort he was stopped by a sentinel calling out to him "Taboo!" and learned that access was prohibited to all strangers, "particularly Europeans." [29]

To Kotzebue, there was no question of supporting Schäffer. As he wrote afterwards: "the Sandwich Islands will remain what they are—the free port and staple of all the navigators of the seas. But should any foreign power conceive the foolish idea of taking possession of them the jealous vigilance of the Americans, who possess the almost exclusive commerce of these seas, and the secure protection of England, would not be wanting to frustrate the undertaking." [30] Thus persuaded, Kotzebue sailed from Honolulu on December 14, 1816, without making any effort to go to Kauai to investigate matters himself.

This evident official disavowal of Schäffer—soon combined, in all probability, with word of Baranov's attitude, borne by Captain Brown of the *Cossack,* and later by Whittemore of the *Avon*—must have greatly encouraged

Kamehameha and his ministers, and their allies the American skippers.

Exactly how the opposition then took shape, and who directed it, may only be surmised from the scanty references in Schäffer's journal and reports, and several other sources. Alexander Adams, in his journal for January 19, writes of sailing on the *Kaahumanu* (*Forester*) from Hawaii to Oahu: "At 1 PM saw a strange sail to the southward, standing in for Kairua [Kailua]. On being told she was a Russian brig, and apprehensive of some harm, cleared away for quarters and bore up after her. She proved to be the brig *Almyra* [*Il'mena?*] from Attoi [Kauai], bound for Kairua for hogs." [31]

Schäffer, meanwhile, carried on seemingly oblivious to the clouds gathering on the horizon. Returning to Waimea on April 9 from a prolonged stay at Hanalei, he found that the brig *Kaahumanu* (*Forester*) had stopped while en route to Canton with a cargo of sandalwood, and that Captain Adams had tried to destroy the Russian flag. Adams had been prevented from doing this, but had sent word back to Oahu before sailing.

Adams' version of this is as follows:

Mar. 7— . . . at 4 P.M. got under way for Attoi. Arrived off the island and delivered our orders to the king from Tamehameha [Kamehameha]. 11th.—Getting off hogs and taro on board, etc. Some Russian gentlemen dined with us.

12th.—N.E. winds. Got off all our stock. Gave the King our ensign to hoist in lieu of the Russian, who said it was on account of his having no other. At 2 P.M. got under way . . .[32]

Calling on the King after his return, Schäffer was well received, but noted that for the first time the King did not raise the Russian flag or salute. He noted further that the King and his chief minister, Kamahalolani, had taken much more goods from the Company warehouse than they should have.

About this time, an ingenious form of psychological warfare against Schäffer seems to have been devised in Honolulu, undoubtedly by the American shipmasters in the port. Schäffer's first inkling of this came on April 16, when the *Columbia* (Captain Jennings) called at Waimea. Peter Corney, on board the vessel, writes merely that they "were surprised at not seeing any of the natives push off. Doctor Shefham [Schäffer], the Russian, came on board in a bodarkee [baidarka]; he would not allow us to have any communication with the shore, and through policy we did not press the point, but made all sail to the northward towards Norfolk Sound."[33]

Schäffer, however, describing the same visit, states: "Captain Jennings told me of the arrival on the island of Oahu of Captain Ebbets the elder, from China, and also that on Oahu there is talk of disagreements between Russia and the United States, and that the Russian Minister has left America."

It is not clear who had concocted this tale, evidently designed to create apprehension, but the scanty data concerning ships then in the area at least indicates some of the principal antagonists of Schäffer. "Old Ebbets," who had arrived at Honolulu from Canton on the *Enterprise* on April 13, was certainly on hand. Caleb Brintnell, with the *Zephyr,* was there; so was Dixey Wildes, of Boston, with the *Paragon;* Isaac Whittemore had arrived from California with the *Avon* in May; and William Heath Davis, out of Boston on the *Eagle,* may also have been present in May. These alone would have constituted formidable opposition once a decision was reached that the interloper must go.

Jennings also told Schäffer of an earlier agreement he had made with Kaumualii, to exchange the *Columbia* for sandalwood, but now void because not acted upon. When he went ashore Schäffer chided the King about the agreement, of which he had not been told, and "again" asked him to load the Russian ships so that they could be sent to Sitka. The King promised to do so, and on April 23, 1817, placed his mark on a new convention reaffirming his agreement of May 21, 1816 (No. 30).

Apparently reassured, Schäffer went to Hanapepe to look after work begun there in the spring. There, on May 7, he heard that "five boats" (elsewhere referred to as "ships," so it is uncertain whether these were native or foreign vessels) had arrived from Oahu "with news of war."

Schäffer hastened back to Waimea, and early on the morning of May 8, visited the King. He found him at the river at a gathering of his ministers, surrounded by "a thousand men." Schäffer again demanded that the Russian ships be loaded and dispatched as soon as possible. Turning to go back to the factory, however, he was seized by a native and "six American seamen" and told that he and all the other Russians must leave Kauai at once. He protested, but was set in a leaky boat and forced to paddle out to the *Kad'iak*. From its deck he heard cannon shots and saw "a pirate flag"—a blue and white ensign of mysterious origin, but deserving to be ranked among the earliest Hawaiian flags—raised to a cannon salute.

There followed a futile wait in the harbor at Waimea, watching the "pirate flag" raised daily ashore. Captain Wadsworth, still a prisoner on the *Kad'iak,* pretended insanity, jumped overboard, and was picked up by a native and taken ashore.

Finding they could do nothing more at Waimea, Schäffer and his men sailed the *Il'mena* and the *Kad'iak* around the island to Hanalei, in hope of making a stand at Fort Alexander. On the way Schäffer wrote to Kaumualii, scolding him and warning him of dire consequences for not keeping faith (No. 32).

At Hanalei, Schäffer made formal claim to the whole island of Kauai in the name of the Emperor of Russia, and ordered the Russian flag raised over Fort Alexander, to a three-gun salute. He hoped to make a stand, and had the men sign a compact to that effect (No. 34), but hostility of the local natives, capped by an order from Waimea to leave Hanalei or suffer the consequences, left Schäffer no choice but to comply.

The *Kad'iak,* up to then under Captain George Young, was unseaworthy for the voyage to Alaska. Schäffer accordingly placed the loyal Young in command of the *Il'mena* and sent it, with tidings of the debacle, to Baranov. As passengers went Madson, previously in command, and the still faithful Chief "Hanalei" (Kallavatti), his wife Mitina, and their servants.

Schäffer himself took command of the leaky *Kad'iak,* and with the remaining Russians and more than forty Aleuts sailed for uncertain sanctuary in Honolulu, apparently hoping to stay there until reinforcements arrived.

After five days the *Kad'iak* dropped anchor outside the harbor of Honolulu. The Russian flag was placed upside down on the mizzenmast to indicate distress, and a cannon shot brought a pilot, who brought the ship to the inner harbor.

Ashore there was uncertainty what to do with the unwelcome guests, none of whom were permitted to land. Finally it was proposed that if Schäffer went as a prisoner to Hawaii, and if the ship gave up all arms and ammunition, the others on board would be allowed to stay. Schäffer agreed to give up the arms, but declined to be "a caught fish" himself and in this was backed up by Tarakanov and the others.

On July 4 flags were flying from all the ships in the harbor in honor of the American Independence Day. At noon Schäffer ordered the Russian flag flown, but upside down, which caused "a great commotion on the American ships." A "Captain Wills" (probably Captain Dixey Wildes, of the ship *Paragon*), sent word to Schäffer to turn his flag around, but he refused on the ground that his ship was still in distress.

On the same day, the brig *Panther* arrived. Its captain, Isaiah Lewis, grateful for medical aid Schäffer had rendered the previous year, offered a way out of the dilemma in the form of passage to Canton.

Schäffer put the matter before a committee of his men. They, probably eager to be rid of him, urged that he accept, on the grounds that he should go on to Europe and report directly to the Company heads and the Russian government. Leaving a committee, headed by Tarakanov, to look after the stricken *Kad'iak* and the men, Schäffer sailed on the *Panther* on July 7. Taking with him an Aleut, Grigorii Iskakov, and a Russian promyshlennik, Filip Osipov, he left the islands as he had come, in an American ship with only two companions.

The voyage was uneventful. The brig touched at Kauai for supplies, but Schäffer was kept in quarters out of sight of the natives. Schäffer records in his journal some observations by the mate—a Mr. Marshal (Merschel?), a nephew of John Jacob Astor and former second officer of Astor's ill-fated ship *Lark*, wrecked off Kahoolawe in 1813—regarding the fur trade on the Northwest coast and the unscrupulous methods pursued.

The *Panther* arrived at Macao on August 26. There Schäffer stayed with Anders Ljungstedt, the Swedish consul, long a friend of the Russian-American Company. Again exceeding his powers, Schäffer made Ljungstedt official representative of the Company at Macao.

On December 4/5, 1817, Schäffer left Macao on the

Portuguese ship *Luconia,* bound for Rio de Janeiro, arriving March 8, 1818. A month later, in April, he sailed for Riga on a Russian ship, the *Natalia Petrovna.*

Reactions to the fiasco, in Sitka and St. Petersburg, were much delayed. In these days of instant communications it is easy to forget the lag which formerly took place in the spread of information. Russian America was particularly subject to this. The fastest of vessels took about a month between Sitka and San Francisco, Honolulu, or Okhotsk. From Okhotsk the post, operated on a relay system, could get a message to St. Petersburg in about three months. However, all depended on the season and the availability of ships. Months might pass before a message could even start on its way. A year was the usual time between Sitka and St. Petersburg, whether by round-the-world ship or across Siberia.

Contrary to the impression given in some accounts, therefore, Schäffer's venture could only have been a one-man show. Baranov, in Sitka, appears to have heard nothing about the fate of his agent from the time of Schäffer's departure for the Islands in November, 1815, until the return of the *Otkrytie* in the following June. The displeasure and uneasiness he then felt at the turn events had taken could not be communicated for some months. When Whittemore arrived early in October, 1816, with a 200,000-piastre claim for the *Avon* and further evidence of Schäffer's misguided zeal, Baranov still could not communicate with the Islands until the departure of the brig *Cossack* late in December. He could not inform St. Petersburg of the situation and of his demands on Schäffer until the brig *Brutus* left for Siberia in May, 1817, bearing dispatches to be sent to the capital on the long overland journey via Okhotsk.

The Company directors in St. Petersburg, half a world

away, were scarcely in the picture at all. They seem to have heard of Schäffer's dispatch on the mission (November, 1815) only in March, 1817. In a dispatch of March 22, 1817, they reminded Baranov that he had earlier stated that Schäffer would likely be of no use, yet now he was sending him on an important mission. They cautioned Baranov against carrying out a proposal he had apparently made, of employing Schäffer to set up a school or distillery at Fort Ross, in California, on grounds that such activity might arouse the Spaniards (No. 40).

The Company heads seem to have heard of Schäffer's successes of May 21/June 2, 1816, via Canton, only in August, 1817, over two months after the game was already up and Schäffer had left the Islands. In a postscript to a dispatch of August 14, 1817, to be sent with Lieutenant V. M. Golovnin, commander of the frigate *Kamchatka,* soon to depart for Russian America, they mention receipt of Dr. Schäffer's "very interesting and pleasant report" (No. 41). In instructions to Golovnin they urged that everything possible be done "to establish Russian authority and to develop factories" on Kauai (No. 42), and sent with him a number of presents for the King (No. 44). They wrote Schäffer instructing him to protect Kaumualii and his people, to give the King due honors and respect, and to avoid quarrels between the Russians and natives, any oppression or mistreatment of natives, or their use as forced laborers (No. 43). At about the same time the naval historian V. N. Berkh, who had visited the Hawaiian Islands with the *Neva* in 1805, prepared a lengthy memorandum on the Islands, evidently for Company use, summarizing his own observations and other information about the area. An interesting adjunct to this report is a letter from I. A. Kuskov, manager of the Company outpost of Fort Ross, in California, dated

August 12, 1816, lauding Schäffer's achievement on the basis of information he had just received, and enclosing a copy of Kaumualii's act of submission (No. 45).

Official circles, however, took a different view of the matter. On August 15, the Company informed Count Nesselrode, Minister of Foreign Affairs, of the developments in the Pacific, enclosing a copy of Schäffer's report of August, 1816 (No. 19), and a copy of Kaumualii's submission (No. 12; cf. No. 45), for transmittal to the Emperor. Nesselrode, unimpressed, sent the Company a short note directing it to take no action concerning the cession of Kauai until receipt of additional information.[34]

Copies of Kaumualii's conventions with Schäffer, Schäffer's proposal that the Company buy the *Avon,* and a report of Baranov's refusal and subsequent orders to Schäffer, sent by Baranov about May, 1817, via the *Brutus* and the overland post from Okhotsk, reached St. Petersburg about October 15, 1817.[35]

The matter then rested until January, 1818, when the Company dispatched a report, accompanied by copies of all pertinent documents, to the Minister of Foreign Affairs, for forwarding to the Emperor (No. 47).

The Emperor threw cold water on the project, informing Nesselrode that acquisition of the Islands would be useless, and could actually lead to "unpleasantness" in the country's relations with other powers. Therefore, Kaumualii's act of submission was not to be accepted, although the Company should try to keep the King's esteem and good will. On February 24, 1818, Nesselrode informed the Minister of Interior, Kozodavlev, of the Emperor's decision, which Kozodavlev relayed to the Council of the Russian-American Company in a letter of March 13.[36]

Upon receiving the Emperor's directive, the Company on March 15, 1818, wrote Baranov at length, telling him to recall Schäffer as soon as possible and, in consultation with Hagemeister and Golovnin, to replace him with someone more able.[37] Meeting on March 26, the Council of the Russian-American Company decided that steps should be taken (1) to return to Kaumualii his act of submission, with the explanation that the Emperor already had enough possessions, but with due regard for the King's feelings; (2) to ask the Ministry of the Interior to strike a gold medal inscribed "To Kaumualii, King of the Sandwich Island of Kauai, as a mark of Russian friendship," to be given him on a ribbon of St. Anna along with a jewelled cutlass; and (3) to get word to Baranov to recall Schäffer as soon as possible, and to put the matter of Company trade with the Sandwich Islands in the hands of a wiser person.[38]

Another lag followed, until August 5, 1818, when at the Company's request, Alexander granted the gold medal for Kaumualii which had been proposed in March.[39]

Then, also in August, the Company received Schäffer's letter of September 20, 1817, from Macao, telling of the evacuation of Kauai. All was lost. On August 13, the Company passed on the sorry information to the Minister of the Interior.[40]

All the while, Schäffer had been on his way to Europe. Late in July he and his two companions finally arrived at Helsingor, Denmark. On July 30 he wrote the Main Office from that port, stating that he must report in person to the Emperor. He had learned that the Emperor had gone to attend the Congress of Aachen, so had sent a message to him there (No. 49). Evidently no invitation to Aachen was forthcoming, for on August 18 he wrote the Main Office from Berlin, complaining of lack of funds, and asked the Company to send him a draft (No. 49).

Schäffer's erstwhile traveling companion, the promysh-lennik Filip Osipov (there is no indication of what ever happened to the other, an Aleut) had meanwhile arrived in St. Petersburg, where he delivered a lengthy report to the Main Office (No. 50). Schäffer, however, failed to appear, so upon hearing that he was at Riga, the Company finally wrote the governor-general of Riga on November 23, 1818, asking that he be sent to St. Petersburg (No. 51).

In the capital, Schäffer appears to have had a cool reception. He wrote the Company on February 6, 1819, stating dissatisfaction with the payment he had received (No. 52). Later in the month he directed a lengthy memorial to the Emperor, setting forth a glowing description of the Hawaiian Islands, the rights of Russia to them, and the political and economic advantages which would accrue from their acquisition.[41]

Although forwarded with some skepticism by the Ministry of Interior's Department of Manufactures and Internal Trade, judging by appended comments, the memorial appears to have reopened the entire question. Evidently there were those in Company or government circles who still favored the project. On February 27, 1819, the Department of Manufactures and Internal Trade asked the Company its opinion of the memorial.[42]

On March 2, 1819, evidently in reply to criticisms of his proposals, Schäffer submitted an "Appendix" to the memorial, amplifying some of its points. A Company memorandum on the project, prepared for the Department of Manufactures and Internal Trade on March 18, 1819, expounded on the benefits that could derive from acquisition of the Islands, and gave grounds for the Russian claim.[43]

However, the hopes of Schäffer and his adherents were soon dashed. On April 1, 1819, the Main Office of the

Company informed Captain L. A. Hagemeister, who had succeeded Baranov as the Chief Manager at Sitka, that the proposals set forth in Schäffer's memorial should be achieved only by peaceful means.[44] There is then a curt letter from Schäffer to the Company, dated April 22, 1819, reviewing his expenditures, and criticizing the Company for handicapping its representatives in the Pacific with inadequate means, especially shipping (No. 53). The Company minutes of May 17, 1819, mention that Schäffer had left for Germany in April, and record efforts to account for amounts still outstanding (No. 54). The coup de grâce was given to the idea of dominion in Hawaii on June 24, when Foreign Minister Nesselrode wrote Minister of the Interior Kozodavlev, passing on a reminder by the Emperor that he had refused annexation from the first and now wanted good relations with the Sandwich Islands restored as soon and as well as possible, and no new adventures.[45] On July 15, 1819, this directive was passed on word for word through the Department of Manufactures and Internal Trade to the Company (No. 55).

That settled the matter. On August 12, 1819, the Main Office stated in a letter to Captain Hagemeister, dispatched via the *Borodino,* departing for Russian America on September 29, that in accordance with the Emperor's will he was to visit the Islands, try to mollify the King, and—showing that all hope of concessions had not been extinguished—try to obtain permission for Russians to settle there (No. 56).

In the Pacific, meanwhile, Hagemeister had arrived at Sitka on the *Kutuzov* on November 21, 1817. He bore orders from the Main Office, concerned over Baranov's capability in the light of reports of his fracas with Lieutenant Lazarev in July, 1815, to supplant, himself, the aging Chief Manager in office if he thought it necessary. Six weeks later, Hagemeister abruptly and tactlessly informed Baranov of his dismissal, and took over his post. He inherited the Hawaiian fiasco along with other problems.

On January 28, 1818, Hagemeister wrote Kuskov, manager at Fort Ross, that "matters have been decided in the Islands—the Doctor has left." He then described how Tarakanov, evidently just arrived in Sitka, had arranged with an American shipmaster for the latter to take two Russians and forty-one Aleuts, then on Oahu, back to Sitka, the men paying their passage home by hunting on the California coast (No. 57). In February Hagemeister directed Podushkin to take the *Otkrytie* to the Islands and settle affairs with Kamehameha and Kaumualii (Nos. 58, 59, 60). On April 6 Hagemeister wrote the Main Office a sarcastic description of Schäffer's transactions (No. 61).

The voyage of the *Otkrytie* was evidently inconclusive,[46] for over a year later, on April 20, 1820, Hagemeister's successor as Chief Manager, Lieutenant-Captain S. I. Ianovskii, wrote the Main Office that he had sent the ship *Brutus* (purchased by the Company from her American owner in 1819) to the Islands to straighten out matters once and for all. However, no satisfaction had been obtained from Kaumualii, causing Ianovskii to observe that "much more might be obtained from the King by threats, if one or two well-armed ships were sent there . . ." (No. 62).

The warships were never sent. Russia was involved in European affairs. Alaska was adequately provided for by the now almost annual round-the-world ships, by foreign shipping, and by the produce of Fort Ross, borne to the north on Company vessels. The Company evidently wrote off the losses incurred by the wreck of the *Bering* and by Schäffer's machinations, and Russian interest in the Hawaiian Islands all but ceased.

Two other foreigners, however, kept Schäffer's dream alive for a little longer. Anders Ljungstedt, the Swedish consul in Macao, caught the idea from Schäffer and passed it on to Peter Dobell, an Irish-American who had made a fortune in the China trade and taken Russian citizenship. Each wrote memorials to the Russian government urging Russian acquisition of Hawaii as the key to trade and power in the Pacific, and each was ignored.[47] Neither Company nor government personnel were inclined to act in the face of the Emperor's expressed opinion.

In the Islands, Kamehameha died in 1819, and with him an era. His son and successor, Liholiho (Kamehameha II), before sinking into a life of debauchery, renounced the old gods and their taboos, put down rebellions, and demanded and received Kaumualii's abject submission. The latter, married, strangely enough, Kamehameha's widow, Kaahumanu, and lived out his remaining years in Honolulu, as a royal prisoner, until his death in 1824.

Schäffer, meanwhile, seeking to repair his fortunes, left Germany for Brazil early in 1821. He had already become acquainted with the Emperor Dom Pedro I and his young Hapsburg Empress, Leopoldina, during a stop at Rio de Janeiro on the outward voyage of the *Suvorov* in May, 1814. From them he received an estate, which he named "Frankenthal," and joined the parvenu nobility of the Brazilian capital as Count von Frankenthal. In 1823 he returned to Europe to recruit German colonists and mercenary troops, gaining the sobriquet of "the soul-buyer" (*Seelenverkaufer*) because of the hardships suffered by the colonists. His book *Brasilien als unabhängiges Reich, in historicher, mercantilischer und politischer Beziehung* . . . (Altona, 1824) is a propaganda piece but is also a competent description of the country.[48] In about 1827 he returned to Brazil. He settled on his estate, his roamings at an end, and died there in 1836.

Any evaluation of Schäffer must depend on clues in his writings and career. They reveal a restless personality, more at home among peoples of distant places than with his own kind. There is an urge to achieve status, hence the miller's son sometimes signs himself as "de Sheffer" and "von Schäffer," Hanalei becomes "Schäffer valley" without apparent resistance on his part, and his career doubtless reaches its pinnacle when he becomes "Count von Frankenthal."

There also appears an almost paranoid suspicion and persecution complex in his references to "old Young," and to "the Americans," typified in his eyes by W. P. Hunt, the elder and younger Ebbets, the Winships, and others. Although these figures doubtless had their faults, his virulent characterizations are not corroborated by other writers of the time, and must be regarded as rising from bafflement and frustration at the thwarting of his own aims.

Likewise, one cannot overlook the opportunism and personal ambition behind his rash disregard of instructions, the deception occasionally evident in his reports to the Company or his deals with Kaumualii, the hypocrisy and self-seeking of his too-fervent love for Russia ("my second home"), the vanity and self-delusion which led him into a hopeless predicament, and the legalistic mind which caused him to place naïve reliance on the symbols rather than the reality of power. Outraged at Kaumualii's fickleness, he lacked the realism which led the native monarch to change sides quickly when the pleasant game of signing treaties and bills of sale, building forts, and giving cannon salutes promised unfavorable results. He had nothing to match the resourcefulness, practicality, and flinty resolve of the Yankee traders, and no understanding of the sea power they represented, upon which he and the Company were dependent at every turn.

On the other hand, this ship's surgeon turned empire-builder managed to get surprisingly far on slender resources. Lengthy survey tours of Hawaii, Oahu, and Kauai, and his attention to local products and to planting testify to a zeal and energy which could have shown good results if properly channeled. Had his gains on Kauai been taken over by some soberer head—Kotzebue could have played this role—Russia might have salvaged at least a foothold in the Islands to the benefit of her possessions in Eastern Siberia and Alaska.

As it was, however, Schaffer's fleeting success merely typified Russia's own brief rise in the North Pacific, due largely to the temporary absence of competition. Baranov's forced retirement in 1819 ended the forward policy he had pursued almost single-handedly for the Russian-American Company. The death of Kamehameha later in the same year, and the arrival of the missionaries, spelled the end of "Old Hawaii." Political change and rapid economic development throughout the Pacific Basin signaled a new era in which Russia could take only a limited part.

Documents

1. *Two Letters of Lieutenant-Captain Hagemeister to the Directors of the Russian-American Company, 1809 (Paraphrased), describing the Sandwich Islands.*

Mr. Hagemeister, in command of the second expedition around the world, made reports to the directors of the Company [which contain the following information].

One letter, dated May 1, 1809, from the ship *Neva* on the Pacific Ocean, contains the following historical observations about the Sandwich Islands:

There is nothing certain about trade with the islands; King Kamehameha, who lives on the main island, Hawaii, did not allow his subjects to engage in trade. He did all the trading himself, maintaining large warehouses filled with European goods. He was not willing to sell his goods at a reasonable price. Because of the climate, one of these islands with small harbors can produce foods in quantities sufficient to supply [the population of] a large part of Asiatic Russia: sugar-cane, from which rum as well as sugar can be obtained; rice, which has been planted as an experiment and has yielded a good crop; also the bread plant, taro, which is similar to flour and is an important item.

King Kamehameha was at first the ruler of only a small northern part of the island of Hawaii, but he conquered the rest of this island and also Maui, Molokai, and Oahu, other islands in the group. The father of King Kaumualii, the ruler of the island of Kauai, had been openly hostile to his progress. King Kamehameha always planned to take vengeance on him but, upon the advice of the Europeans, he abandoned his plan. [On the other hand] King Kaumualii, who constantly anticipated such an act of vengeance on the part of Kamehameha, gladly welcomed newcomers who might help in his defense.

The inhabitants of this island, Kauai (27 N.L. and 169 E.L. from Greenwich)* are not as advanced as those of Hawaii and everywhere suffer from lack of organization. The port Waimea (about which Sheffer has written) is quite good, but dangerous during southern winds, which, however, are very violent only on rare occasions. The Bostonians spread rumors on these islands that the Russians wanted to come and settle there. At first King Kamehameha was afraid of us, but now he says: "Let the Russians come; we have lived without them, we can also live with them."

The English frigate *Cornwallis,* sent at the end of the previous year from East India to the shore of Peru, purposely entered the bay of Kealakekua in order to find out whether we had made any territorial claims.†

If we were to undertake a settlement, we should start it on the island of Molokai, which is more fertile than the others. In the southern part there is a port for small boats. Near this island are the best fisheries. The king would be willing to sell us either this or some other island. The inhabitants are lazy by nature, but, if enlightened by faith, they would learn to lead better lives and improve [their habits]. He [Hagemeister] held a long conversation about their superstitions with the king, Kamehameha, during the latter's sickness, which was purely imaginary. Finally the king remarked, "Our fathers taught us that way, but if you know better, why don't you teach us?"

If we cannot occupy the whole island now, it is possible to buy a part of the land from the king. The Europeans who have settled there have a great many natives working for them for food alone.

The first year's profits could be used for the purchase of taro from private dealers and this will be well worth our attention in the future. Also, wheat would surely grow here very well.

For defense in this locality, it would be sufficient to maintain one or two towers with one or more cannons each.

King Kamehameha has plenty of gunpowder and about twenty different cannons (nine-pounders). But they [the islanders] do not know how to use them; the king keeps them only for display in

---

* Kauai is now placed at 22.0 N. 159.30 W.

† H. M. S. *Cornwallis* actually called at Hawaii in December, 1807, *before* Hagemeister's visit.

front of his little residence. On the other islands they do not even have guns.

To occupy this territory would require only about twenty Russians for defense and about the same number for agriculture.

He [Hagemeister] is sure that these islands can be occupied by friendly methods; but if force is necessary, then two ships would be sufficient. He wonders, however, whether it would not be necessary first to take up that matter with the English government. Although Englishmen own only one island, Hawaii, they may claim the rest of the islands by right of first discovery.

The best of these islands is Oahu. It has an excellent harbor and the most moderate climate.

In the second letter of June 20, 1809, [Hagemeister] wrote from Petropavlovsk, port of Kamchatka:

He repeated the circumstances under which he was sent to the Sandwich Islands and explained that he had stopped at the island Maui at the village of Lahaina and, having found out that there were no European ships there, he went to the island of Oahu, to the port of Honolulu, which served as a port for this as well as for other islands, namely Maui, Molokai, Lanai, and Kahoolawe.* The king has his residence there. This harbor was described in 1796 by Captain Broughton. The entrance to this harbor between the reefs is somewhat dangerous, but the harbor itself is good.

During his [Hagemeister's] stay there were no North American ships there, a fact which all the European residents interpreted as a sign of conflict between the Republic [U. S.] and the English.

On account of frequent visits to the Sandwich Islands by the Bostonians on their way to Canton, food on the islands has become very expensive. Moreover, it is being sold by the king alone. He, himself, determines the prices and to whom the Bostonians shall sell their leftover goods for a mere trifle. They deliver to the king iron, sailcloth, nails and other simple articles, wool cloth, red and blue thread, muskets, and gunpowder. Besides, the residents, the Eng-

---

* Tribesmen of King Kreiona [?], called Tergobu by Captain Cook. [Note in original.] The latter name is probably a copyist's slip in rendering the Russian version of Terreeoboo (Kalaniopuu), king of Hawaii at the time of Cook's visit.

lishmen and North Americans, in order to win the favor of the king, tell him stories about the superior qualities of the island's products and thus turn his head.

According to the journal which he [Hagemeister] has enclosed, he arrived at Maui on January 6, 1809, and at the island of Oahu January 12. On March 8 he departed from this island.

2. Letter of King Kaumualii, Through Captain J. Bennett, to Chief Manager A. A. Baranov, December 27, 1814, Asking for Trade. [in English]

Atooi [Kauai,] December 27 [,] 1814
Letter of King Tamari [Kaumualii] to the Governor Baranoff, per C. [sic.] Bennett.

Dear Sir:

I have the honour of presenting you with these few lines if they are acceptable [.] Sir [,] I received from Captn Bennett 50 muskets and 42 rifles but my people not being used to rifles [,] I would much rather have muskets with a large bore and long [;] withall I should like to have two hundred muskets and one hundred kegs of Powder and 40 Boxes of musket balls and 20 from Cannon of different sizes and 2 long Brass do and 20 Brass Muskets and please to send the cannon in good order with carriages, rammers [,] springer ladles [?] and worms [;] and I want 4 more such stills as I got the last time but rather bigger and I want 10 pieces of blue broad cloth and 5 pieces of red do and 5 pieces of blue duffel and 4 pieces of green cloth and 2 forges and 2 anvils and 2 pr of bellowses with the tools fit for a blacksmiths use and some carpenter tools such as saws & gimbles of different sizes etc. etc. [:] and when the ship comes down again I will have everything in readiness for her such as dry tarrow [taro], kukuees [candle nuts], salt and everything that the island affords without it is sandal wood and that I want to keep to buy a vessel with and I dare say we wont [sic] fall out about that and I should like to have a snug brick [brig] about 90 or 100 tons that was strong built with sails [,] rigging etc. I should like you to have the sandle [*sic*] wood and I should like to have her copperd [*sic*] and anything that is on the island that you want all you have to do is to send word and you shall have it for I take you for a friend if you will accept me as one and I should like to see you down to the island once as I have heard tell of you a great many times [.] Some of my people have seen you [.] my wife sends her best respects to you [.] So no more at present. from your sincere friend Towmoree King of Atooi & Onehaw [Niihau]

for Send, and answer the next return

X his mark

3. *Instructions, Baranov to Dr. G. A. Schäffer, October 1, 1815, on eve of Latter's Departure for Hawaii.*

From the Collegiate Councilor and Cavalier Baranov, Manager of the Novo-Arkhangel'sk Factory of the Russian-American Company under protection of His Imperial Majesty.
To the Collegiate Assessor, Egor Sheffer, Doctor of Medicine and Natural Science.*

INSTRUCTIONS

You have been informed of the unfortunate accident which occurred to the [Company's] three-masted ship, the *Bering,* how it was wrecked on the island of Kauai, and how the local king, Kaumualii, and his chief or minister, seized the cargo salvaged from the sea. The company thereby suffered a considerable loss of capital. It was proposed last July to use the ships *Suvorov* and *Otkrytie* for its recovery. But the first-named ship left this port without notice. So far as the other ship is concerned, the circumstances and profits of the Company prevented its despatch before completing the trade

---

* The titles of all persons serving the Russian state in civil, court, and military capacities were arranged in parallel columns in fourteen equivalent ranks. As a collegiate assessor, Schäffer had rank corresponding to that of an army captain; as a collegiate counsellor, Baranov was equivalent to a colonel.

with the natives along the straits. The ship left for there early in August, and may not return until December, unless the trade is very brisk. In the meanwhile, a way was discovered to reach the [Sandwich] islands by an American vessel. There, while waiting for our ships and using political means, you may win the favor of the chief king, Kamehameha. Through the latter it may be possible either to recover our cargo seized by King Kaumualii, or to obtain compensation in the form of local sandalwood. You are [already] in possession of certain information in regard to this possibility.

Until the return of the ships *Otkrytie* and *Chirikov*, and the repairing of the *Mirt-Kad'iak*, you will lose considerable time from the standpoint of profit and pleasure as regards any useful and scientific research in the three kingdoms of nature. The severity of the climate here will not allow you to continue your scientific work this fall and later in the winter. [In the meanwhile] the Sandwich Islands, situated in the best climate on earth, have an abundance of various water and land animals; you will find there extensive opportunities for discovering many rare things, because the eyes of the curious have not as yet penetrated the works of nature there.

For these reasons I am offering you a commission on the Pacific Sandwich Islands. You will proceed now on the American-Bostonian ship *Isabella*, under the command of Captain Tyler, who is going to Canton and intends to stop on the islands for supplies. If you reach the islands in safety, kindly undertake the fulfilment of the following commission:

1. You are to report to King Kamehameha and in my name ask his immediate protection until the arrival of our ships. Explain to him the position you hold, your rank of doctor of medical science, and your standing as a scholar of natural science and an investigator of the various forms of natural life, and tell him that it is in the latter capacity that you visit the islands and himself. You will have to prove it by devoting all your time in the beginning to this [scientific] work. From the very beginning try to win his [the king's] favor and to make him a friend. Not until you have done so are you to reveal to him the commission entrusted to you by me concerning either the restoration of our cargo by King Kaumualii or the payment of compensation for the cargo and copper taken from

the ship's sheathing, bolts, and nails. This payment is to be made in sandalwood, which, at the time of the arrival of our ships, should be in the harbor ready for delivery.

2. When you have gained the full confidence of the king, then bring to his attention the question of trading in sandalwood, either on the same basis and conditions as were granted to the American citizens Davis and the two Winship brothers, or under any other conditions which will be profitable to the Company and advantageous to the king. It should be kept in mind that during the last sale in Canton sandalwood was sold at nine dollars for a *pikul*. We here do not know as yet whether they have been selling it by weight or by amount, and you can find it out easier as soon as you have become acquainted with the foreigners and their families who have settled over there, as well as with the natives of the better class.

Among the latter, many travelers praise the king's minister highly for his cleverness, good nature, and courage. They call him Pitt, comparing him to the famous English minister. It will be useful to win the good will and friendship of this clever member of the court. It is also desirable to pay homage to the wives of the king, because here, as in Europe, they direct the king's wishes according to their own plans and intentions. Under all circumstances, however, be on guard against thievery from anybody, high or low, because none of them see anything wrong in it.

For such purposes as the drawing up of contracts and the purchase of sandalwood from King Kamehameha, you will receive some of the goods listed in the inventory, as well as one thousand piastres for payment of deposits. When our ships go there, they will carry goods and money from California. We cannot send much goods on foreign ships carrying many passengers, who may start intrigues, thus destroying all our plans in regard to the Sandwich Islands, with the possibility of bringing the English into competition with us.

3. I am not explaining to you the scientific work [you are to undertake] there—research and the discovery of new curiosities. I leave that to your knowledge and ability. By the discoveries you will make, you will demonstrate your gifts to the scholarly world. But also be sure to give credit to the Russian-American Company for its participation in this work of enlightenment.

In addition, I ask you to remember the request of His Excellency, Count Nikolai Petrovich Rumiantsev. You have a copy of his letter. This request must be fulfilled to his complete satisfaction. I will not waste words in regard to the policy you should adopt toward the subjects of many nations who are there engaged in different types of competition and are jealous of each other. I shall rely upon your good sense and ability not to miss any opportunity to advance the interests of the Company and the fatherland. You will not let yourself be caught by the clever tricks of such foreigners.

I am sending as presents to Kings Kamehameha and Kaumualii pieces for each of red fustian and to the first also a large silver medal attached to the ribbon of the order of St. Vladimir. These gifts are to be delivered on a proper occasion, but with caution, lest the foreigners give the king a malicious interpretation of their acceptance as a symbol of imposed subjection to Russia.

(On the original)
Collegiate Councilor and Cavalier
ALEXANDER BARANOV

Please find enclosed one large and three medium-sized medals with the ribbons of St. Vladimir.

No. 82
October 1, 1815
In comparison with the original, which was sent to the department of the Minister of the Interior, this copy is correct.
EGOR SHEFFER

4. *Letter, Baranov to King Kamehameha, about October 1, 1816, to be Delivered by Schäffer.*

1816
Most enlightened king, the sovereign ruler of all the Sandwich Islands, and the nearest neighbor of the Russian settlements, the great Kamehameha.

Dear Sir:
Perhaps you have been informed that at the end of the year 1814, the Russian ship named *Bering,* under the honored flag of Russia,

entrusted to an American, Captain Bennett, with the cargo in charge of the agent of the Company, Verkhovinskii, came to your island to buy provisions on its way from Okhotsk. At the island of Kauai, which is under the rule of Kaumualii and his chiefs, a storm drove it ashore. The whole cargo was saved and placed in local storehouses. There it was seized by Kaumualii and his chiefs, the owners of this island, who also plundered the wrecked ship. The crew was allowed to depart on another American boat for the Russian port Novo-Arkhangel'sk, which is under my control, and reached it safely.

We are sending the enclosed inventory of Russian property seized by the ruler Kaumualii and his chiefs, and, in addition to this, we want you to know that on these ships the bolts and nails, instead of being made of iron, were of copper. The [interior] was finished in velvet and the hull of the ship alone, with its reinforced ties, cost me 10,000 piastres, not counting the articles mentioned in the inventory.

Contrary to international usage, violence and insult were offered to the Russian nation, to its Autocrat, Sovereign, and Emperor, as well as to the so-called Russian-American Company on the Northwestern shores [of America], which is under his [the Emperor's] protection and my management. If a satisfactory compensation for the above-mentioned injury is not forthcoming, I shall consider it my duty to report to the Emperor. But first, I am addressing your Magnificence with the complaint and the following request:

As we have already mentioned, we are the closest neighbors because all other nations are separated from you by a great expanse of sea. It is most appropriate that we, rather than anyone else, should establish with you friendly and mutually advantageous commercial relations, as there are no obstacles to the conduct of extensive negotiations based on mutual profit.

Hoping that it will meet with your approval, I am purposely sending Egor Nikolaevich Sheffer, staff officer, third class, of the Russian Imperial Service, Collegiate Assessor, Doctor of Medicine and Natural Science. I am asking you to assist him within your power in the collection of scientific specimens and other works of nature found on your islands. For that I shall be duly grateful to you. Meanwhile, I am also asking you to order the above-mentioned ruler, Kaumualii, and his chiefs to return the property of the Company which they so insolently seized, namely, the actual articles stolen from the ship. If this property is scattered among the natives, it should be gathered as completely as possible. If it is lost irretrievably, compensation can be made in form of sandalwood. Mr. Sheffer has authority to act as an agent of the company in this matter. Otherwise, I shall know that you have no authority over this ruler [Kaumualii] and that you have no means of curtailing the insolence [with which he] breaks the peaceful law of hospitality and friendship.

You, the King, know yourself that no Russian ever gave you cause for dissatisfaction in regard to the treatment of the lowest of your islanders and that here your men are always accepted and treated benevolently and kindly. If Kaumualii does not satisfy our just demands, I shall be obliged to take measures myself in order to obtain just satisfaction and, with your permission, I shall treat him as an enemy.

Remaining as ever very respectfully an obedient servant of your Highness, I am
ALEXANDER BARANOV

5. Instructions, Baranov to Lieutenant I. A. Podushkin, February 15, 1816, on Departure for Hawaii.

February 15, 1816
To Iakov Anikievich [Podushkin], Lieutenant of the Russian Imperial Navy and Cavalier in the service of the Russian-American Company under the protection of His Imperial Majesty.

INSTRUCTIONS

To His Honor, Mr. Podushkin   February 15, 1816
My dear Sir:
Some time ago your Honor was given an oral request to prepare the armed ship *Otkrytie* for the journey to the Sandwich Islands.

You already know the purpose of the expedition. It has to do with the return of the property seized from the company's vessel *Bering* in January, 1815, by Kaumualii, the ruler of the island Kauai, and which consisted of the cargo, arms, and the copper parts of the ship. The ship, but slightly damaged, was cast ashore by the storm close to the very residence of the ruler of the island and it remained there. On board were an American master, Bennett, and a supercargo, Verkhovinskii, who left the island in May of the same year on the American ship *Albatross*. [The *Bering*] with but slight damages, aside from what was stolen by the islanders, remained intact on the shore. The cargo, instead of being stored in the ruler's storehouse, was retained by the latter and by his assistant, the so-called chief. Such an outrage is contrary to the usages of all enlightened nations. Therefore, in order to demand the return of the cargo and ship, Mr. Sheffer, Collegiate Assessor and Doctor of Medicine, was sent there on the American-Bostonian ship *Isabella,* which was en route to Canton.

He [Sheffer] was instructed to remain on the island belonging to King Kamehameha and the residence of the latter. He was to present a complaint in my name against the outrageous conduct of the above-mentioned ruler, Kaumualii, and he was to ask aid or mediation, so that the company could get back its property, which was illegally seized. At the same time he was to try to induce the king [Kamehameha] to conclude an agreement for mutual trade in sandal- or aromatic-wood in Canton and Manila. The agreement was to be of advantage to both sides; the conditions were to be the same as those agreed on with Davis and Winship, on the basis of a limited period of time. The term for the agreements [with Davis and Winship] lapsed a long time ago, and they are now prohibited by King Kamehameha and the ruler, Kaumualii, either to acquire or to export the wood from the islands. They [Davis and Winship] traded for four years and made very large profits. If the king would not consent to a similar agreement [with the Company] then [Sheffer] was to make some temporary arrangements which would protect the interests of the Company.

At the present time we do not know what concessions, if any, Dr. Sheffer was able to secure in the above-mentioned matters. He has had no opportunity to write to inform us.

Under such circumstances, I decided, in order not to lose valuable time, to hasten the departure of ships to the islands, although they [our ships] are also needed for other profitable expeditions. Otherwise the American-Bostonian ships, by their intrigues, may entirely destroy our plan with regard to sandalwood trade, because they are also interested in this business. The ship *Otkrytie,* under your command, is already armed, loaded with cargo and ballast, filled with provisions, and ready for sailing. I recommend that you pull up anchor and leave this port. Kindly take advantage of the first favorable wind and raise sail. Your destination is [to go] directly to the above-mentioned islands. In a short time, as soon as it is ready, the ship *Mirt-Kad'iak* will follow you.

When you reach these islands in safety, I recommend that you make use of the following suggestions, provided the circumstances do not prevent it.

1. When, with God's help, you reach the above-mentioned islands, try to get to the residence of King Kamehameha. Perhaps you will find Dr. Sheffer there. When you see Sheffer, gather from him information about all the events which have occurred there. A copy of our letter to Sheffer is enclosed. Take it into consideration when you receive information from Dr. Sheffer about the local situation. Hold a general council. Also invite Verkhovinskii. If our ship *Mirt-Kad'iak* is there, also ask George Young and Toropogritskii to the council. Then decide what measures it will be necessary to undertake. If the ruler Kaumualii will not consent peacefully to pay for the ship *Bering* and its cargo, which he seized by force, then try to persuade King Kamehameha to render you such assistance as is in his power. Bring him to your side by pointing out the advantages he could secure over the ruler Kaumualii. When you arrive on the island Kauai, join forces with the *Mirt-Kad'iak.* If Dr. Sheffer has not succeeded in negotiating peacefully with Kaumualii before your arrival, then approach the island with united forces and demand from the ruler the peaceful satisfaction of our just pretensions—[compensation] for the outrageous seizure of the company's property and for the insult to the flag of the Russian nation.

At first, exhaust all methods which might achieve your ends

peacefully. But if he [Kaumualii] fails to respond to peaceful negotiations, then it might be necessary to give him a lesson in the form of military chastisement. Its nature should be determined by your strength and by general considerations. Spare, however, as much as possible, human beings and blood, not only for your men, but of the enemies as well, if God will help you to defeat them. In such an event, the whole island Kauai should be taken in the name of our Sovereign Emperor of all the Russias and become a part of his possessions. It seems that neither the English nor any other nations have rights there and [Englishmen] consider only the islands of Kamehameha as their own, on a weak claim that these islands were first discovered by Englishmen.

2. But if you are lucky and if God helps you, you will persuade the ruler to settle matters peacefully by the voluntary return of the entire cargo and the ship. The ship is then to be taken apart or burned right there; all the copper, as well as the iron, used in the equipment is to be gathered and loaded on our ships. In addition, these ships [*Otkrytie* and *Mirt-Kad'iak*] are to be loaded with the returned cargo from the *Bering* or with sandalwood. Payment for the wood is to be made according to the written estimates given to supercargo Verkhovinskii. Value the wood according to prices exacted by King Kamehameha from Davis and Winship. This wood was last sold in Canton by these mariners at the rate of one *pikul,* or our 3¾ *puds,* for nine dollars.

There are good and bad varieties of sandalwood. Because of that it will be necessary to find out from the residents of long standing, Europeans and American-Bostonians, about different sorts of wood, provided that our doctor in his capacity of naturalist has not learned as yet about them during his stay on the islands. Besides, you can experiment. Reduce the wood pulp to powder and put it on a glowing coal. The odor will indicate which is the better kind. That with the stronger odor is better; the one with the weak odor is poor. There are also ways of judging the quality of growing trees by their bark.

As soon as you succeed in persuading this ruler, Kaumualii, and King Kamehameha to use the wood as compensation, try to enter into negotiations with them about a contract for the next few years for the delivery of wood to be sold in China and Manila.

3. When you have enough to load both ships fully with the aromatic wood obtained as compensation, by purchase or by virtue of contract, then send one of them to Macao, and another here. It is suggested that you send the ship *Kad'iak* to Macao. Send Toropogritskii on this ship, because he has been in China and knows the Swedish consul [in Macao], Mr. Ljungstedt, who will act as commissioner for the whole cargo sent to Macao.

4. It is possible that you may suffer bad luck in all the matters mentioned above because of intrigues of Americans and Englishmen, who suspect rivalry everywhere. They might prejudice King Kamehameha and the ruler, Kaumualii, so that the latter would not be willing to enter into contract with us. In that case, provided that no Americans have gone to visit our northwestern shores, send the ship *Mirt-Kad'iak* for the purpose of buying furs. Proceed into the straits where you already have been and visit places abundant in furs. The ship is to be supplied with proper goods. But if some of the American merchants have already gone to our shores, then continue the voyage of the *Mirt-Kad'iak* toward the shores of New Albion into the small port of Little Bodega, below our new settlement, Ross. Deposit there the remaining cargo and exchange it for local goods. There are probably enough wheat, salt, and other articles which you could bring here by sea.

And you [the ship *Otkrytie*] are to come here directly from the Sandwich Islands so as not to miss the navigation to Okhotsk during the summer of the current year. Use the goods shipped with supercargo Verkhovinskii and supplied by Dr. Sheffer, which are on the ship entrusted to you, for trade. In addition to sandalwood, get local products in every place you may happen to be. We need most of all: pork, hemp or the grass used by the islanders to make their fish-nets, combustible nuts for [——] oil, a small amount of dry taro, garden vegetables and, as a trial, a small quantity of tobacco and rum, also ropes made of bark for tow ropes and halyards. There is an abundance of salt, but get only as much as will be necessary for salting meat. We do not need [salt] because big supplies of it are stored in California and there is plenty of it in the storehouses here. An exception can be made if the cost of it is very low—less than 50 kopeks per pud. In that case, you can take 500 to 2,000 puds. It will be necessary to prepare supplies of beef, salted and dried. After asking permission of the owners, use your own men for shooting cattle, of which great numbers have become wild there.

In case of a shortage of barrels, you can salt the meat on ship by making boxes in the interior foot waling. The Americans are doing that in California and the meat does not spoil for a long time. These provisions, especially pork, would be useful not only in our American-Company regions, but in Kamchatka and Okhotsk as well.

5. You have twenty-seven hunters with thirteen baidarkas from Kad'iak and Alaska, who can add to the appearance and increase the number of the ship's crew. They are all efficient and courageous men, hunting animals and birds. In the event that peaceful and pleasant relationships prevail, they can entertain the rulers of the islands by their dress and exploits; in case of hostilities, they will be useful with firearms, especially if it is necessary to undertake an attack at night, in fog or darkness.

After the completion of business on the islands, if the ship *Kad'iak* does not sail to Macao and the straits along our shores but takes the course to the Albion coast instead, then send all these hunters there, with the exception of the translator, Andrei Aiagvik Aleksinskii from Nikitynankov. All these hunters are heavily in debt, and they will be able to improve their fortunes because of the abundance of animals there. If, however, [the departure of the *Mirt-Kad'iak* toward Albion] does not take place, then send them all back here, while the guns and pistols of the Company may be sold if there is a demand for them and if they can be sold with profit.

6. You are accompanied by two boys from the school of Filip Kashevarov: Petr Malakov and Ivan Chumovitskii. They write and know arithmetic. Let the apprentice in navigation, Ivan Chernov, who is with you, teach them navigation. Instruct that they be taught theory and practice gradually, and begin it with the study of the compass, heaving the log, and marking the course according to the rhumb. The boys should help him [Chernov] in navigation by taking the watch in turn. When at anchor they should study the rules and the theory of navigation. If necessary, they should assist supercargo Verkhovinskii in trade and in the inspection and protection of the cargo. Since they have reached maturity, and

cannot stay in school any longer, they should try to apply themselves toward being useful to the Company and not to be parasites, because enough money has been spent for their schooling. They should also be taught the use of firearms.

7. Check the provisions and supplies according to the inventory in possession of Verkhovinskii. He has been told to use first those supplies which are likely to spoil, especially in a hot climate, such as salted [——] California dried meat, and especially herrings, which are for the use of hunters, who must use them together with boiled wheat and fat. The biscuits, grits, and flour are to be used economically by everybody. Wheat is to be used daily, until you get the proper substitute [for bread] produced on the Sandwich Islands, and once over there, having stored pork and other products, you will have to provide special food rations for the crew. You will give directions to the supercargo about the quantity and kind of daily rations according to what you have stored and what provisions will be available at that time. Everybody must have the same kind of provisions; no personal discrimination should be allowed among the crew, with the exception of the apprentice and supercargo or [——] , if anybody must have them.

8. The crew and passengers on the ship entrusted to you will be under your command and under your humane and sympathetic care. If, by God's will, anybody becomes ill or as a result of the weakness of human nature commits unintentional errors, such men should be excused. The greater number of the men are without much experience, and not used to strict military and naval discipline. They should learn it, however, and the careless and lazy should be punished. Sick men, if, God forbid, you have them, should be put under the care of Dr. Sheffer as soon as you arrive in the islands.

May the all-powerful God help you to succeed in your important expedition, to your great honor.

Very respectfully, I am and shall remain,
my dear sir, your obedient servant,
(The original signed) ALEXANDER BARANOV
Verified in the office of A. Baranov

P.S. If during your stay on the Sandwich Island, our Russian-American Company ships and those of Count Rumiantsev chance to come there to get provisions, ask their commanders and officers for help, if local circumstances require such action.

6. Further Instructions, Baranov to Podushkin, February 15, 1816, on Departure for Hawaii.

Instructions by Alexander Baranov to Captain [!] Podushkin, February 15, 1816, concerning the case of the ship *Bering,* wrecked on the Island of Kauai.

I am sending to you the bill of sale for this ship [issued] by Captain Bennett, drawn up in the English language, and signed by him and by three witnesses, commanders of other ships. In case of inquiry, this document is to be presented to the commanders of foreign and Russian ships as proof of ownership by the Russian-American Company of the ship *Bering,* together with its cargo. Enclosed find the clearance papers from the commandant of Okhotsk, testifying that the Sandwich Islands were the ship's destination.

I am sending Your Honor copies of the documents containing information in regard to the capital invested by the Company in the ship, the cost of the cargo, provisions, and other items seized by Kaumualii, the ruler of the island Kauai; the originals are being sent to Dr. Sheffer. These documents are to be used when circumstances require and if the ruler, Kaumualii, is willing to negotiate peacefully. I am confident that you, together with Dr. Sheffer, will liquidate this disagreeable incident.

If, God willing, you succeed in winning the favor of King Kamehameha, then ask his permission for us to start a factory on the island of Oahu, where the Americans, the Winship brothers, used to have one. In the past, the king showed many favors to the latter, but now he is not well disposed toward them. Taking advantage of these circumstances, reach an agreement with the king about the sale of sandalwood for a number of years. You may leave Verkhovinskii there [in Oahu], with about six Russians and about as many hunters. Later you may add to them as many more men as will be necessary. Perhaps if he is sufficiently friendly, the king himself may attach some of his subjects [to your factory], a favor previously granted to many others.

On the same island of Oahu, there have lived for many years with their families a Spaniard named Marina [Marin] and either an American or Englishman named Mr. Holm. Both enjoy the not inconsiderable confidence of the king. Therefore, it might be worth while to show kindness to them, for otherwise they might prejudice the king [against you] by their intrigues. The king has our girl Barbara from Kad'iak, who speaks both the Russian and Sandwich languages well. She was taken there from Kad'iak by Captain O'Cain at the end of the year 1806 or about nine and a half years ago, and she served as a translator between Kuzminov and the king. Win her over with presents because she might be trusted better as a translator than foreigners during the negotiations with the king. With the king's consent you might take her also to Kaumualii, where she also might be useful.

Manager
(The original signed)
GOVERNOR BARANOV

The copy, as compared with the original which was sent to the Ministry of the Interior, is true.

EGOR SHEFFER

7. *Letter, Baranov to Schäffer, February 10, 16, 26, 1816, to be Delivered by Lieutenant Podushkin.*

To His Honor, Mr. Sheffer, Collegiate Assessor, Doctor of Medicine and Natural Science

From the port of Novo-Arkhangel'sk
February 10/22, 1816

My dear Sir, Egor Nikolaevich.

Excuse me for delaying the departure of the ships up to the present time. Contrary to [our] wishes, the *Otkrytie* returned from the straits as early as October 9, after accomplishing very little of any value, because the attacks of the savage natives made trade impossible. The ship itself required serious overhauling: the rigging had to be repaired and many new sails had to be put on. The repair, armament, and loading of ballast continued until nearly the end of January. Meanwhile, another ship, the *Mirt-Kad'iak,* also required repairs and needed new rigging and sails. The *Mirt-Kad'iak* will proceed to you [to the Sandwich Islands] following the *Otkrytie,* after being loaded with timber for sailyards, top masts, etc., which probably could be used in barter trade on the islands or in Macao when the ship is sent there. The order to Lieutenant and Cavalier Podushkin, advising him to hasten to [join] you with the ship *Otkrytie,* remains in force. After his arrival, kindly give him the local news and tell him about the commission which was entrusted to you. If there is a hope of satisfying the claim against Kaumualii, the owner of the island Kauai, then take the *Otkrytie* to that island. This claim consists of the demand for compensation for the cargo and the ship with its armaments, copper ties, and planks. At the time that Bennett and Verkhovinskii left the island, the ship was still intact, with only slight damage caused by the wreck during the storm. The cargo, however, was looted and plundered by the above-mentioned owner of the island, Kaumualii, and his chief. Kaumualii must pay for his loot and for the ship, if the latter has been destroyed and the copper parts removed. The payment may consist of sandalwood, as I have already explained in previous instructions, and by [return of] anchors and other articles mentioned in the inventory, of which we are in great need. Return immediately with the cargo, because in May or June the ship *Otkrytie* is supposed to take a cargo of furs from this port and from the seal islands directly to Okhotsk. An early return is imperative in order [that the ship] may be here when the time is favorable for navigation. You can remain there a little longer until the arrival of the other ship, the *Mirt-Kad'iak,* which is also to be loaded. If circumstances are favorable, either obtain sandalwood in payment for the damages, or purchase various local products. For such purchases, you have for sale goods listed in the enclosed inventory. In addition, more goods of a high quality will be sent to you, as listed in the enclosed copy of the account of supercargo Pavel

Verkhovinskii. The latter, under your supervision, is to be in charge of the examination and evaluation of the goods [used in trade] because he already has some experience from his work with Captain Bennett.

If the situation is different from what was anticipated above—if there is no hope of securing satisfaction and settlement of our claims for the ship and cargo from the ruler Kaumualii—then wait for the ship *Mirt-Kad'iak* near the islands belonging to King Kamehameha. [Then] with both ships proceed to the island Kauai and first propose to Kaumualii and his chief peaceful terms for the satisfaction of our claims, which are in accordance with international law. If Kaumualii consents to meet our demands, then the best method would be to induce him and his chief to visit the ship and to detain him there until payment is made. But if these naturally arrogant savages are obstinate, then treat them as enemies, taking into consideration the circumstances and forces at your disposal. God will assist the just cause. It may not be a bad idea to ask King Kamehameha for aid, in case there is no close friendship or agreement [between Kamehameha and Kaumualii]. Reassure Kamehameha with promises and, if necessary, conquer Kaumualii by force of arms. Consult Iakov Anikievich [Podushkin] about it. If, with the Lord's aid, our peaceful intentions are brought to the desired end by peaceful measures, without spilling human blood, which is what I sincerely desire, then use every possible and persistent effort to make contacts with both rulers, Kamehameha and Kaumualii, in regard to providing for the sale of sandal- or [other] fragrant wood on the basis of their former agreements with the American-Bostonian navigators Davis and Winship. Upon your departure you received instructions to this effect and if you succeed in reaching an agreement, then give them all the remaining property in return for cash and promise to pay for the [sandalwood] thus provided either in Russian or Chinese goods, as they prefer, and guarantee the certain delivery of these goods.

In addition, if you find yourself at a disadvantage and in serious need of help, [remember] that, as you already know, the Main Office of the Russian-American Company informed us in its instructions that last year, 1815, two ships were to be sent from St.

Petersburg into these regions, one a large Company vessel, the other a small vessel belonging to His Excellency Count Nikolai Petrovich Rumiantsev. It is likely that they will arrive here in April or May and before that time they will visit the Sandwich Islands to get fresh supplies of food, as is being done by ships making a round-the-world journey. When these ships arrive safely at these [Sandwich] islands, you will have the pleasure of meeting the commanders and officers. In case of need, show them all my instructions, because they [the instructions] do not contain anything except concern over the advantages for the fatherland and the Company to be gained if a new branch of [our] trade is established on these islands which will be profitable to the parties involved [the Russians and the Sandwich natives].

Our schooner *Chirikov,* under the command of Mr. Benzemann, arrived here from Albion and the Spanish port of San Francisco soon after your departure last year, on October 6, 1815. The *Chirikov* brought a cargo of wheat, some dried beef, a small amount of furs, but no piastres, because the brig *Il'mena* had not visited the shores of California but was being repaired in the port of Rumiantsev. For this purpose [to obtain cash in piastres] and to obtain furs, it went again in September almost at the same time that the *Chirikov* left for here.

Glory be to God, everything there is well, the relations with the Spaniards are good, and only the English near the coast have started competition with our trade. As to local news, you will be interested to learn that our ship *Suvorov* was there, stopping at San Francisco on August 8, just when Benzemann on the *Chirikov* awaited there the cargo bought by Mr. Kuskov. Benzemann was told that [the *Suvorov*] was there for overhauling, purchasing food, obtaining fresh water and wood [fuel] for the long journey to Lima, where it was to sell the ship's cargo, and thence to Cape Horn. I hear only from Lieutenant Shveikovskii, and then but briefly. There is a letter from Krasil'nikov to G. Molvo; apparently he has received German's post of imbibing freely and easily. He did not write either to Mr. Kuskov or to me.

On the same day the *Chirikov* arrived, the brig *Finlandia* from Okhotsk stopped here en route to the Andreianov islands. The ship is not of much value but, thank the Lord, it has enough men, including fifty who have just entered the service. It brought me a great deal of pleasant and unpleasant correspondence which is, however, without any interest to you, and besides almost all is the old news of Russia and Europe received on the *Suvorov* and the *Otkrytie* [and] from the *Bering*.

I send you my regards and wish you good health. [I hope] for your safe return and success in the matters entrusted to you.

Dear Sir, your obedient servant,
ALEXANDER BARANOV

February 16, 1816
Port Novo-Arkhangel'sk

P.S. Enclosed find copies of the instructions given to Lieutenant Cavalier Podushkin. Kindly follow such directions which you find therein as are not included in your own instructions, particularly in regard to the sending of the ship [*Mirt*] *Kad'iak* to the straits or to the port of Small Bodega [Rumiantsev] in Albion in case it is not able to obtain sandalwood. If, however, you get enough sandalwood to load both ships, then, if you do not deem it desirable to go there yourself and would prefer to go on the *Otkrytie,* send the [*Mirt*] *Kad'iak* to Macao with Toropogritskii in charge. I am sending you exact copies of the letters of Krasil'nikov and Lieutenant Shveikovskii from the ship *Suvorov* in San Francisco, as well as the instructions given by Mr. Lazarev to Krasil'nikov. [These letters] will satisfy your curiosity and will serve to explain certain happenings. I must add that possibly letters from these men were sent through Mr. Kuskov or on our brig *Il'mena,* which I am daily expecting. Perhaps its arrival will explain the letter from [——].

Your obedient servant
A. BARANOV

February 26, 1816

In comparison with the original sent to the department of the Minister of the Interior, it is correct.

EGOR SHEFFER

8. *Letter, Baranov to Schäffer, February 26, 1816.*

February 26, 1816

My dear Sir, Egor Nikolaevich.

In my official letter to you which was given to Iakov Anikievich [Podushkin] in an envelope sealed with the seal of the office and which he will forward to you, I have mentioned briefly the letters from the *Suvorov;* a copy of them was also given to Mr. Podushkin. In addition to the postscript of the letter, the copies of the letters from the *Suvorov* and the instructions to Mr. Podushkin were given in a special envelope to Verkhovinskii, whom I am asking you to take under your protection.

If, with God's help, you win the favor of King Kamehameha, then obtain permission to start our factory on the island Oahu, where the Americans, the Winships, had theirs. The king was very favorably disposed toward them for several years but their accord was destroyed, possibly through the intrigues of the English. Under such circumstances, it might be possible to induce the king to let us have sandalwood for some years to come. Then leave Verkhovinskii there with about six men from the crew and an equal number of hunters; later increase their number, if necessary. Perhaps the king will assign some of his subjects to you, if you win his favor. He does it for others. There are on the same island, together with their families, a Spaniard, Marina [Marin], and either an American or Englishman, Gom [Holmes]. They enjoy the full confidence of the king; therefore be nice to them, so that they will not attempt to influence the ruler by intrigues [hostile to us].

There is also at the king's court a Kad'iak girl, Barbara, who speaks Russian fluently and the Sandwich languages well. She acted as a translator between Kuzminov and the king. She was carried away from Kad'iak by Captain O'Cain at the end of 1806, or about nine and one-half years ago. She ought to be given presents and used in negotiations with the king. That will be better than to rely on foreigners. You can also take her for the negotiations with Kaumualii, if such take place.

I have the honor to remain, with proper regards for you,

My dear Sir, your obedient servant

ALEXANDER BARANOV

February 26, 1816
Port Novo-Arkhangel'sk

In comparison with the original sent to the department of the Minister of Interior, this copy is correct.

EGOR SHEFFER

9. *Letter, Schäffer to the Main Office, January 1, 1816, Describing Affairs at Hawaii.*

Received January 8, 1817
To the State Russian-American Company in St. Petersburg.
Report of Dr., Assessor Egor de Sheffer.

In undertaking the journey on the ship *Suvorov,* my chief objective was scientific research. After Captain Lazarev frustrated my plans, with the aid of the governor of Novo-Arkhangel'sk, Collegiate Councilor Baranov, I found other means to achieve my wishes. This is the reason why I am here at present on the island Hawaii, which is the largest of the Sandwich Islands. I am now [at the court of] King Kamehameha, not only as a naturalist but [also] as an agent of the Imperial Russian-American Company, which last January lost the ship *Bering* on another of these islands, Kauai. I have every confidence that I shall recover the [vessel's] valuable cargo, worth about 20,000 piastres. Already I have gained the friendship and confidence of the great King Kamehameha, whom I am treating for heart trouble. I also succeeded in curing his favorite wife, Queen Kaahumanu, of yellow fever.

I shall send a part of every collection of [specimens of] natural history, which I am preparing, to the main office in St. Petersburg; today I have sent the first shipment to Canton on the American vessel *Millwood* under Captain Bailey, and you will receive it through the Swedish Consul in Canton, Mr. Anders Ljungstedt, and through Mr. Wertin in Lisbon. Kindly pay the latter the expenses of transportation according to his estimate. I am sending similar collections to His Excellency Count Nikolai Petrovich and His Excellency, Minister of the Interior Kozodavlev. [From the Company's collection] kindly spare one bread plant for State Councilor and Court Physician Mr. Stofregen.

If I receive instructions to remain here for some time, I hope I shall be able to acquire the trade monopoly in sandalwood for the Company. I arrived here from Novo-Arkhangel'sk about four weeks ago on the American ship *Isabella*. Since my arrival I have succeeded in offsetting the effect of malicious information spread here by William [!] B. Hunt of the Astor Company and by other Americans, and I restored the confidence of the king and the people. I would have had difficulty in defending the honor of the Russians and one of the Company were it not for the aid of several decent people; among them I must recommend to you specially Mr. Jennings, the captain of the English schooner *Columbia*.

The ship *Suvorov* was in the port of San Francisco and was about to depart for Lima.

DR. EGOR DE SHEFFER

Hawaii, January 1, 1817 [!—1816]

10. *Letter, King Kaumualii, Through Captain John Ebbets, "to any Russian Ship Commander," February 5, 1816, Stating That Furs on the* Bering *Were to be Taken to Sitka by Ebbets* [*in English*].

Atooi [Kauai] 5th February, 1816

Copies

Sir.

At the desire of Tomooerrie [Kaumualii], King of this island[,] I have left with him these few lines to inform you that the King has delivered me on account of Governor Baranoff what furs were in the Russian Ship *Behring* at the time she was lost.—and has promised to give up what property he has in his possession that was saved from the wreck and for that lost to pay for in the produce of the island.—this offer *I hope* will *prevent* any measures that may lead to hostilities from being *adopted*—the King assuring me of his sincere desire to be in peace with your nation and to carry on a friendly commerce with Governor Baranoff[.]

Yours

JOHN EBBETS

Commander of the Ship *Enterprise* of New York to the Commander of any Russian ship that may arrive at Atooi.—

11. *Letter, King Kaumualii to Baranov, February 5, 1816, Offering Restitution for cargo of the* Bering [*in English*].

Atooi [Kauai], 5th February, 1816

Governor Baranov, Sir:

It being my sincere desire to be in peace with your nation and [in order] that you may not think otherwise I have thought proper to write you a few lines by our mutual friend Cpt. Ebbets & by him have sent you that you may be convinced of my sincerity what furs were in the ship Behring at the time she was wrecked—much of the property on board her such as salt, the oil nuts, vegetables etc. was lost: but if your excellency will send a ship direct to this island I will on application made from you deliver her commander what Russian property I have and for that lost will repay him in the produce of this island. This you cannot consider but very fair it being my wish to be in amity with you and to carry on a trade to our mutual advantage. In this business it is my desire to treat solely with your agent—none of the Chiefs of the other islands having any concern therein.

I am—etc.

TOMARREE   X   his mark

TOANAUHE   X   his mark

12. *Act of Allegiance of King Kaumualii to Emperor Alexander I of Russia, May 21, 1816.*

Copy

His Majesty, Kaumualii, the king of the Sandwich Islands in the North Pacific Ocean, Kauai, and Niihau, and hereditary prince of the islands Oahu, Lanai, and Maui, asks His Majesty, Sovereign Emperor Alexander Pavlovich, Autocrat of All the Russias, etc., etc., etc., to accept under his protection the above-mentioned islands. He [Kaumualii], for himself and for his successor, wishes to profess loyalty to the Russian scepter. As a sign of his faithfulness and devotion he [Kaumualii] accepts the Russian flag from the ship *Otkrytie,* which belongs to the Russian-American Company.

Sign of the king   X   KAUMUALII

Translated into the Sandwich language and announced by the king himself to the inhabitants of the islands Kauai and Niihau.

Russian Imperial Collegiate Assessor,
Commissioner of the Russian-American Company,
Doctor of Medicine and Surgery
EGOR DE SHEFFER

Read on the ship *Otkrytie* in the presence of the total crew—thirty-eight men.

Naval Lieutenant and Cavalier PODUSHKIN

May 21, 1816, Island Kauai, port Waimea, ship *Otkrytie*

13. *Award of Honorary Naval Rank to King Kaumualii, May 21, 1816.*

According to the voluntary alliance of Kaumualii, king of the Sandwich Islands Kauai and Niihau, with Alexander Pavlovich, the Sovereign Emperor, Autocrat of all the Russias, etc., etc., etc., on the occasions of visits by foreigners who come to these islands, as well as on any other occasions, King Kaumualii is to be given all honors which belong to the rank of a line-staff officer of His Imperial Majesty's navy.

(Original signed) *Russian Commissioners*
EGOR SHEFFER
GRIGORII TERENT'EV

May 21, 1816

14. *Contract Between King Kaumualii and Schäffer, May 21, 1816.*

No. 3 (Copy)

The undersigned has concluded the following contract:

1. King Kaumualii will deliver to the Russian-American Company whatever cargo of the wrecked ship *Bering* he was able to salvage.

2. King Kaumualii promises to trade exclusively with the Russian-American Company. In the case of American ships, he is to sell them only provisions.

3. The king will allow the Company to establish factories everywhere in his possessions and he will aid with his men in the erection of buildings and in the development of plantations.

4. The king will furnish provisions for any Russian vessel. For a small payment to the Russian-American Company the king will receive as much goods from the cargo as he needs, and besides he will receive from the cargo of the *Otkrytie* as much goods as will cover the year's delivery of sandalwood. I, myself, will judge how much sandalwood can be loaded on the *Otkrytie*. In six months the cargo should be ready and the Company undertakes to supply the king with a fully armed ship, and in return the king will again deliver as much sandalwood as the *Otkrytie* or a similar ship can carry. This delivery should be ready a year after the first one has been made. The next load should be ready in eighteen months, and for every stipulated delivery of sandalwood the king will receive

whatever goods he is pleased to take. The Company will leave the vessel at the Sandwich Islands until the king receives [——] taro-roots which the king will deliver free. The Company will immediately send a messenger to St. Petersburg to make a report to the Emperor and to deliver the king's request for protection. The king gave permission for preparations here of mineralogical, botanical, and zoological collections.

> *The Russian staff officer, Commissioner*
> *of the Russian-American Company*
> Dr. Egor de Sheffer
> (Seal) Sign X Kaumualii

May 21, 1816, Island Kauai, port Waimea, ship *Otkrytie*

15. *Award of Medal to Prince Kaukari Tautuno of Kauai, May 21, 1816.*

A large silver medal, on the ribbon of St. Vladimir, is bestowed upon Kaukari Tautuno, prince of the Sandwich Island of Kauai, as a sign of his loyalty and alliance. This medal, to be worn on all occasions of visits by foreign and Russian ships and at all assemblies, entitles its owner to all privileges which are established for its bearers by his Imperial Majesty Alexander Pavlovich.

> (The original signed) *Staff officer of the Russian Imperial Service,*
> *Commissioner of the Russian-American Company*
> Egor Sheffer

May 21, 1816

16. *Journal Kept by Lieutenant Podushkin, March 9–June 2, 1816 (Extract).*

> 1816
> June

The ship *Otkrytie* of the Russian-American Company, under the protection of His Imperial Majesty.

On March 3, 1816, at nine o'clock in the morning, under a strong northeasterly wind, I weighed the anchor with only one fluke and left the port of Novo-Arkhangel'sk [———]. Because of strong squalls we held to 50 latitude and then took a course toward the Sandwich Islands. During the journey there was nothing worth mentioning except that we saw a large herd of seals about 29° 28' north latitude and 141° 20' longitude from Greenwich, from which I conclude that there must be an island in this vicinity. Crossed the North Tropic [of Cancer]. Took direction toward the island of Hawaii. Arrived there on April 13 and dropped anchor on the northwestern side of the island, opposite the village of Kawaihae, where King Kamehameha, ruler of almost all of the islands, has his residence.

The next morning I sent a man to request a meeting with the king. He could not refuse me and so I went ashore in a boat with six oarsmen who composed my retinue and who made a great impression on the king. He also liked my uniform so much that he shamelessly asked for it, whereupon I told him that I could not give it to him without the permission of our emperor. The king frankly stated that he had heard that Russian ships would arrive soon to take over his possessions. I reassured him in this respect as far as I could, [but] in the end he was still in doubt. I asked him to give me a man through whom I could obtain provisions on the islands of Maui and Oahu. He agreed and asked me to send some Aleuts ashore the next day to show him their dances. I took my leave. Using signs and without touching [each other] we expressed mutual friendship.

The king's first councilor, a middle-aged Englishman named Young, invited me to his house. After spending about half an hour there I asked him to visit the ship. We went together and had a dinner for which his own pigs were slaughtered. I had only to keep pouring him more grog as an appetizer and invent new toasts in his honor. As a result he became quite intoxicated. After dinner he looked over [our] goods, received a few gifts, and departed in the best of spirits.

The next morning I went ashore accompanied by a convoy of

twenty baidarkas and a boat, with the oarsmen in red caps. The men fell into military formation, and an enormous crowd accompanied us to the residence of the king. The wild exclamations of the Aleuts and their spectacular dancing delighted both the king and the crowd. After staying there for an hour, I ordered the men to return to the beach and told the king that I proposed to lift anchor, which was done. The king sent a messenger asking me to stay another day and to come ashore [again]. I complied with the request and he received us very kindly, even, I might say, cordially. I received from him ten large fishes, taro, and potatoes. The king, however, insisted on our bringing a howitzer [*edinorog*] ashore. I tried to dissuade him from that by telling him that I had no rowing boat which could hold it. The king then offered to send his double canoe the following day and I had to make the concession.

On the sixteenth [of April] a boat came to take the howitzer. We put it on the boat and went ashore ourselves. When the cannon was ready for action, it was discharged. A grenade was shot toward the sea, where it exploded. The king was so delighted that he wanted to buy the howitzer immediately, but we sternly refused to sell it, telling him that there would be no trade, because our commissioner was not present. [I told him that I] would go and return as soon as possible. The king told me he would wait for me and promised to abstain from trading with anyone else until my return. For ten pieces of sailcloth [raven's duck] I bought forty pigs and for sixty axes I got thirty bundles of bast fiber. During the trading I entertained the king [——]: the sailors sang songs. But as the hour struck, I told the king that it was time to return to the ship. The king bade me a friendly farewell and, what was especially pleasant, we exchanged kisses, in the Russian manner.

Although I took my leave, I had to spend the night at anchor by request of the king, and wait because the next night was taboo. At ten o'clock a northeasterly wind caused a strong squall, forcing us to drift all night, and at eleven o'clock in the morning we had to drop anchor on the corals.

On the seventeenth [of April] at five o'clock in the morning we raised anchor and went to the island of Maui, and at seven o'clock in the evening of the eighteenth we dropped anchor in Lahaina. The beautiful appearance and abundance [of natural products?] of this place made it seem to us a paradise in comparison with the northwestern coast of America, but we did not stay there long. I should have obtained thirty pigs there, but to get them would have required seven days. I did not want to remain there [so long] and, after filling five barrels with water and obtaining only six pigs, I raised anchor on the twenty-first and dropped it again at eleven o'clock in the morning at the island of Oahu; on the twenty-third I came to the harbor of Honolulu. Here I lowered the top mast, repaired the rigging, calked the deck, repaired the hull of the ship as far as possible, and replenished the water supply.

On May 5 we left the harbor with Dr. Sheffer on board, and went to pick up his cargo from Hawaii. On May 11 we reached the village of Kailua, where we dropped anchor and went ashore. The king met me again with a kiss in the Russian manner and showed signs of affection for me. Because I was under orders to follow the doctor's instructions, I obeyed his commands, lowered the long boat, picked up his cargo, and on May 14 at seven o'clock in the evening I lifted anchor and went to the island of Kauai, where, on May 17, I dropped anchor at the mouth of the small river Waimea.

The bottom of this harbor is of sand mixed with clay, reaching to a depth of about twenty *sazhens*. This port has no wharf for rowboats and presents difficulties in obtaining water and fuel.

The provisions available there consist of pork, taro, and other products found on the rest of the islands. There is sandal- or fragrant wood there, but the king values it very highly. If the Americans could be driven out, this island would become ours. The Americans are liars and calumniators. The captains of their ships flatter the chief manager of Novo-Arkhangel'sk when they see him, but behind his back spread tales about him as well as about the Russians in general, blackening their characters in every possible way. These tales are so vile that one cannot listen without revulsion to what they have said on the Sandwich Islands about my countrymen. All I could do was to catch my breath, murmuring to myself the proverb: "Be patient, Cossack, and you will become an ataman."

The next day the doctor went ashore and was kindly received by the king. The third day, the twentieth [of May], was a "Taboo"

day. I went ashore myself, saw the king, and invited him for dinner
on the ship on [May] 21, the birthday of His Highness Constantine Pavlovich. The king accepted the invitation with pleasure; on
the twenty-first at ten o'clock by request of the king I sent a boat
ashore with twenty men to attend the raising of the Russian flag.
At eleven o'clock the messengers of the king brought some liquor
and said that the king would be absent, as the result of intrigues on
the part of the Americans. This was an insult to the Russian flag.
So I sent back the messengers with their liquor and ordered them
to tell the king that [previously] he had wanted to accept voluntarily the Russian flag and the protection of our emperor and now,
if he refused all that, then I would make him keep his promises by
the use of force. In the meanwhile, I sent a boat ashore with an
order to bring back all the Russians immediately. That was done
by twelve o'clock. The members of the crew were given a small
glass of vodka apiece and they greeted the health of our Grand
Duke Constantine Pavlovich with hurrahs. Cannons were discharged in salute. Afterwards I sent a baidarka to bring back three
boys who had remained on shore.

At one o'clock the baidarka came back, and who was there but the
king himself. I met him in the cabin and at first treated him in a
very reserved fashion, telling him that we had almost quarreled but
now must become friends again. He replied that he had been seeking our friendship for a long time and that he was pleased to have
an opportunity to receive the protection of our sovereign emperor.

To reward him for his voluntary consent, the doctor put on him
the uniform of a staff officer of the navy and then asked him to
proceed to the quarterdeck. There the king accepted the Russian
flag and announced to the whole crew of the ship *Otkrytie* his
decision to become a subject of the Russian crown. Afterwards, at
five o'clock in the evening, the king went ashore with the flag. At
his departure a seven-gun salute was fired. When he reached shore,
he raised the Russian flag on a spot already prepared, to the
accompaniment of a fourteen-gun salute. The people surrounding
the king greeted it with hurrahs and the ship answered with
twenty-one guns. After that I went ashore to congratulate the king
on the exalted protection of the Emperor of all the Russias,

Alexander Pavlovich. The king was very pleased and asked me to dine with him the next day.

The next day at twelve o'clock we went ashore and were met by a crowd of people who accompanied me to the king. The king and his wives met me under the trees, where the king seated me in an armchair near to himself. The square where the meal was served was covered with grasses and flowers. Thirty men of the king's guard, somewhat resembling soldiers, stood in orderly formation in front of the king's residence. The crowd grew gradually on all sides until there were about one thousand or more people standing at a distance of about thirty feet from us. At one o'clock we were seated at the table, which was similar to our officers' table. The wives went away, and with the exception of the king, no one shared our table. The king himself offered a toast to our Imperial Majesty, while cannons were discharged and his guard shouted "Hurrah!" After that we drank the king's health. Three Sandwich men performed a rifle drill, the Aleuts sang songs and danced, and one man gave an exhibition of horsemanship, which filled the Sandwich natives with wonder. Thus the whole day passed and apparently a full accord was reached with Kaumualii, who agreed to all the doctor's demands and gave his consent for the opening of a good trading branch by the Company and for the establishment of a colony in this rich land and wonderful climate.

On the twenty-third I started unloading the cargo under the direction of the doctor. No one could entertain the king better than the doctor himself. The people on the ship *Otkrytie* [——] the cannon, which the people carried from the longboat to the shore, getting in water up to their necks. The cannon was placed on a carriage and there was no need to encourage anybody to drag it to the palace. Such was the excitement that everybody wanted to participate in the task. Sand and rocks were no obstacle. One man got under the wheel and lost a leg, but the cannon was brought to the king without any time lost. The natives did not know how to handle the cannon and wanted to learn its action. The king sent a messenger to me on the ship. I went ashore and discharged a grenade which exploded with a great noise. The king was pleased and I increased his pleasure when I said that three grenades sent in the direction of the *Otkrytie* would drive it from the port, and that a shot from the other side of the river (250 sazhens) would kill a man and disperse all the crowd. The king immediately ordered that a barrel filled with grapeshot be placed alongside [the cannon]. The king was so pleased with the cannon that the doctor might have bartered it for almost a full cargo of fragrant wood. This commerce, however, is not my business, so I went back to the ship and took charge of unloading its cargo and loading it with the cargo of the wrecked ship *Bering*, which was seized [by the natives]. The items received [back from the natives] are listed in the ship's journal. The work continued until May 31.

On May 31 at ten o'clock in the morning I raised anchor, unfurled the topsails and set the foresail and mainsail. At two o'clock in the morning reefed the topsails; at eleven o'clock turned before the wind . . . (storm) . . . to the island of Niihau, where I dropped anchor at a depth of nine sazhen. This is how we got there: The doctor ordered me to go to Oahu, taking along fifty Sandwich natives as passengers. [He told me that] if it were impossible to go to this island [Oahu], then to go directly to Sitka. There was no water or provisions, so we spent the night there [at Niihau?], but could not take off the passengers on account of their cursed taboo. A boat came to our ship, the occupant said the place of anchorage was "taboo!" and went away again. You can imagine my position, with the dangerous rocky bottom, the high rocks all around, the heavy rocking of the ship, and strong winds which threatened danger every minute. The night passed, day came; we put up false masts from topgallants of the mainmast and mizzen-mast, on which were placed appropriate sails, in order to go from the southern cape toward the north [to a point] almost in the middle of the western side of the island of Niihau, where there is a convenient place for anchorage.

On June 2, at nine o'clock, I lifted the anchor without a fluke and went along the shore toward the north. The depth was from five to nine sazhens. The wind freshened from the northeast, but the sea was calm. There was a coral bottom. When we came to where it was sandy we began to pull away from the shore.

        . . . etc. etc. etc. . . . back to Sitka . . .

    Fleet Lieutenant and Cavalier IAKOV PODUSHKIN

July 20, 1816

17. Secret Treaty Between King Kaumualii and Schäffer, July 1, 1816.

Secret treaty, concluded and ratified between His Majesty Kaumualii, King of Kauai, etc., etc., and Doctor von Sheffer, Collegiate Assessor of the Russian Empire.

Port Waimea, Island of Kauai, July 1, 1816

His Majesty, King Kaumualii sends his army to those Sandwich Islands that formerly belonged to him and were taken away [from him] by force, namely, Oahu, Lanai, Maui, Molokai, etc. The king asks [Dr. Sheffer] to reconquer them [these islands], entrusting the command of the expedition to Dr. Sheffer.

The king demands from Dr. Sheffer the delivery of necessary ammunition and clothing [for the army]. For transportation of troops, the king demands from Dr. Sheffer a sufficient number of ships [from those] which might be at his [Sheffer's] disposal at the Sandwich Islands.

The king [———] and offers all islands in his possession to his Majesty, Alexander Pavlovich. Dr. Sheffer, through the Russian-American Company, is to use every effort to enable King Kaumualii and his successors to enjoy peaceful possession of the above-mentioned islands.

The king at first will put on the field five hundred men and will supply his own men as well as the Russian ships with necessary food.

The king will give full authority (carte blanche) to Dr. Sheffer in regard to this expedition; he will also give aid for constructing a Russian fort on every island. These forts are to be placed in charge of Russian commanders, as has been done in the case of the fort in the port of Honolulu on the island Oahu.

On behalf of himself and his successors, the king cedes one-half of the island Oahu, with everything found there, to the Russian-American Company, which is to choose the half it wishes.

King Kaumualii cedes [to the Russians] forever all sandalwood on the island Oahu.

King Kaumualii promises to pay in sandalwood from the island of Kauai for arms, ammunition, a brig or schooners, whether already received or to be received. He will also refuse to trade with the citizens of the United States.

King Kaumualii promises to give permission to the Russian-American Company for the establishment of factories on all his islands; in addition to one-half of the island Oahu, the Company is to receive a strip of land on each [of the king's] other islands.

King Kaumualii promises to sell sandalwood to no one but the Russians.

In ten years, King Kaumualii is to establish on the newly acquired islands an army of two thousand warriors and Dr. Sheffer will undertake to bring a supply of fish from Russian North America. Doctor Sheffer is to arrange for the islanders sent by the king to Sitka to cut as much lumber as the king needs and Doctor Sheffer will take care that Russian ships bring most of this lumber to Kauai.

Doctor Sheffer undertakes to build factories on the Sandwich Islands and to introduce a better economy, which will make the natives educated and wealthy.

Graciously approved by His Majesty and signed by His Honor, Doctor Sheffer.

KING KAUMUALII X

Russian Imperial Collegiate Assessor

DR. EGOR DE SHEFFER

18. *Award of Chief's Rank to Baranov by King Kaumualii, July 1, 1816.*

We, by the grace of God and the protection of his Imperial Majesty, the Emperor of Russia, Kaumualii, King of the Sandwich Islands, etc., etc., elevate His Honor, the Russian Imperial Collegiate Councilor and Cavalier Alexander Andreevich Baranov to the rank of first chief of the Sandwich islands, as a token of our great appreciation of the protection of His Majesty Alexander Pavlovich, the Emperor of Russia. This is done for the special service rendered [by Baranov] to the subjects [of Kaumualii] and to the islands. We also grant to him and his family, free from taxes for all time, a royal village in the district of Okougrena [?] at the port of Honolulu.

KING KAUMUALII

Given in our capital
Waimea on Kauai
July 1, 1816

19. *Report, Schäffer to Main Office, August, 1816.*

August, 1816
To the Main Office [of the Russian-American Company]
Report of Collegiate Assessor Sheffer

Two years ago, through the misfortune of Captain Bennett, a Company ship, the *Bering,* was wrecked on one of the Sandwich Islands, Kauai. His Honor, Collegiate Councilor Baranov, sent me there as chief commissioner to investigate this matter on the spot and to demand from the Indians [Sandwich natives] the return of the cargo which they had carried away. I finished this business to my complete satisfaction in twenty-four hours and saved the company 20,000 piastres. At my departure, Mr. Baranov expressed a wish to establish a factory on the Sandwich Islands. King Kamehameha, however, under the influence of an old English sailor, Peel, and of some Americans, categorically refused. On the other hand, Kaumualii, king of the island Kauai, not only consented to [our] establishment of a factory, but asked for the protection of the Russian Empire. In a formal written declaration he made the islands a part of the possessions of His Majesty, Sovereign Alexander Pavlovich. I am enclosing a copy of this act; I shall send the original to the Main Office in St. Petersburg by way of Sitka, to submit it to His Majesty and to ask his most gracious consent. At the first opportunity send notice of his consent here by way of Sitka. In the name of the Company I also concluded a commercial contract with King Kaumualii by virtue of which the Company gains a permanent monopoly of the sandalwood trade. The king also granted to the Company a whole gubernia [province] on the island of Kauai as a permanent possession. This province has a population of about four hundred Indian families, who can be used in plantations, factories, etc. There is also a port, Hanalei, in this province. I shall forward all the chief documents to St. Petersburg on some Russian ship or through Okhotsk, and I shall give detailed reports. My chief desire now is to have sent here from St. Petersburg two good ships with reliable crews and well armed. In Sitka there are no such ships or seamen with the exception of the Lieutenant of the Navy, Podushkin.

[In Sitka] there is always need of men and skilled workers. In addition, the Russian settlement in New Albion is in danger of being destroyed by the Spaniards. I have reliable information that the governor of Monterey asked permission from the Mexican Viceroy to bring about [its destruction]. As a result, thirty of our baidarkas were captured, together with some Aleuts, a few Russians, and Doctor Elliot. The captives were seized and sent into the interior of the country.

Would not His Imperial Majesty consent to send a frigate into the Pacific? Such ships would be very useful along the Spanish Coast and even in Norfolk Sound and would serve the welfare of the Russian Empire. It would be desirable to have also 400-ton ships for the Company. The ship *Otkrytie* which arrived here lost two masts and we almost perished.

The brig *Maria* was sent last year to Okhotsk, but I have received the very unpleasant news that it apparently has gone down. German Molvo returned to St. Petersburg through Okhotsk. He left Sitka in September, 1815, and Kad'iak in April, 1816.—The officers from the *Suvorov* are great rascals.

I hope that my letter will reach St. Petersburg four or five months earlier than the original documents. I am using for this an American ship *Otseana* [*O'Cain?*], which is leaving for Canton the beginning of September, 1816.

EGOR SHEFFER

Kauai, Sandwich Islands
August, 1816

20. *Contract Between King Kaumualii and Schäffer,*
August 22 [*September 3, N.S.?*], *1816, Concerning*
Purchase of the Ship Avon.

His Majesty Kaumualii, the king of the Sandwich Islands,
Kauai, Niihau, etc., on one side, and His Honor, Collegiate
Assessor, Egor Nikolaievich Sheffer, in the name of the Russian-
American Company on the other, on August 22, 1816, concluded a
contract. His Majesty requested Mr. Sheffer to buy at any price for
the Russian-American Company the armed ship *Avon* from a
citizen of the United States, Captain Isaac Whittemore. Mr.
Sheffer told King Kaumualii that he would buy this ship for the
benefit of the king and his islands, as well as of the Russian-
American Company, to which it shall belong. Because of the outlay
of so much capital by the Russian-American Company for the
protection of King Kaumualii and his islands, the latter pledges his
royal word that the Russian-American Company will receive three
cargoes of sandalwood. The king undertakes to pay for the goods
received and for the boat within five years, according to the first
contract concluded here on May 21, while every year the Russian-
American Company will cut sandalwood free as a partial payment
on the part [of the king]. The king also undertakes to furnish men
to aid [in cutting sandalwood]. On the other hand, Mr. Sheffer
undertakes to aid the king and provide him with Russians and
Aleuts under his [Schäffer's] command. This document is signed by
His Majesty and by Mr. Sheffer.

KING KAUMUALII   X
EGOR SHEFFER

Island Kauai
Waimea Bay
August 22, 1816

21. *Affidavit by Captains Whittemore, Smith, and Gyzelaar Substantiating Transfer of the Schooner* Lydia *to King Kaumualii, September 4* [*August 23, O.S.?*], *1816.*

A la suite d'un act de vente du schooner "Lydia" à Georges Schäffer—se trouve—

Island of Kauai Sept. 4, 1816 We the subscribers do hereby certify that George Schaffer a staff officer with the Russian Imperial service and agent of the Russian American Cy. gave in our presence the schooner "Lydia" and her appartenances as expressed in the annexed bill of sale to Tamooree, king of the island of Atooi, for his, the said King's, use thereof forever, this present made in consequence of a contract made on the 21st [of] May, 1816, between the said George Schaffer & Tamoorie, King of the island, the terms of said contract are to us unknown.

ISAAC WHITTEMORE, master, Ship *Avon,* Boston

WM SMITH M. R. [?] Ship *Albatross*

HENRY GYZELAAR f¹ʸ master of *Lydia*

Correct, EGOR DE SHEFFER

22. *Deed of Hanalei Province to Schäffer by King Kaumualii, September 21, 1816.*

By the grace of God and by the protection of the Great Russian Emperor Alexander Pavlovich, we, Kaumualii, king of Kauai and Niihau, prince of Oahu, Lanai, Maui, etc., etc. [declare the following]:

According to the contract which I concluded with the commissioner of the Russian-American Company, Mr. Egor Sheffer, on May 21 of this year, on the ship *Otkrytie,* I, King Kaumualii, ordered my toion [chief] * Ovana to proceed instead of myself and hand over to the commissioner, Mr. Sheffer, our province [*gubernia*] which is located on the northern side of the island of Kauai, in the place called Hanalei where Sheffer acquired the rights I granted to him as representative of the Russian-American Company, including my [sovereign] rights, my property, my land, and my peasants. I renounce the above-mentioned part of the island in his [Sheffer's] favor or [of] whoever will rule there [his successors] so they [may] do whatever they please there. I renounce it also in the name of my successors who will not have any right to claim as their own this land, the rivers, port, sea, peasants, or any other former possessions [of mine].

This, my order and act in regard to this province, was made public through my toion Ovana and through the commissioner and witnessed by the chiefs of this province and handed to the commissioner, Mr. Sheffer, and his secretary Charles [Fox-] Bonnick.

The witnesses present: The chiefs of this province—Kallavatti Hanalei, Toion Vorontsov; the names of the other chiefs are:

1. Vaimeri Primeri	11. Aganemor	23. Iurko
2. Tuvaori	12. Turoli	24. Paviti
3. Inavi	13. Tapuri	25. Orogu
4. Lavaia	14. Chait	26. Tagana
5. Magoi	15. Voata	27. Tapech
6. Tuvatea	16. Tateri	28. Mikamu
7. Tuvagerani	17. Teaitavo	29. Puagavu
8. Tomataori	18. Agurusuru	30. Tanaguna
9. Nateoro	19. Makalevo	31. Pechu
10. Tupigea	20. Paraori	32. Lapochitu
	21. Uvara	33. Bogitirova
	22. Tavuiri	

For the sake of greater security, this act was made in two copies with my name and sign [cross]: One copy is given to the

---

* *Toion* or *toen* was a Siberian term for chief, carried to Alaska and later, as we see, applied to Hawaii.

Commissioner, Mr. Sheffer, and another is to be placed in our archives.

[On the original]
KAUMUALII   X

September 24, 1816
Island Kauai

23. Declaration of Friendship and Deed of land, Chief Kamahalolani to Schäffer, October 1, 1816.

Copy

Contrary to false rumors coming from many seamen and other citizens of the United States of America, I may assure His Honor, Doctor and Collegiate Assessor of the Russian Empire, Commissioner of the Russian-American Company Egor von Sheffer, that myself and King Kaumualii never wished anything other than friendship with the Russians and especially with the Russian-American Company. From the Russians, we never heard anything that was not good. From the Americans we have heard a great deal of evil. As an evidence of my friendship, I am making to Dr. von Sheffer for the Company's factory a present of two strips of land, one in this harbor on the right bank of the river Waimea, which is called Guramaia, for a building and vegetable gardens, and another strip on the left bank of the Waimea, with twenty peasants, at the place called Vaikari. This is given permanently. I assure you of my service to the great Russian [Emperor?] and shall do for the Russians all I can.

(On the original)
KAMAHALOLANI—*minister*
X

Waimea, Sandwich Islands
October 1, 1816

24. Grant of Land by Princess Naoa of Kauai to Schäffer, October 1, 1816.

Copy

To His Honor, Doctor, Collegiate Assessor, Commissioner of the Russian-American Company, as a token of friendship and appreciation of various presents received from him, I am granting him a strip of land, called Gamalea, on the river Mattaveri in the gubernia of Waimea, together with thirteen peasants and everything else pertaining to it. Dr. Sheffer, or whoever succeeds him, can own this land permanently and do there whatever he pleases.

He received the whole Bat [?] Mainauri at a distance of 8 versts from Waimea.

(On the original)
NAOA, (mark)
Princess of Kauai

Waimea on the Sandwich Islands,
Island Kauai
October 1, 1816

25. Grant of Land by Chief Ovana Platov to Schäffer, October 1, 1816.

Copy

To His Honor, Commissioner of the Russian-American Company, Doctor, Collegiate Assessor Egor von Sheffer as a token of regard, friendship, and gratitude for many gifts received from him, I am granting a strip of land called Tuiloa on the river Don in the province Hanapepe on the island Kauai, together with eleven peasants. The boundary line goes from the river Don and as far as the sea. Everybody else is prohibited from fishing in this river. Whenever any peasant of Kauai sees his [Sheffer's] canoe while fishing, he must approach this canoe without expecting any fish.

This canoe [Sheffer's] is called taboo. This strip of land is also made taboo by King Kaumualii and is free from any taxes. Doctor von Sheffer or whoever takes his place can possess it permanently and do with it whatever he pleases.

(On the original)
OVANA PLATOV
X

Waimea, Island Kauai.
October 1, 1816.

26. Letter, Schäffer to Baranov, November 25, 1816.

November 25, 1816
Received November 23, 1817,
through Albion on the *Kutuzov*
A.B.

Your Honor, My dear Sir:
Alexander Andreevich

I suppose that the ship *Avon* with Antipatr Andreevich [Baranov] on board has arrived safely at Sitka. You must excuse me for bargaining with Whittemore. Circumstances here required that; all the American captains were set against us, and when I accomplished that [the deal with Whittemore?], I ceased to be afraid of them. However, everything here is well. All the sandalwood on this island belongs to the Company. As soon as I receive information and orders from you, I think I shall send the brig *Il'mena* for such goods as the king might require. In five days I expect the Russian ship which is now in Oahu. It is the same ship about which I told you two years ago, the one which His Excellency, Count Rumiantsev, wanted to send around the world. The name of the captain of this brig is [Otto von] Kotzebue. He is the son of the great and famous Russian writer, Collegiate Councilor Kotzebue. Last summer he went north much further than other navigators [have succeeded in doing] and he has discovered a great deal of new [information]. Next summer he will go north again and later will call on you at Sitka. He [Kotzebue] visited the port of San Francisco, met Mr. Kuskov there, settled former hostilities between the Russians and the Spaniards, and liberated the Russian prisoners. Among them he liberated the former commissioner on the *Il'mena,* Dr. Elliot, who at present is on the island of Hawaii, and whom I shall bring here.

I wrote a short letter to Mr. Kuskov about the local situation; I am also writing briefly to you. I now have almost ready here one fortress of stone and two fortifications of earth, with palisades. I am now waiting for men from Sitka; only do not send such men as Verkhovinskii and Toropogritskii, who did nothing except disgrace themselves [and us]. I must also report that we absolutely must have Russian captains for the Company ships which are to be assigned here. English and Americans will not do. They are too treacherous. Also send me a man who could take care of the office work here, and send some paper because otherwise we shall not have anything to write on. Mr. James Wilcocks, the American consul in Canton, [!] promised to forward this letter to you. I think you should consider establishing a friendship with him, which is very important, because through him we could carry on business in Canton. According to rumors, even the governor of New Holland paid him high honors. He [Wilcocks] treated me in a manner suggesting a kind and noble character; he is entirely different in his behavior from other Americans. Myself and the local king supplied him with provisions, giving him taro-roots and ten pigs without any charge. You will see [from that] for yourself how honest he is. I do not think that there ever was in Sitka an American captain as honest as he is. Cavalier Ljungstedt in Macao, whose letters he [Wilcocks] will bring you, is also his friend. I have sold him a few trifles: 15 female and 10 young [seals?] and 77 sea bears [?], both females and young. Females and young were sold at the same price because the larger skins were spoiled by worms. The drunkard Toropogritskii left them with me and I did not want to trade them but Mr. Tarakanov asked me to sell them before they were altogether ruined by worms.

I am planning to send the ship, the *Mirt-Kad'iak,* to Sitka or some other place. It leaks very badly; while in port they have to pump out of it 24 feet of water every day. At the first opportunity send here horses, cows, and about ten silver medals for distribution among the prominent natives who are serving us faithfully in the provinces which belong to us. Our first cargo of sandalwood is ready; I am only awaiting a ship to send it to Canton. Mr. Wilcocks gave me a great deal of information in regard to the sandalwood and other trade in Canton and apparently he told me the truth. He told me that he would return to us, and I am anxious to hear how far you carried out your negotiations with him, especially because I know that he and Cavalier Ljungstedt are very friendly. I should like to know your policies [a line of broken, incomprehensible Russian] and I remain with great respect

Your Honor's obedient servant
EGOR SHEFFER

November 25, 1816
Sandwich Island Kauai.

27. Letter, George Young, et al., to Schäffer, December 29, 1816, Asking for Protection After Native Attack at Hanalei.

Copy

Delivered by Tarakanov, December 20, 1817, at Novo-Arkhangel'sk.

Your Honor, Dear Sir, Egor Nikolaevich:

We, your humble and obedient servants, take the liberty of asking you to extend your protection to us as your children because we are placed here at your orders. We depend on you and expect you to defend us, for there have been grave happenings in the place called Sheffer [valley]. As you will learn from this letter, an Aleut was murdered here on the twenty-sixth [of December?]. According to Mr. Young and others, you should investigate it. The boat with your messenger Fedor Leshchinskii was ready, as was the boat loaded with chalk and clay. Mr. George Young was then on the

beach about to send off a letter to you. The natives left their houses
and went somewhere near our buildings, which include a winery, by
the lake, with [——] and masses of calabashes. They took two
butts of wine and a large quantity of roots used in making alcohol.
We, Mr. Young, myself, and Bologov, decided that we needed a
watchman so no one, whether an Aleut, a Russian, or a kanaka,
would dare to steal or rob [us of] anything. We thought we could
avoid trouble that way, but just as we handed the sealed envelope to
Leshchinskii, suddenly we heard a gunshot from the guard posted in
the kanaka [——]. We—Captain Young, myself, Bologov, and
Leshchinskii—rushed from the room. We found two men from Mr.
Young's boat whom we sent to inquire as to the cause of the
shooting. We followed them ourselves and started to run along the
shore; before we had covered half of the distance we met the
returning men, who told us that the watchman was dead. As soon
as we heard that, we saw the building burning on all sides, although
there was not one Sandwich Islander to be seen. In ten minutes this
unusual fire was over. The grass was burned out and we could see
the dead body. Using water brought from the lake in calabashes,
Mr. Young, I, and the others put out the rest of the fire. We
examined the body of the dead man in the presence of a large crowd.
We found the cause of death—a large wound in the chest and two
more in [——]. We brought the body to the house and called
Chiefs Hanalei and Ovana Platov. In order to complete the
investigation we went to Platov, who was sick with an injured foot.
He said that he would use all his influence in our favor and asked
Captain George Young, myself, Bologov, and all the Russians and
Aleuts to carry guns. He [Platov] offered us armed kanakas to aid
us in catching the kanakas of Hanalei, and if the latter refused to
surrender, to shoot them. He [Platov] asked to be allowed to
subdue them [the men of Hanalei] by force of arms so that in the
future they would not dare to provoke the Russian Empire, but we
hesitated to begin the conquest of the savages without Your
Honor's command. Even the chief Hanalei himself, with tears in his
eyes, requested us to conquer the savages, so that the latter would
feel the might of the Russian people.

On the original, signed:
GEORGE YOUNG

This statement is correct—IVAN BOLOGOV
This statement is correct—IVAN FELENIN
This statement is correct—signed in person by
NIKOLAI PONOMAREV
This statement is true—PETR KYCHEROV
December 29, 1816

28. Letter, John Elliot d'Castro to Schäffer, January 7, 1817, Reporting Arrival at Oahu [in English].

Waohoo [Oahu] Jan. 7th 1817

Dear Friend.

You will perhaps think it strange that at last I am arrived here—After having been twice through California & to St. Blas, the city of Tepic and as far as Acapulco. I received my liberty when I was at St. Blas and from theron [*sic*] I had to go in the Spanish brig of war *St. Carlos* to Acapulco & from then to Monterey [;] from Monterey I went on board of the Russian brig *Rurik* [,] Capt. Kotzebue [,] who is on discovery & he landed me here on these islands. I should be happy if you would land all my things here with me & receive my letter for Gov.ʳ Baranoff.—In case you cannot I shall be obliged to proceed in the first vessel bound for Sitka & I do not wish to go at present as I have the venereal upon me & the cold wth.ʳ would be too much for my weak constitution at present.—After being thirteen months a prisoner & at St. Blas it has brought me down exceedingly—In case I cannot go to the North I shall write to G.ʳ Baranoff for all my things and my pay.—I should wish very much to see you.—They inform me that Antipatr is gone with Whittemore to Sitka give my best love to all friend and let me see you as soon as possible.—I hope in God Gov.ʳ Baranoff is well—the people that was taken with me is now at Monterey & Mr. Kuskoff was at S Francisco but I did not see him—I shall let you know everything when I see [you] which I hope will be before long so God bless you & keep you in good health is the sincere wish of your sincere friend

JOHN ELLIOT D'CASTRO

to Dr. Schäffer

29. Letter, John Elliot d'Castro to Schäffer, February 3, 1817, Refusing Invitation to Come to Kauai.

Illmo Sir.

I Rec^d your kind letter inviting me to come down to the island of Atooi, I am Dear Sir, at present in a bad state of health, but in case I am better, I shall proceed to Shitka [*sic*] this summer, in case I cannot I write to G^r Baranoff for my clothes, wages, writing desk——that I left on board the *Ilmania* [*Il'mena*], another thing I do not want to forfeit the friendship of King Tamaamaha by going to Atooi therefore when I do go to Shitka it will be in an American vessel.

As the Russian-American Company owes me for my Commission upwards of two thousand dollars and as I am now very short of every thing . . .

> Dr Sir your humb & Devot.
> JOHN ELLIOT D'CASTRO

Insula Waohoo [Oahu]
3 febr. 1817

30. Trade Agreement, King Kaumualii and Schäffer, April 23, 1817.

By the grace of God and the protection of the Great Sovereign of all the Russias, Alexander Pavlovich, we, Kaumualii, king of Kauai, Niihau, etc., etc., etc., enter into the following contract with the Russian Collegiate Assessor, Commissioner of the Russian-American Company, Mr. Egor Sheffer.

1. King Kaumualii shall not trade in any articles with anybody but the Russians, unless he has the consent of Dr. Sheffer, or his successor.

2. Every year King Kaumualii is to provide the Russian factory on the island Kauai with one hundred pigs, five hundred puds of salt, about 15,000 dry taro-roots, bast fibers, coconuts in whatever

amount the king is able to gather, also other products and fruits growing on this island—yam-roots, etc. In exchange Dr. Sheffer undertakes in the name of the Company to provide King Kaumualii with such articles and goods as His Majesty, King Kaumualii may demand, provided it [the value thereof] will not be in excess of 12,000 rubles. If there are none of the required goods in the factory, then Dr. Sheffer will obtain them with all possible speed from Sitka.

3. King Kaumualii gives away forever all the sandalwood, whether cut or still growing in the forests, on the whole island of Kauai, and he and his people undertake to prepare every year two cargoes for ships such as the *Otkrytie* and the *Mirt-Kad'iak*. In case the Company requires more than these two cargoes, then the cutting of the wood is to be done by the Company's own men. For the wood, land, and the port Hanalei, for the four hundred peasants ceded permanently to the Company, for the food supplies delivered by the king and still to be delivered until May 21, 1817, the king has been paid in full and does not demand anything further. Likewise, for the food supplies delivered and to be delivered until May 21, 1817, for the Company's ships, the king does not claim any payment. Both sides mutually reassure each other in the friendship established on May 21, 1816.

(On the original)

KING KAUMUALII   X

KAMAHALOLANI, MINISTER,   X

EGOR SHEFFER

TIMOFEI TARAKANOV

Waimea, on the
Sandwich Island of Kauai
April 23, 1817

31. *Letter, King Kaumualii to Baranov, May 15, 1817, After Expulsion of Schäffer* [*in English*].

Copy   Atooi May 15th 1817.

To his Excelency Elexandr Baranoff a fewlines [*sic*] from his Majesty King Tomaree The King says that the Doctor came to his

Island and has heard a great of [sic] disturbance heare. And titeled himself as a governor above all. and Hoisted Rushe [Russian] colours. All the Chiefs and—Natives of the Isslands alway a comming to His Majesty and telling him that the Doctor is not good, to stop heare and it is good they say it to send of the Issland is [his] people & all is things that belongs to him—while the Doctor was heare he would not let me trade with any Nationals ships, as I use to do—and I meane to have a free trade as I use to do as before. the King says that he will let the Company have as much in Return as he as [has] from them. but the things is not Ready at present. but he will have it ready in the Course of 16 Months time such things as he Produces. The Doctor has keep all the people buisey so that they have had not time to get any thing more at present. His Majesty says a free trad with all nations but no Settelers.

I am Your Humble Majesty etc.

TOMOREE   X mark

THE COMMANDER IN CHIEF

TORORORNEYS   X mark

Copy certified for Hagemeister

32. Letter, Schäffer to King Kaumualii, May 25, 1817, Urging Reconsideration of Policy [in English].

Copy

Under his Emperial Majestys [sic] the emperor of all the Russias etc. etc. etc. protection to the Russian-American Company from the Russian Emperial Staff officer and agent to said Company [,] Georges Schaffer to King Tamooree, Island Atooi.

Your majesty. After a couple of days I hope to be in Hanaray [Hanalei], the same as you wrote to me yesterday, to get the rest of our property [.] at present you have a few days time, to consider to change yours oppinion, concerning the Russians; Every thing may be settled for the best for you, your people and Island. I know

very well, that the Revolution against the Russians was against
your will and wishes, and you know very well that all my wishes
was for the best for you and your people; if we go away from
Hannaray, it will be too late to consider afterwards, and you and
your Island must expect the greatest ingratitude from the Russian
Empire. Never mind that three or four of your men is bad. dont
believe that the great Russian Empire will allow you to make only
play with him with his flag and people [.] dont believe that he wont
assist and demand the Rights of his Company. You made an
agreement with me for land for the Company. You got all our
property and now you have drove us off the Island—without paying
anything that you have agreed with me [,] for you asked the
Russian protection and flag [;] at last I gave it to you and your
petition to his Emperial Majesty the Emperor is gone to St.
Petersburg [.] I protected you with my people and two ships for
one year [;] the third vessel [,] the schooner *Lydia* [,] I gave you
for your own use[.] Nobody has troubled you or your island all this
time. You promised that the Emperial Russian-American Company
should have all the sandal wood on this Island of Atooi Eternally
[,] dont forget it, dont forget it, that you have given to the said
company the state and harbour of Hannaray! dont forget it, that
the same Company was master of other lands and plantations for
which I payed several of your chiefs; dont forget what agreements
you made with me and what papers you have signed, dont forget,
that I told you many times, if you did not intend to fulfil your
promises, you had better not signed, principally because you said
you forgot the agreement that you made with Mr. Natron [?] and
Captn Jennings [——] about buying the schooner *Columbia*. dont
forget what bad success you will meet with if you dont fulfill your
agreement. Consider seriously Every thing I have wrote here. if
you wish to get clear of the greatest shame that man could be
guilty of, and keep off the punishment that threatens you I am
ready to settle with you in peace and friendship Every thing. I wont
stop in Hannaray any longer than what is necessary to take in the
property, if in that time I receive an answer from you I will
write to you again.

GEORGE SCHAFFER

25th of May 1817

33. *Letter, Schäffer to Baranov, About End of May, 1817, Reporting Expulsion.*

Copy

Received from the *Il'mena,* July 9, 1817, via George [Young?]

Your Honor, My dear Sir, Alexander Andreevich [Baranov]:

More than half a year ago I wanted to send the brig *Il'mena* to you with local products, but, as every sailor knows, I had the hardest kind of a time getting Captain Wadsworth away from the port of Hanalei. He stayed here for a long time without any results. He spent on drinks whatever articles he could steal. When he left Hanalei he tried to run aground and destroy the brig. Great thanks are due to Captain Young. The brig would have been lost if he had not speedily come to the rescue, offering two anchors, ropes, boats, etc.

Captain Wadsworth went to Waimea, where he demanded different articles and instruments for the brig, without which he said he could not sail. I ordered that he be supplied with what he requested. He received the things himself, but not a single item ever reached the brig.

The next day Stepan Nikiforov came to Timofei Tarakanov and told him that, according to one of the sailors, Captain Wadsworth had called King Kaumualii a fool for trusting the Russians. He said the Russians were deceiving the king and that in the future they would kill all the Indians and build fortresses. He said the Russians were so poor that they would die of starvation without the aid of the Americans. He told him that the brig *Il'mena* is not a Russian ship, but belongs to him [Wadsworth] and that he [Wadsworth] wants to help the king drive the Russians from Kauai.

When I had heard all this I went to the king and said to him: "Your Majesty! I know everything that Captain Wadsworth told you; I want to hear it from you." The king repeated word for word what I had heard from Nikiforov. I immediately went back home and found Wadsworth there. He wanted to shake hands, but I told him that I was not shaking hands with pirates and ordered his arrest.

Meanwhile, Mr. Wilcocks came here, and told me that Dr. Elliot was on [the island of] Oahu. I thought that perhaps he did not know about our circumstances. In order to bring him [Elliot] here I had to send Mr. Matson as captain of the brig; in addition he [Matson] was to bring the pigs, goats, and sheep which we had left there [on Oahu]. After thirty days he returned with [only] the pigs, goats, and sheep. Mr. Elliot refused to come and merely wrote me [February 3, 1817; No. 29] to ask that I send him three thousand piastres. I did not reply.

Upon his return, Mr. Matson told me that during his voyage he had discovered an island which one could reach from Kauai in thirty-six hours. I heard from Captains Smith and Winship that there is a small island not very far from here where there are a great many [sea?] elephants. I decided to go there and see if this island was worth taking and to prepare food supplies and fat for the Aleuts. Thanks to an unfavorable wind and the inexperience of Mr. Matson the trip took forty-two hours instead of thirty-six. The island has been known to seafarers for more than a hundred years.

Meanwhile, the brig *Forester* arrived at Waimea, and Captain Adams demanded the lowering of the Russian flag. The king refused to do this and he [Adams?] sent a letter to Oahu. When Captain Young and his crew arrived at Hanalei I asked if they would like to undertake an expedition that summer, and everybody agreed. Our [ships], the *Mirt-Kad'iak* and the brig *Il'mena,* arrived at Waimea for provisions. The king promised to supply them according to our last contract, No. 9. I presented Tarakanov's silver watch to the first chief so that he would hurry, thus enabling the ships to leave. On April 25, Chief Platov came and told me of the arrival of five canoes from Oahu with news that the Americans wanted to make war on the Russians. I heard that old Ebbets had returned from Canton. I had heard about him, as I wrote you, from Captain Jennings.

I wanted to go to the king and ask him to fulfil his written obligations in order that our ships could depart. I went ashore and there were the king, the chief, and about one thousand Indians.

They were busy with the schooner. I made my request to the king, who agreed. Then I said to him, "You are busy; I shall come later," and when I had walked about one hundred feet away, one Indian and six American sailors seized me and sent me to the ship in a badly leaking canoe, with orders not to return to the shore. I could hardly keep the leakage down long enough to reach the ship.

On the shore a cannon was discharged and they ran up a pirate flag. They sent back to the ship the unopened [cases with?] the remainder of the Company's goods. They also sent out to the brig a small amount of dry taro, salt, and kukui nuts, as well as some provisions. In the meanwhile, Captain Wadsworth escaped to the shore in an Indian canoe. On the same day Captain Young asked [the natives?] to deliver him back or else pay his [Wadsworth's?] obligations [to the Company?], but the chief refused to do so. Wadsworth told the chief that the Russians would kill him when he returned to Sitka. Captain Matson also testified that [———] the American [———]. I and many of the others noticed that he was against us. He told Thomas [?] that "The Russians will take the country [but] I will live to see the day when the Russians will be on the bottom and the Americans on top." Today I told him that Captain Young would have command over the *Il'mena* and that he [Matson] would be his assistant. He at once quit. I told him to go as a passenger and serve under Nikiforov.

We went to Hanalei, with the ship *Kad'iak* taking in forty-eight [cubic?] feet [of water] in twenty-four hours. The captain and entire crew condemned her.

I sent Mr. Tarakanov to King Kaumualii with a letter, and the barbarian sent back an answer without his royal signature. On shore I raised the Russian flag. I asked the garrison at Fort Alexander and they all agreed to hold out here until the arrival of help from you. I am holding the island in the name of our great sovereign until we shall be strong enough to administer punishment. All is in the hands of the Lord, and if I die or am killed, please send the news of it to the Frankfurt newspapers. I intend to show that I deserve your confidence and the rank of a Russian staff officer. Timofei Tarakanov, Odnoriadkin, and Filip Osipovich, as well as Mr. Wallace, were among the first to support me. Also, all the crew except Stepan Likhachev was with me. Send me as soon as possible a few hundred Russian Aleuts, two or three ships, Captains Podushkin and Young, a few twelve and eighteen pounders, and as much fish as possible to feed the Aleuts. When you send me to St. Petersburg, I can assure you that all the Sandwich Islands will be Russian. The protectorate of England is not yet established over Hawaii, and the other islands are still unoccupied. I have copies of letters which came from England to Kamehameha. I shall send the papers with Nikiforov, whom I especially recommend to you. All this business came about thanks to old Ebbets and, so to speak, through the Russian-American Company. Do not worry; when we get help the Russians will be on top again and everything will be settled.

I am the obedient servant of Your Honor,

EGOR SHEFFER

34. *Declaration, Schäffer et al., June 1, 1817, of Decision to Make a Stand at Hanalei.*

Copy

Brothers! The last hope of settling matters peacefully with the bandits of Kauai is lost. We have orders to leave here tomorrow. If we stay longer, they threaten to attack our ships and to refuse provisions. On the one hand, there is the barbarous and brutal treatment to which we are subjected; [on the other is the fact that] our ship, the *Mirt-Kad'iak*, is not in a condition to venture into the open sea. Consequently I intend to show these Indian bandits what Russian honor is and that it cannot be treated lightly. The Russian flag is not a toy and the name of our great sovereign is not to be scorned. Particularly I will show these barbarians that a Russian staff officer can put down rebellion. Who among you will join the good cause? Who is willing to follow me and fight in the face of privation and suffering? Let those yell hurrah, hurrah.

Be assured that I shall always be with you and leading you and that within a short time I expect large reënforcements from Sitka from our father Alexander Andreevich.

The original signed: EGOR SHEFFER
Everybody agreed, except Stepan Likhachev
In the name of the crew and Captain Young, signed:
TIMOFEI TARAKANOV
GEORGE YOUNG
In the name of the crew and Captain Young, signed:
ALEKSEI ODNORIADKIN

Hanalei
June 1 [7th?], 1817

35. Letter, Schäffer to Baranov, June 6, 1817, Announcing Departure from Hanalei.

Copy
Received per the *Il'mena,* July 11, 1817 from George [Young]

Your Honor, My dear Sir, Aleksander Andreevich:

This morning I sent about a dozen picked Russians by long boat [with orders] to bring [back] eight pigs and sixteen sheep which belong to the Company. Six men had rifles. Our pigs had already been driven away by the Indians, and, when our men started to chase the sheep, the Indians attacked them and wounded the hand of one Aleut. Our men fired several shots. I ordered them to return because we saw a large crowd of the Indians approaching. We then sent three shells from the cannons over their heads. Although all our men returned safely, today the whole crew refused to stay here any longer and, after a council with Captain Young and our captains, we decided to go to the island Oahu, there to repair our ships as well as possible and to wait for your decisions. Your further orders in such a case [incomprehensible phrase] and what we still have left. I am sending you the chief Hanalei and his wife, Mitina of Hanalei. [——] was in our province and always served faithfully, but the other [——] is a great bandit.

Your Honor, etc., etc.,
EGOR SHEFFER

Hanalei, June 6, 1817

Checked in the office: MANAGER BARANOV

36. *Report, Timofei Tarakanov to Lieutenant-Captain Hagemeister, at Sitka, February 12, 1818, Reviewing Departure of* Il'mena *from California, and Proceedings on Oahu and Kauai.*

Received February 12, 1818

To the Governor of the Russian-American Colonies of the Russian-American Company under the exalted protection of His Imperial Majesty, Lieutenant-Captain of the Navy and Cavalier Leontii Andreianovich Hagemeister.

From the servant of the Company, Timofei Tarakanov. A most respectful explanation—

In accordance with the verbal order given to me by Your Honor, I have the honor to explain the details concerning my departure from Bodega on the ship *Il'mena,* and how the ship sprung a leak during its stay in the Sandwich Islands. On November 3, 1815, at the entrance into the port Bodega, the ship lost its false keel. Until April, 1816, we stayed there [in Bodega] and were busy with repairs. Upon completion of the repairs we were assigned by His Honor, Commerce Councilor Ivan Alexandrovich Kuskov, to the port of Novo-Arkhangel'sk. Upon leaving the harbor we ran aground, but got the ship off and for several days were stationed at anchor within the harbor and loaded all the remaining cargo and no one noticed any leakage [in the ship]. In the meanwhile we lived on shore with Mr. Kuskov. When all the cargo was loaded, Mr. Wadsworth, the commander, gave the signal for departure. Immediately Mr. Kuskov and I went to the ship. Mr. Kuskov handed over the papers and returned, and we raised anchor and set out toward our destination under a northwesterly wind.

We covered a considerable distance and in the evening went down into the captain's cabin, where we mutually congratulated each other upon the departure. Then the servant, Balashov, came in asking for a candle. Because there were none in the cabin, Wadsworth went down into the hold to get the candles. After he had gone down, he asked for a light. I told him that it would be dangerous to have anything burning there because there was gunpowder there. He said there was no danger any longer because the gunpowder was already under water. When we took a candle to him, we saw that there actually was water. The captain immediately ordered both pumps put into operation, which pumped out water which also carried [with it] the wheat loaded in the ship. The whole crew took turns at pumping water.

We had to change our course because the first examination of the hold had revealed leakage on the left side. The next day we went toward the coast. Then we asked the captain where he intended to go to prevent disaster. We advised him to return to Bodega, but he said that it was impossible because we were much lower to the west [?] and besides, California did not have facilities for repair. [He said] that we had no other choice but to proceed with the favorable winds to the Sandwich Islands. We held a long discussion and decided to put ourselves in his hands in order to save ourselves from imminent peril. So he gave orders to turn in the direction he preferred. He assured us that, if favorable winds continued, we should reach [the Sandwich islands] in twelve days.

With favorable winds, but sometimes in calm weather, we reached the island of Hawaii in twenty days. There, not without difficulty, we obtained permission from King Kamehameha to enter the harbor in order to repair the ship and to dry up the cargo. We heard there about the ship *Otkrytie*, which had arrived there and then sailed for Oahu. We received news of Doctor [Sheffer], who had stayed with the king for a long time and then had left on a foreign ship for Oahu a day before the arrival of the *Otkrytie*.

After spending one day [at Hawaii] we went to Oahu and found there the frigate *Otkrytie*, under the command of His Honor, Lieutenant of the Navy and Cavalier Iakov [A]nikeich

Podushkin. When I met him I explained the reasons for our arrival. He [Podushkin] remained five days and then left for his destination, while we were busy with unloading the wet cargo and all provisions in Oahu. Although I did not have the honor of knowing Iakov [A]nikeich before, he treated me very kindly and at times would converse with me. Likewise I saw the Doctor for the first time; but he treated me like a stranger—never talked with me, never asked anything. Upon his departure for the island of Kauai he gave written instructions to Captain Wadsworth to get everything ready for the expedition but not to sail until the twentieth [of June, 1816?].

We were almost ready to start when, on June 21 [1816], the Company's ship, the *Mirt-Kad'iak,* arrived with a strong leak. We were detained again because we had to tow it for repairs. In the meanwhile, the Doctor returned on the newly purchased schooner. He stopped at the commissioner's house, which was close to that occupied by Toropogritskii and myself, where our lodgings were separated only by curtains. Doctor [Sheffer] often called on Toropogritskii in his part of the house. They held conversations there and as I was not acquainted with the Doctor, sometimes I used to go out in order not to interfere with them. Once he called me in and asked me how many beaver furs we had. I told him. Suddenly a former commander of the schooner came with orders from Doctor Sheffer to unpack the bales [of furs] which were in charge of Nikiforov. I said that I had no authority over them. Then they called in Nikiforov and, seeing that they needed more men, ordered me also to help in the unpacking. After finding out the number of whole beaver skins and tails, [Sheffer?] gave instructions (whether oral or written, I do not know) to Toropogritskii to accept from Nikiforov the goods from the *Il'mena.* That was done and the goods were brought to the storehouse occupied by Kicherov. Mr. Maditsyn [Madson] was appointed as commander of the schooner. Toropogritskii at first loaded iron and everything [else that was] heavy on the *Kad'iak.* I concluded that he was going to be the manager there.

About this time Toropogritskii told me that Doctor [Sheffer] asked him about my conduct. Finally he [the doctor] called me in and talked a great deal about my business in beavers. He explained to me the reason for his being in the Sandwich Islands; he was commissioned by His Honor, Governor, Collegiate Councilor and Cavalier, Alexander Andreevich Baranov; he was sent there [to the islands] to gain advantages for the Sovereign and profits for the Company. Therefore he [Sheffer] had a full right to detain there all the Company's ships and to order the crews at his own discretion. I gave him my respectful attention and accepted for my future guidance all that was said to me. Then he ordered me to receive the goods from Toropogritskii, to load them on the schooner, and to proceed to the island of Kauai. He promised, too, to go there in the near future.

Seeing that he was the commander of our ships and men, I obediently acted on his wishes and went to the island of Kauai. I arrived there safely. The ship Il'mena followed us in arriving there and brought news that the doctor had remained on Whittemore's ship. Later I received information [by land] from across the mountains that Captain Whittemore with his ship was on the northern side of Kauai in the harbor of Hanalei. Two days later the doctor arrived on Whittemore's ship. He went ashore and to the Company house and ordered me to unload the schooner. He obtained a storehouse from the king. They brought to me there various articles from Whittemore's ship. He [Sheffer] announced then that he had bought this [Whittemore's] ship and that he would send it to Sitka to get the money [to cover the purchase]. He appointed Antipatr Alexandrovich and Toropogritskii [to go] on this ship, while I was to stay [here] and copy the papers for him. He ordered Toropogritskii to move on the ship but added that the ship was to remain here for a few days. The next day he told me that the papers must be ready the following day because Whittemore was to leave then. I reported to him that the remaining beavers would be spoiled by moths; that it was impossible to trade in skins in a warm climate, and asked him to be so kind as to send the skins to Sitka. Late that evening he called on me and ordered me to go to the ship Il'mena and to deliver them [the remaining furs] to Toropogritskii. When I came on board the vessel I saw that Toropogritskii was sick. Mr. Whittemore was in a hurry to lift anchor, so I delivered the bales [of furs] to Antipatr Alexand-rovich so they would not be left with us on Kauai, and, as soon as the furs were transported [from the *Il'mena* to the newly purchased ship], the sails were set and the ship departed. I left the *Il'mena,* went ashore, and remained there for a long time. By order [of Sheffer] I assumed the duties of manager (*prikashchik*) and was ordered to supervise the men.

Later, on January 20, 1817, a schooner arrived at Kauai and dropped anchor. Doctor [Sheffer] sent me to the ship to ask whence it came and who was in command. I boarded the ship and found that it was the *Cossack* and its captain a Mr. Brown. I had known him before, in 1810, when he rescued me from captivity. He told me that he had been at Sitka and brought letters which about fifteen minutes before my arrival he had sent ashore by some natives in a canoe. There was nothing else for me to do on the ship, so I took a baidarka and went ashore. Upon my arrival there, I received from the Doctor [Sheffer] a letter from His Honor, Alexander Andreevich [Baranov], who wrote, among other things: "It is better for you to hunt beavers than to till the soil; report with all [your] Aleuts to Sitka." I showed the letter to the doctor, who read it and gave it back and said with contempt: "Go on foot, if you wish. I will not give you a ship and I will keep all the Aleuts; I will hold you until Alexander Andreevich sends an intelligent, sober, and experienced man in your place."

Until this time my conduct was as desirable as he could have wished and he hardly ever saw me drunk. I now saw myself confined to a narrow space from which, with my simple soul, I could not find any way out. How was I to escape this pigheadedness? My superiors would consider any action on my own initiative as insubordination. Life was very hard. So when I went back to my home, I asked for a glass of vodka, and then for another, and went to bed. The next day I did the same; and so it went for over a week. The doctor often asked for me and always received the answer that I was drunk. At first they [the other men] said that I was not a young man and should not be ashamed of a little relaxation after having served the Company for such a long time. Later, people started to wonder because of the excess [of my drinking], knowing that I had always considered drunkenness as one of the worst vices. [My excuse was] that everything I undertook [in the interest of the Company] was done in vain.

When we were driven from the island of Kauai, the doctor went on board the *Kad'iak* while I remained on shore supervising the loading of the property. When the last party was leaving, I wrote to the doctor asking for permission to board the ship *Il'mena*, but was refused; I received an order to put all my property on the *Kad'iak*, but I was to remain behind.

In the above statement, submitted to your Honor, I have tried to present my explanations conscientiously and truly.

[Signed] T<small>IMOFEI</small> T<small>ARAKANOV</small>

February 12, 1818

37. Affidavit, Charles Fox Bennick, June 16, 1817, Attesting to Agreements Concluded by King Kaumualii.

The undersigned testifies that he acted as a translator between the two contracting parties and heard the contract between His Majesty, Kaumualii, on the island Kauai, on one side, and the Commissioner of the Russian-American Company, Egor Sheffer. May 21, 1816, the king among other things asked the above-mentioned Commissioner and Captain Podushkin of the ship *Otkrytie* for a Russian flag and for the protection of the Russian Empire. I testify that King Kaumualii concluded several contracts with Mr. Sheffer, who represented the Russian-American Company. The king promised to deliver to the Company every year a small ship's cargo of dry taro and other products of Kauai. The king also handed over to the Company for all future time all the sandalwood on the island Kauai. The king also gave the Company the whole province of Hanalei, together with its port, and he allowed the Company to maintain a factory in Kauai. For the provision given by the king, extending to May 21, 1817, for all the sandalwood on the island Kauai, for the province and port of Hanalei, the king consented to accept a schooner, the *Lydia*, and goods from the *Bering*, [———], *Otkrytie*, *Il'mena*, and *Kad'iak*. In addition to that, the king received goods from Mr. Silnoks [Wilcocks?] which were placed in the storehouse of the Russian-American Company on Kauai. For the great future cargoes [of sandalwood?] and for yearly provisions, Mr. Sheffer promised to bring every year whatever goods the king would need, to the value of 12,000 rubles.

All these conditions were included in the contracts and I, as a Christian and a subject of Great Britain, am a witness thereof, so help me God—

Wittness [sic] CHAS. FOX BENNICK

Kauai

June 16, 1817

Vient à la suite la legalisation de Chas. Fox Bennick par devant Jose Gabriel Masda, Tabellão, a la ville de la cividade de Nome de Dios de Macao 15 de Sept. 1817[.]

A la suite l'approbation Miguel de Arriaga Brum da Silveria[,] Governeur de Macao[,] du 16 de Sept. 1817 & sceau aux armes de Portugal—.

38. Report, Timofei Tarakanov, et al., to Main Office, July 7, 1817, on Events up to Departure of Schäffer.

To the Main Office of the Russian-American Company, under the exalted protection of His Imperial Majesty.

REPORT

Because of hatred and jealousy [toward us], almost all the seamen of the United States of America who trade along the Northwest coast, have tried previously, and are still trying, to incite the Indians of the Sandwich Islands to rebel against us. In order to oppose the Russians and the Russian-American Company, in 1816 they started their factories on the island Kauai, ruled by King Kaumualii . . . and his chiefs. They bought plantations from the king and all the sandalwood on the island. They paid the king whatever price the latter demanded. They also bought a year's supply of provisions, namely, dry taro, salt, coconuts, etc., which the king was under contract to deliver to the Russians in exchange for a cargo of 12/t [12,000 rubles worth] of such goods as he might have needed. We have the list of what was demanded by the king.

When the Company ship *Otkrytie* arrived at Kauai the king asked Sheffer, the Chief Commissioner of the Company, and Iakov Anikeevich Podushkin, Lieutenant of the Russian Navy, the commander of the ship, to grant him a Russian flag and to accept him under the protection of His Majesty, the Emperor of All the Russias. In consequence of that, on May 21, 1816, the king was given a Russian flag, and his request for protection was sent to the Sovereign Emperor at St. Petersburg. The king himself took the flag from the ship to the shore, and it was raised there on a mast. A thirteen-gun salute was fired by the ship's cannon, and was followed by one of twenty-one guns. Before he made his decision, the king *gathered together all the images* [stress in original] which served him as gods and called in all the priests and chiefs and asked their advice. Gods and men gave answer: "It was good to receive the flag." After the contracts were concluded with the Russian-American Company, they constructed, as a sign of gratitude, a new "morea" or temple and made sacrifices of various kinds—fruits, and, if reports are correct, two men. After these events took place the commanders of every American ship which called at Kauai tried by every means to revile the Russian flag, which the king raised every time a foreign vessel called at his port. They [the Americans] urged the king to lower the Russian flag and they discredited the Russians in his opinion.

What they tried to persuade the king to do [on Kauai], the Americans did themselves on Oahu, where there were also Russian factories and several plantations. They succeeded there so much more easily because John Young, the commissioner of King Kamehameha, used to receive valuable gifts from them and so worked with them hand in glove. They destroyed the Russian factory there, and we had to take off the Russians who were there. After the failure of their [the Americans'] evil plans on Kauai on August 25, 1816,* they sent five boats there from Oahu, with a

---

* Evidently an error. The reference may be to the September 24, 1816 landing from the *O'Cain*.

letter falsely stating that the Americans were at war with the Russians. The letter contained threats that unless King Kaumualii immediately drove the Russians from Kauai, five American vessels would go there and kill him and all his natives.

At that time the Americans in the Russian service rebelled against the Russians. When the revolution started on the island, an American, William Wadsworth, who was captain of our ship, the *Il'mena,* fled to the Indians on shore. The Indians sided with the Americans and sent all the Russians from the shore to their ships. At that time we almost lost the manager of the factory, Egor Nikolaevich Sheffer. The barbarians drilled holes in his boat and then sent him along in his boat to the ship *Mirt-Kad'iak,* which he reached at great personal danger.

In the meanwhile, on shore they discharged the cannon and raised a flag which did not belong to any known nation. They [the Americans] refused to give us any provisions and prohibited the Indians from trading with us or from visiting our ships. They even refused to give us our own pigs, goats, and sheep. When our men were sent to Hanalei to take care of our property, the Indians, at the sight of the arriving Russians, started to shoot at them from the bushes and wounded one of the Aleuts from Kad'iak. The Indians even refused to allow us to get water and grass for the cattle. After that we received a letter containing a threat that unless we left the island in twenty-four hours, or if anybody dared to go ashore, then we should suffer dearly. The letter was written in the name of the king but it lacked his mark. The Company men on the ship *Mirt-Kad'iak* were in a most pitiful state. There were sixty men on board, while the leakage of the ship was forty-eight feet a day.

The chief commissioner sent a letter from Hanalei by Tarakanov to the king, reminding him of our rights and our property. The king, after reading the letter, at first said that he would keep his word. "It is true that the sandalwood belongs to you. However, farewell to you, Tarakanov, farewell to you, Doctor. You will have to excuse me, but I cannot let you stay on the island; circumstances force me to act so." His words show that only because of fear of force and really against his own will he had to treat the Russians so dishonorably. We could not resist our enemies. Our forces are

weak, and all the Englishmen and Americans in our service
betrayed us, with the exception of George Young, commander of
the *Mirt-Kad'iak*. Because this vessel was unfit for the long voyage
to Sitka, it was decided by general agreement that George Young
should take command of the *Il'mena* and take her and necessary
papers to Sitka. The rest would go on the *Mirt-Kad'iak* to Oahu, so
as to make necessary repairs there before going to Sitka. The port of
Honolulu is the only one in the Sandwich islands where it is possible
to dry and repair ships.

We reached Honolulu in five days by the incessant efforts of Mr.
Sheffer, without aid from any other navigator. We dropped anchor
two miles from the entrance to the port on its eastern side, as well
as we could with the unfavorable wind. Then we discharged a
cannon as a sign of distress. In answer to this signal, a pilot arrived.
As it was already evening, we asked him to leave us there until
morning, sending back with him a letter written by George Young
truthfully describing our misfortunes. The next day we sent to the
port a request for a pilot, but we received an answer that they
questioned our condition and thought that we had drilled holes in
our ship on purpose. Soon they sent a carpenter to inspect our ship.
The carpenter looked it over and declared that it was leaking
everywhere. Then we received a letter from old John Young to the
effect that if we should remove our cannons, muskets, sabers, pikes,
and other weapons, as well as gunpowder, from the ship, they
would then let us enter the port. We agreed to this and waited to
learn what they wanted us to do. Still, under different pretexts, we
were not admitted to the port for eight whole days. It seems that
Mr. Veils [Wildes?], the captain of a Bostonian ship then in the
harbor, had the utmost influence there.

In the meantime, some of the Russians visited the port and went
to see John Young. They were told to deliver Dr. Sheffer, who
was to be put in irons and sent on the first ship to America. To that
Tarakanov answered that under such circumstances all the Russians and Aleuts should be sent along with the doctor! An American
sailor, Beckley, a long-time resident on the island who was present,
said to Tarakanov, "It is better that one man should die rather than
sixty-six." This view was supported by Francis Voles [Wallace?],

an Englishman and former boatswain of the Russian-American Company, who added that old Young had told him that if we brought the ship into port, and Dr. Sheffer, Filip Osipov, or Foka Boniga [Fox Bennick?] came ashore, they would be shot.

The above-mentioned Beckley, who knew Tarakanov, told him that the Americans spoke so much evil of the Russians to the king that the latter had begun to doubt their [?] word. The American captains sailing near these shores [of the Sandwich Islands] do not care if the Russian ship and its crew perish; all they are concerned with is how to get another piece of sandalwood. Their attitude is based on their acceptance, as a fact, of the stories told about us by Francis Voles, the former employee of our Company who afterward deserted us. He described the Russians in the worst possible colors. His stories had such an effect that the Americans, with the help of the Indians, decided to capture Dr. Sheffer and to send him to the king of Hawaii, where he might be executed, a fate which the local barbarians might be expected to mete out. The Americans hated Dr. Sheffer because, when he was on Kauai, he tried to establish Russian factories there on the basis of contracts with the local king, Kaumualii. The Americans were very much opposed to this and incited the Indians to kill Sheffer and to destroy the [Russian] ship. Such an attempt was made when the Indians towed the ship to a sand bank with the intention of grounding it, and if the Russians had not noticed it and dropped anchor, the ship would have been lost. Fortunately an American vessel arrived there, whose captain, Lewis, was a goodhearted man. He agreed to take Sheffer on his ship and to take him to Canton, from where Sheffer could easily travel to St. Petersburg and there report to the Main Office how the Americans had dishonored the Russian flag and how much of the Company's property they had seized. Under these circumstances it seemed advisable that Filip Osipov, a servant of the Company, should accompany Sheffer to make sure that the papers would reach the company.

From Sitka we have had no news for a long time and when it finally does come it may be too late and Sheffer may not be alive. For these reasons we have decided, against his wishes, to send him to Canton, from whence he may go wherever he likes. We have advised, however, that he go to St. Petersburg, where we hope to find support for our rights on these islands.

We remain the servants of the Company:

TIMOFEI TARAKANOV
IVAN BOLOKOV
ALEXEI ODNORRIADKIN
PETR KICHEROV

Island Oahu,
July 7, 1817

39. Letter, Schäffer to Baranov, July 7[?], 1817, Concerning Reception at Oahu, and Departure for Canton.

Received November 15, 1817 from the brig *Brutus,* per A. Larionov.

Your Honor, my dear Sir, Alexander Andreevich [Baranov]:

Circumstances turned against us on Kauai before I had a lengthy report ready for you; I sent the *Il'mena* to you and had no opportunity to write more. I left this letter of explanation with Mr. Tarakanov, who will send it to you at the first good opportunity, or will bring it himself. Here on Oahu everything is clear. Trustworthy men have explained everything to us. I can assure you that there is nothing left for me to do, except to make as speedy a journey as possible to St. Petersburg, and there report to the Main Office and to all Ministries everything that is demanded by Russian [national] honor and by the interests of the Company. They [the St. Petersburg authorities] must take immediate action. We have no opportunity to communicate with you now. Lord knows when we shall have it. It will be too late to travel this year to St. Petersburg by way of Okhotsk. All our fellows here understand the situation. They have asked me to go along with Captain Lewis, who plans to make another trip to Canton, and from there to proceed to St. Petersburg. I hope that His Honor, Mr. Ljungstedt, in Macao, has the money I shall need for traveling expenses.

One can do little with the ships you now have on hand. King Kaumualii now has Whittemore's ship *Avon;* the local king [Kamehameha] has three ships; besides which they will have more ships from the Americans, who are enemies of yours and of all the Russians. Be especially on guard against old Ebbets, who is a crook, and Winship, who is another. Every American arriving here spreads some lies through old Young. Mr. Holmes himself assured us that William [!] Hunt was the first to start trouble for us here.

I can tell you in secret that they [the Americans] incite the old king against the English. Their plan is to put the Sandwich Islands under the American flag, because everybody knows that there is no true English protectorate over Kamehameha. I have copies of all papers which Kamehameha received from England. Two of them concern [incomprehensible phrase in broken Russian] interest against the Americans and the native chiefs. You and I cannot see each other, but be assured that I need neither a soldier's medal nor reward to defend your honor and the Company's interests. I only wish that the ship *Avon* were ours, for we need it twice as badly now as before. [Three incomprehensible sentences.] Meanwhile I shall pray the Lord to grant you strength and a long life and to grant me a chance to see you again and to drink a glass of Russian vodka to your health. I hope to see you in a year and a half. I asked Mr. Tarakanov to take command [over?] Odnoriadkin, Boligov, and Kicherov, and have ordered him, after he delivers reports, ship, and men to Sitka, to send them [the men] back here, because they are familiar with everything here. I can tell you with a great deal of pleasure that they are deserving, honest, and sober men. Perhaps you have known Leshchinskii for a long time, perhaps but a short time, but I can recommend him as a gross scoundrel who even sent to the next world our old Chereglasov.

Once more I wish you many years of health and happiness. I am reduced to nothing more than skin and bones since I assumed the service of the Company. Perhaps you will hear from some honest men the explanation of such lies as were reported to you by the good for nothing Toropogritskii and Verkhovinskii. I have not time to write about them, but I have a ready answer for every one of them.

I send my respects to all the honest men who live in Sitka, and remain, until death itself, with the greatest esteem,

Your Honor My dear Sir
(The original signed:)
Your obedient servant
EGOR SHEFFER

Checked in the Office: AL. BARANOV
Island of Oahu, port of Honolulu
on the ship *Mirt-Kad'iak*
July 7[?], 1817

40. *Directive, Main Office to Baranov, March 22, 1817, Expressing Disapproval of Use of Schäffer on Hawaiian Mission and Forbidding his Employment in California.*

No. 196
Copy
From the Main Office of the Russian-American Company, under protection of His Supreme Imperial Majesty.

To the Chief Manager of the Russian-American colony, Collegiate Councilor and Cavalier Alexander Andreevich Baranov.

In your dispatch of last year you stated that you considered Doctor Sheffer to be of no use, having quitted the ship *Suvorov* because of personal differences with the officers and dissatisfaction because the ship did not put in everywhere that he wanted to collect specimens, not for the Company, but for himself and foreign nations. Now, however, you seem to have entrusted him with an expedition to the Sandwich Islands, whence you sent him on the ship *Otkrytie,* although he has not previously headed an expedition, is a foreigner, and has not acquired his specimens for Russia. If you find it necessary to leave him in his position as physician, then under no account allow him to set up schools and distilleries at Ross. It is too early to start one or the other. It is necessary to wait until the Russians are firmly established there and the Spaniards have become our good neighbors. The monks in California are too numerous and too influential with the local government. Our establishment of schools would cause them to look upon us from an entirely different angle, whereas at present they look upon us merely as trading settlers. As the island of Sitka is at present our chief settlement, all such universally beneficial establishments, especially hospitals, must be promoted at Novo-Arkhangel'sk. Keep that particularly in mind. Leave the village of Ross in such a condition that the Spaniards will have no cause to suspect us of doing more than trading and hunting. Yet, meanwhile, under the pretext of them, increase tillage, cattle breeding, poultry raising, gardening, and planting. Also enlarge the settlement itself with necessary buildings.

Office Director ZELENSKII

March 22, 1817

Checked by Desk Chief LIUBOMUDROV

41. *Main Office to Baranov, August 14, 1817, Expressing Interest in Schäffer's Achievements* (*Extract*).

No. 451 August 14, 1817

P.S. After signing this dispatch we received, as you will see from the attached copies, a most interesting and pleasant report from Dr. Sheffer, from one of the Sandwich Islands, Kauai. The report was transmitted to the Emperor today in case His Majesty will deign to send any orders with the departing frigate *Kamchatka*. We also enclose a copy of our instructions regarding the establishment of a factory on Kauai island, to which in due course you may add your own suggestions.

BENEDICT KRAMER

42. Main Office to Lieutenant V. M. Golovnin, August 14, 1817, Directing Him to Aid at Kauai (Extract).

Case No. 5
No. 472
From the postscript of a letter of August 14, 1817, written to Vasilii Mikhailovich Golovnin [departing on] the sloop *Kamchatka*.

. . . They hope that you will visit the Sandwich Islands and especially the island of Kauai, and that in fulfillment of directions given to you, you will thoroughly investigate that place. You are to do everything possible to establish Russian authority and to develop factories there. You will arrange relations there between the Russians and the inhabitants of this and other islands. You will notify the Main Office of the [Russian-American] Company so that it can take up such measures as might be necessary to make certain the acquisition of this new and important possession, both for the Company and for the Fatherland. English and North American papers have already published news of the fact that the Company has acquired land on Kauai and has fortified its factory.

43. Main Office to Schäffer via Baranov, August 20, 1817.

From the Main Office of the Russian-American Company under His Exalted Majesty's Protection.
To the Manager, commissioned by Mr. Baranov, of the expedition of the Russian-American Company on the island of Kauai.

DIRECTIONS

There has occurred a gratifying and important event for the Russian-American Company and for our country in general. The Collegiate Assessor, Doctor of Medicine and Surgery, Sheffer, reports that Kaumualii, the king of the island Kauai, has placed himself, all the islands in his possession, and all his people under the protection of our Sovereign Emperor and Autocrat of All the Russias. The king also ceded to the Russian-American Company, in full and permanent possession, a whole province with its native population. He also concluded with Sheffer, who represented the Company, a commercial treaty giving the Company exclusive rights in the sandalwood trade.

Concerning this event we do not as yet have detailed information—no description of the island, and its inhabitants, etc. Mr. Sheffer, mentioned above, has promised to send this information to the office of the Company, which regards as its duty and obligation, prior to further considerations, to give preliminary directions to the person who is to be in charge of this new acquisition.

As to the protection of King Kaumualii and his people

It is very likely that King Kaumualii sought the protection of the Russian Emperor, because he [Kaumualii] is weaker than the other kings of these islands, who probably threatened his position. If such is the case, the manager of the expedition on Kauai should protect his [Kaumualii's] life and his people from the evil designs of the other stronger rulers of the islands. He must do so in so far as local circumstances allow it, except when the attack is made by any European nation, directly or indirectly. In such a case, the Company should not interfere.

As to the respect and honors due King Kaumualii

King Kaumualii should be given proper respect as a ruler friendly to us and under the protection of our Sovereign. He should be given such honors as seem to be most suitable, considering his simple and savage life.

How to settle quarrels between our men and the natives

If there should be any dispute with the Indians, his [Kaumualii's] subjects, or any difficulties, then neither the manager of the factory nor his subordinates should settle the affair themselves, but must always consult King Kaumualii and seek his justice. Even if those who have been given into the possession of the Company are found guilty of any crime, the manager of the expedition should not try them himself but should ask advice and justice from the king. These directions should be observed strictly until the receipt of new directions defining the status of the expedition.

To avoid any oppression or mistreatment of the islanders

Most of all, under the threat of unavoidable and strict punishment, any oppression of the islanders, insults, disregard for their property, or violations of women should be prevented. Such base actions always bring trouble to the offenders and to the Company. People who are unfamiliar with the general situation or who bear a grudge are apt to denounce and criticize the Company, even if the latter has not taken the least part in such actions and prohibits them.

The islanders should not be used as laborers
by force or without payment for their work

No islanders, even those who belong to the Company, should be forced into any service or work under compulsion. They ought to be asked and gradually trained to perform different tasks according to local conditions and needs, with remunerations for their work. Take care to develop trade with them and get them used to that. In other words, treat the islanders as your countrymen, as friends and subjects of Russia. Otherwise, you will never do anything with these children of nature; you will fail to unite them with you and only develop obstacles toward permanent rule over them.

About the trade affairs of the expedition

We do not have as yet but are still expecting complete detailed information about the island of Kauai. We do not know as yet what advantages and profits it offers and what sort of trade can be carried on there. Therefore we do not suggest anything in particular and leave it to the judgment of the manager [of the island] to take advantage of his own knowledge and experience, as well as of the suggestions by Mr. Baranov. In time, when the Company learns all the expected details, new directions will be issued.

Director BENEDICT KRAMER
Director ANDREI SEVERIN

Office Director and Court Councilor ZELENSKII
For the Russian-American Company
Main Office Seal
No. 472
August 20, 1817

44. *Memorandum, Main Office, August, 1817, Listing Gifts sent to King Kaumualii.*

Sent with His Excellency Vasilii Mikhailovich Golovnin as gifts, in the name of the Russian-American Company, for King Kaumualii of the island of Kauai:

1	large mirror in a gold frame ....rub.	150
1	cut glass carafe .... "	60
1	" " .... "	40
1	pitcher .... "	60
1	glass . . . with portraits of the Emperor and Empress no. 40 "	35
2	goblets .... "	80
1	large round cup .... "	80
1	" " " .... "	30
2	cups at least 20 rubles each .... "	40
		375

First Secretary of the Main Office
Court Councilor I. ZELENSKII

45. *Memorandum, V. N. Berkh, on the Sandwich Islands, Written About August, 1817, with Letter of I. A. Kuskov, Written at Fort Ross, California, August 12, 1816, Enclosing Copy of King Kaumualii's Act of Allegiance, May 21, 1816.*

Copy

THE SANDWICH ISLANDS

Information about the Sandwich Islands. The famous Cook, the excellent navigator of the eighteenth century, during his third and last trip discovered some islands in the northern part of the Pacific Ocean, which he called the Sandwich Islands in honor of his benefactor, Lord Sandwich. Readers will know very well that he ended his days on one of these islands.

Although Captain Cook brought us information about these remarkable islands, the honor of discovery does not belong to the English. There are proofs that Spanish mariners already knew of these islands by the middle of the sixteenth century.* The English admiral, Lord Anson, during his cruise around the world, captured a Spanish galleon which was going from Acapulco to Manila. On this galleon Anson found a map showing islands on the parallels 18° and 23° N.L. which are the present Sandwich Islands. The chief proof is that the biggest island was named by the Spaniards *La Mesa* (i.e., table). On the largest of these islands, Hawaii, there is a magnificent mountain, Mauna Loa, which has a top like a table board, suggesting the above-mentioned name. After the discovery of these islands by Captain Cook, that is, between 1778 and 1793, they were but little known to the world. At that time [1792–1794] the English government sent Captain Vancouver [on an expedition] for the purpose of getting a description of the Northwestern part of America. During his frequent visits to the Sandwich Islands, Vancouver investigated them thoroughly and in his journal he made known to the world the results. Vancouver, supposing that his country would consider the [Sandwich] islands worthy of occupation, presented the [local] king with a small schooner (a small sailing vessel) and wrote in his journal that the possessor of the Sandwich Islands accepted it with due respect in the name of his Britannic Majesty and declared himself a vassal of England. It was very easy to write such words on paper, for the king did not know anything [about this report] and, as is known to all navigators who have been there, he does not recognize himself as a subject of the English crown.

Great Britain, having by this clever policy acquired the largest and richest portions of the globe, did not feel it necessary to accept the Sandwich Islands, which are outside of its sphere of activity, and [therefore] does not consider the islands as its property. Certain persons even appealed to Parliament suggesting the occupation of the islands, but Parliament disregarded the request.

The entire group of Sandwich Islands belongs to two rulers; the

---

* A Spanish discovery of the Hawaiian Islands in the sixteenth century still remains a possibility.

first of them, Kamehameha, has seven islands: Hawaii, Maui, Kahoolawe, Lanai, Torotou [?], Molokai, and Oahu, and he is very powerful. He has several sailboats and over eighty sailors, deserters from English ships. They surround the king, forming a guard against his own subjects, by whom he is hated because of his cruel temper and the tyrannical murder of all former rulers of the above-mentioned islands. If he had not surrounded himself with these guards, the higher nobility, which has by this time been completely suppressed by him, would find a way to break his power.

The second king, whose name is Kaumualii, is a very clever, courteous, and pleasant man. He owns only four islands: Kauai, Niihau, Lehua, and Kaula. If his possessions had been nearer to the island Hawaii, the permanent residence of the first-named king, then Kaumualii would long ago have become a victim of the insatiable avidity of King Kamehameha.

I had the pleasure of meeting King Kaumualii in 1805, and talked with him a great deal in English, which he knows quite well. The poor king was much elated over the arrival of the ship *Neva*. He explained to us with tears [in his eyes] that every moment he expected an attack from Kamehameha and, having only a weak army, he was afraid of becoming the victim of Kamehameha. Kaumualii said: "If this barbarian should seize my islands, he will put me and all my family to a most cruel death."

His [Kamehameha's] hellish policy is so farsighted that when he took possession of the islands Oahu, Molokai, Lanai, and Maui, he not only killed the kings, but he also had all their relatives and followers put to death in his presence.

King Kaumualii tried very insistently to persuade us to remain here for a while for his protection. He also asked us to give him gunpowder and guns. In spite of our most cordial feelings toward him, we had to refuse his request. As we were taking leave of him, he repeated his request in such a tearful voice that Lieutenant Arbuzov and I presented him with our swords. The grateful Kaumualii accepted them with deepest appreciation and left us highly concerned over his fate.

Wise Providence, however, checks unlimited ambitions, and accordingly it destroyed the plans of the rapacious Kamehameha.

This savage ruler had subjugated to his power all the Sandwich Islands, with the exception of those which belonged to Kaumualii. Repeatedly he sent messengers to Kaumualii demanding the surrender of the latter's possessions. When he failed to receive a satisfactory reply, Kamehameha began to gather a strong army. At the time when we, having parted with our worthy leader, I. F. Krusenstern, landed on the island of Hawaii, Kamehameha had all his army in Oahu. We have heard that he had about seven thousand warriors. Going from there to the island of Kad'iak, we feared very much that Kaumualii would be vanquished, and on several occasions we felt alarmed about his fate.

Upon our arrival the next year in Canton we rejoiced very much upon hearing that the numerous army of Kamehameha had been dispersed because of the spread of disease and that the enterprise had failed. In order better to succeed in his plans Kamehameha went with his army to Oahu and began gathering rocks to fit sling shots and also made other military preparations. The inadequacy of food for such a number of men and the time required to transport additional supplies caused a disease similar to scurvy, which forced him to postpone the conquest of the island Kauai.

According to the latest information, King Kamehameha is now even more powerful [than before]. He has two ships commanded by Europeans. One of these Kamehameha sent to Canton to engage in trade. Another was sent to the Marquesas Islands with the purpose of looking them over. This new "Nadir" * has the intention of conquering for himself one-fifth of the globe.

After 1805 he did not make any new attempts against King Kaumualii. One of my friends who visited the Sandwich Islands much later than we did assured me that only superstition prevents Kamehameha from making another attack. During his first expedition he took along a multitude of idols, which he burned publicly in the market place on his return because they had not helped him. The priests interpreted this circumstance unfavorably for Kamehameha, and the latter lost the courage to attempt another enterprise.

---

* The reference is to Nadir Shah (1688–1747), a Persian conqueror notorious for his cruelty.

These islands, which do not belong to any European power, must belong to Russia. Their location between the eastern shores of Siberia and the American colonies makes them of the utmost importance for keeping communications open between these points, and also as a food base for Kamchatka, [which is] suffering from a shortage of provisions.

Kamchatka, that remote part of the Russian Empire, is placed by nature in such a disadvantageous position in comparison with other parts of Siberia, that all supplies have to be taken there by sea. The coastal communication is very inconvenient because it is possible only during the winter season and then only with the greatest difficulty.

Beginning with the year 1716, transport ships with necessary supplies were sent annually from Okhotsk to Kamchatka. The distance by sea is not very great, but the boats must pass between the various northern Kuril islands, where they encounter unbelievable currents and winds rushing between the mountains. As a result, a number of ships have been wrecked. As long as the transport ships pursuing the course from Okhotsk to Kamchatka have no safe haven when they encounter adverse winds, they have to follow the mountainous shore of Kamchatka and end their existence either there or on the rocks of the Kurils.

Suppose now that the northern islands of the Sandwich group belonged to Russia. Then the above-mentioned government ships, upon encountering adverse winds, could go down to the island of Kauai, and after spending the winter months in this most pleasant climate, would arrive safely in May on the shores of Kamchatka. In this way not only food supplies but other necessities would reach Kamchatka.

The Russian-American Company, which controls the trade of the entire eastern part of Russia and which has important colonies on the northwestern shores of America as far as California itself, is losing ships because it does not have a safe port on the Pacific.

The ships of the Company going back and forth from Okhotsk to America usually sail in August and September, meeting severe adverse winds, which cause the ships to seek refuge on the Aleutian Islands. The volcanic shores of the latter, however, present imminent peril rather than salvation.

The inhabitants of the Sandwich Islands are graceful, of medium height, and in spite of their dark skins are not unattractive like the Kalmuks and other savage tribes. The women here are very pleasant, quick, good-looking, and remind one of the charmers of the Tahiti Islands described in so many [accounts of] sea travels. They like Europeans and seem to be the chief attraction inducing the 150 Englishmen living on the islands to stay there. The women are very imitative, have a great deal of sense, and quickly learn European customs. The well-known Captain Meares had a Sandwich woman on his ship for two years.

She became so accustomed to all the labors, occupations, and clothing of our ladies that it was very difficult to tell that she was not an Englishwoman.

Nevertheless, the women of the Marquesas Islands are much better-looking and, because Europeans do not go there as often, they are much more respectable and moral.

The Sandwich Islanders in many respects are different from the savages inhabiting America. They are very active, capable of doing any work, docile, obedient, and are willing to work on European ships. One American captain told me of stopping once at the island of Hawaii. His ship needed repairs which made it necessary for him to stay there for more than four weeks. During this time his men became acquainted with the Sandwich women, who charmed them to such an extent that when he had to depart again for the open sea, out of eighteen men on his ship, he did not have one-half. Having the intention of spending the winter months near the northwestern shores of America, this navigator did not dare continue the voyage with such a small number of men. So he hired twelve young Sandwich men. He told me that these men in eight weeks became such proficient sailors that he could not want any better.

The Sandwich Islands, being situated between 18° and 23° north latitude, should be very hot, like all countries in the tropics. But because they are situated in the very center of the Pacific and very far from the shores of America, their climate is very pleasant. The sea breezes blowing to the shore, from sunrise to sunset, moderate the burning heat and purify the land of obnoxious vapors. I was there for only six days, so I cannot speak from my own experience about the weather. But from the conversation of those who had stayed there from three to four months, I heard that only during the equinox do they have bad weather and incessant rains.

There is a wealth of plant life on these islands.* The chief plants are sugar cane, sweet potatoes and roots, yams and taro. About thirty years ago Europe made a hubbub about the breadtree, which is not nearly as nourishing as yams and taro; besides, because it suffers easily from slightly cold air, it does not always produce crops. On the other hand these roots (yams and taro) grow in abundance, never spoil, and are so soft that in five minutes one can reduce the biggest root to flour. In my opinion the taro root is the most nourishing substance on earth.

Among the fruits, the most important here are bananas, coconuts, and watermelons.

Quadrupeds are not numerous on these islands. There are cattle there, but they wander in the woods. I have seen the domesticated cow with calf only at the king's [palace]. There are many pigs there. The good climate and ever-ready supply of food account for their large numbers. Pigs and dogs are the favorite foods of the Sandwich Islanders. The dogs are especially appreciated [being considered] a most appetizing dish. With the exception of chickens, there seem to be no domesticated fowl on the island of Hawaii.

The Sandwich Islands, surrounded by the ocean, must have a wealth of fish. The lakes also contain a great deal of fish. No minerals have been found as yet, but the pearl industry promises great profits.

Now Russia has an excellent opportunity to acquire this land, new and indispensable for her. One of my friends who lives in America wrote me the following letter:

---

* The island of Kauai, according to Captain Dixon, is in many respects preferable to Hawaii. There are more pigs there. Taro, bananas, and potatoes are better tasting; it has more coconut trees than on any other island. The water there is very pure and the salt is so good that one needs no better for salting. There are 60 villages on this island. Cook supposed there were 30,000 people there; King thinks there are about 50,000 inhabitants; but Dixon thinks there are no more than 25,000 of them. Dixon's *Voyage,* page 265. [Note in original.]

Dear Sir:

I think you have not forgotten those pleasant moments when we conversed together in these distant parts. We amused ourselves by dreaming imaginary enterprises. We divided the universe. We spread the boundaries of our beloved fatherland from the Amur river to Matsmai [Hokkaido], from California to the Sandwich Islands, and we organized the future prosperity of the Russian colonies.

Ten years have passed since that happy time. Many new enterprises have occupied me during the passing years and have aged me physically. But I am happy, especially because my activity resulted in great profit to the Russian-American Company, the possessions of which, to the glory of our fatherland, spread now as far as the shores of New Albion.

We have sent several ships to the Sandwich Islands. From there we obtained different provisions and other necessary things. Two years ago we had a disaster, very deplorable at the time, which resulted however, in a new and very useful acquisition.

Our ship *Bering,* which sailed in 1814 from Okhotsk to Novo-Arkhangel'sk, stopped at the island Kauai and as the result of an unfortunate accident perished on the rocks. A large part of its cargo was saved but the savages who rushed from all sides to the site of the disaster stole it all by night.

In the summer Alexander Andreevich [Baranov] sent Doctor Sheffer on the ship *Otkrytie* to the king of the island of Kauai to demand compensation for the stolen cargo.

Dr. Sheffer conducted the negotiations very cleverly. The king remunerated him with different articles to the value of 20,000 piastres, and concluded with us a commercial treaty according to the terms of which the Russians acquired the exclusive right of purchasing the sandalwood trees growing on the islands. I have heard from you about the pleasant character of this worthy ruler, so I did not doubt the success of our doctor. But imagine our pleasant surprise when we received the document enclosed here.

Evidently, fearing that he sooner or later would become a victim of the ambitious Kamehameha and having heard

from the Russians who frequently visited the place that
their possessions are not very far away, Kaumualii invited
G. Sheffer to see him and suddenly offered to become a
subject of Russia.

The doctor, our representative, acted very cautiously and
wisely on this occasion. He composed the above-mentioned
document in English and persuaded the king to make known
its contents to his subjects. The king obeyed without any
protest, and his subjects expressed their joyful consent. After
that, Kaumualii put a cross on this document saying "here is
a sign that I and my successors will belong forever to the
Russian throne." In parting, the king asked for the flag of
the Russian-American Company with the two-headed eagle
in the center. Mr. Sheffer gave it to him and the king raised
it above his dwelling.

Now you can see how our former plans came to fulfillment
by accident. We submitted all details to the Main Office
which assuredly will not fail to bring it to the attention of
the Emperor. Because of the wisdom and foresight of our
beloved Monarch, we may hope that he will accept the offer
of Kaumualii and will add to his possessions these islands
which are absolutely essential for us and for the entire Siberian coastal region.

Assuring you of my . . . I have the honor, etc.

IVAN KUSKOV

August 12, 1816
Northwest Coast of America

Although in the past I have written a great deal about our
American colonies, I would never have undertaken this account if I
had not received this letter from my dear friend in America. The
importance of its contents and the benefit which our country would
derive from the acquisition of these islands which are so valuable to
us, forced me to acquaint my countrymen with this new and little
known part of the world.

(Original signed)
VASILII BERKH

Perm
August, 1817

A copy of an act submitted by King Kaumualii to Doctor Collegiate Assessor, Sheffer, after making it known to his subjects.

I, King Kaumualii, ruler of the Sandwich Islands Kauai, Niihau, Lehua, and Kaula, hereditary prince of the islands Oahu, Lanai, and Maui, ask his Majesty, the Emperor Alexander Pavlovich, Autocrat of all the Russias, etc., etc., to receive the above-mentioned islands under his protection, and for myself and for my successors I undertake to remain always faithful to the Russian throne.

Sign of the King   X   KAUMUALII

May 21, 1816
Island Kauai

46. *Newspaper Reports, 1817, Regarding Events in Sandwich Islands.*

The Morning Chronicle (London), Wednesday, July 30, 1817 [in English]:

It was recently stated in a German Paper that Russia was negociating for the cession of California. The possession of this extensive territory, forming a peninsula of 300 leagues in length, bounded on the south and west by the Pacific Ocean, would give to that Power a great influence and controul in that sea, and afford great facilities to trade with North and South America, as well as China. Indeed, with the advantages which so great a line of coast presents, it would be in the power of Russia not only to open new sources of commerce in that region of the world, but command a complete monopoly of the commerce of those seas. The American Papers, of which we have received a mass at our Office, further the policy of Russia and its commercial speculations. One of these, *The National Advocate,* says: "The Russians, whom we have imagined to be a heavy and dull people, without spirit or Enterprise, are giving us daily proofs to the Contrary. They have taken possession of one of the Islands in the Pacific Ocean not far from the Sandwich Islands and have already fortified themselves. They will now derive the advantages of the whaling trade, one of the most profitable and necessary pursuits for the Russians, who consume a great quantity of oil. We will shortly find that nation with their Renown and active government in every part of the world."

[In Russian]

In the *Severnaia Pochta* [Northern Post], No. 76, September 22, 1817, it was mentioned that American newspapers have written that one of the islands in the Pacific near the Sandwich Islands has been taken [by the Russians] in the name of the Emperor.

47. *Minutes, Council of the Russian-American Company, January 19, 1818.*

January 19, 1818.

The council of the R. A. Co. [Russian-American Company], under the exalted protection of His Imperial Majesty, heard the draft of the Company's report to the Chief of the Ministry of Foreign Affairs, to be used for the information of His Imperial Majesty. The report contained the deed by Kaumualii, king of the Sandwich Islands of Kauai and Oahu, which was given by him to the Commissioner of the Company, Dr. Sheffer. According to this deed, the ruler [Kaumualii] handed over to the exalted protection of His Imperial Majesty all the islands belonging to him [Kaumualii]. At the same time he granted to the Company for colonization one-half of the island Oahu, with a few Indian families, and he granted permission to the Company to build factories on the island Kauai. One plantation there has aleady been started by Dr. Sheffer. In addition, this ruler concluded other negotiations with the Company concerning trade in sandalwood.

The Council decided to send the report to His Imperial Majesty through the Chief of the Ministry of Foreign Affairs.

GAVRIIL SARYCHEV
IVAN VENDEMEIER
IAKOV DRUZHININ

48. *Letter, Main Office to Baranov, March 15, 1818, Praising his Refusal to Buy the* Avon (*Extract*).

. . . You are to be thanked for your refusal to pay Wilcocks in Canton in sealskins for the cargo which he expected to foist off on the Company, but must now let spoil in storage. Also [for telling him that] the cargo bought from him in the Sandwich Islands, along with his vessel *Lydia,* for 21,000 rubles by Dr. Sheffer, who was unauthorized by you to make such transactions, can be paid for in sandalwood if Dr. Sheffer has acquired it already in the Sandwich Islands. And for your reply to Skipper Whittemore, who expected 200,000 rubles in furs, at the lowest prices, for sale of the three-masted vessel *Avon,* with fifteen guns, arranged by Sheffer for King Kaumualii. You have thus punished the boaster Sheffer for his arbitrary action, and have made the skippers feel that it is time for them to stop robbing the Company of beavers and seals at cheap prices set by them. . . .

MIKHAILO BULDAKOV
BENEDIKT KRAMER
ANDREI SEVERIN
Office Director ZELENSKII

No. 120
March 15, 1818.

49. *Letter, Schäffer to Main Office, July 30, 1818, upon Arrival in Denmark, and Notation Regarding his Letter of August 18, from Berlin.*

Dear Sirs:

Justice, the interest of the Company, and particularly the special advantages which might be derived by the Russian State, all necessitate my reporting in person to His Majesty, Our Most Enlightened Alexander Pavlovich. I found out here through our ambassador, however, that His Majesty had gone to attend a Congress, and that consequently I shall not be able to see him in St. Petersburg. In order not to lose any time, I am sending a message from here to Aachen, but in order to keep you informed, my dear Sir, about the main events which have taken place, I am sending you, by the promyshlennik Filip Osipov, some of my notes, as well as some of my reports to the Department of Foreign Affairs.

EGOR V. SHEFFER

Helsingor
July 30, 1818

[There follows a notation in French:]

In another letter, dated August 18, 1818, from Berlin, he complains of being without money and asks the Company to send him 100 *chervontsy*. He also states that the chief Grigorii Iskakov of Unalaska is with him.

50. *Report, Filip Osipov to Main Office, about September, 1818, Reviewing Operations in the Islands.*

Report of the promyshlennik Osipov who arrived at St. Petersburg from the Sandwich Islands with dispatches concerning Russian enterprise on the Islands and of the expulsion of the Russians from these Islands.

Doctor Egor Sheffer went to the Sandwich Islands with the two creole boys, on an American ship. Soon afterwards, the ship *Otkrytie,* under the command of Mr. Podushkin, went there also.

The ship arrived at the islands and found Mr. Sheffer on one of them called Oahu, which belonged to King Kamehameha.

As soon as the *Otkrytie* arrived at Oahu, Sheffer immediately came on board and sailed to the island of Kauai, whose king, Kaumualii, received him kindly and graciously. On the third day the king came out to the ship. They asked the king for the return of the pillaged cargo of the Company's ship *Bering,* which had been wrecked on the island of Niihau[!]. The king answered that he could not return the cargo, because all of the spoils had already been used up, but he consented to compensate the Company by delivery of the sandalwood on the island of Kauai. That satisfied Sheffer, who concluded an agreement with the king whereby the Company acquired the sandalwood. Upon that occasion the king requested Sheffer and Podushkin that he be accepted under the protection of the Russian Emperor. He wanted to adopt the Russian flag to signify that he enjoyed such protection. Although Sheffer and Podushkin were very willing to satisfy this wish, they wanted nevertheless to be assured first as to the sincerity of the king, and the support [of this scheme] by the subjects of the king. This is why they did not satisfy the king's request for three days. The king, in order to convince them of the sincerity of his intentions, finally gathered all his people in the port of Waimea and solemnly asked them if they would agree to his wish. The people, with no objections, approved his proposals. Then the agreement was concluded and announcement was made that the request of the king to be accepted under the protection of Russia would be forwarded to St. Petersburg to the Emperor, and the king could obtain a flag from the ship. In the presence of all the people who gathered there Kaumualii came aboard and they [Sheffer and Podushkin] handed him the flag. In order to win him over to Russia and to demonstrate that he [the king] had become an ally of Russia, Lieutenant Podushkin dressed him in his uniform with epaulets, hat, and cutlass. In this solemn dress he went ashore with the flag, and accompanied by all the people went to his house and raised the flag there, while a salute was fired from the ship. Three days passed during which Kaumualii was very friendly. After that they [the Russians] obtained an interpretor from Kaumualii and sailed on the *Otkrytie* to the island of Niihau. This was done to survey the island and to obtain fowl and yams for the ship. The king issued orders to this effect. During this voyage the masts were damaged. They were repaired [on the island] and after the food was obtained, the *Otkrytie* went toward Sitka while Sheffer himself, in the company of the two Aleuts, Osipov and Odnoriadkin, went back in a baidarka to Kauai, where two promyshlenniks had been left.

The king was overjoyed at Sheffer's return, and at that time granted to the Company some land at Waimea, where he himself had a residence. Sheffer gave orders to have this land cultivated. On it were planted cabbage, potatoes, turnips, carrots, beans, peas, and other garden vegetables, as well as corn, mustard, pineapple, watermelon, grapes, cotton, wheat, etc. Everything planted came up well except the wheat. Why the wheat crop failed is not known; perhaps the soil there is not fit for wheat cultivation, or possibly the seed was not good.

The cultivation of so many plants, many of them unknown to him, pleased the king greatly, and he granted to the Company two more lots of land; situated on both sides of a small river which flows into the harbor of Waimea. On these new lots the crop was just as good as on the first ones. The new successes pleased the king even more and he granted to the Company a large piece of land on the same island, nine versts in length and fifteen versts in width. That was between the port of Waimea and the province of Hanapepe, along the seashore where one could gather a great deal of salt.

At first they [the Russians] cultivated land with [illegible word], then after the ship *Il'mena* arrived at the island of Kauai they used small shovels taken from it. During the cultivation of land and harvesting of the crop the king voluntarily supplied his own men to help, according to the need, so that they also would learn how to cultivate the land.

While they were still cultivating the first lot of land the vessel *Mirt-Kad'iak* came to Kauai and two months later the *Il'mena* arrived. The *Mirt-Kad'iak* arrived directly from the colony, but the *Il'mena* came en route from the coast of California to Sitka. It had had to change its course because of a big leak and had steered for the Sandwich Islands. This vessel was in charge of Elliot de Castro [!—Wadsworth] who had contracted large debts in the name of the Company and had proved himself to be an incompetent sailor. For this reason he was dismissed from the *Il'mena* at Kauai. Both these ships, the *Mirt-Kad'iak* and the *Il'mena,* remained in Kauai until the expulsion of the Russians. The crew was divided into shifts, who alternated in going ashore to help cultivate the land.

While the land granted to the Company was being cultivated,

Kaumualii maintained uninterrupted friendly relations with Sheffer, and repeatedly told him that the other Sandwich Island king, Kamehameha, had two war ships, and that he, Kaumualii, would like to have at least one. This desire finally became so strong that he incessantly urged Sheffer to buy a ship, promising in exchange a whole province, Hanalei, with all its inhabitants and everything that was there. At that time there arrived at Kauai a ship belonging to an American, Gazli [Gyzelaar]. Sheffer, persuaded by the requests of the king, offered to buy this Gazli's vessel. Gazli agreed, and they decided on the conditions. They went to the island of Oahu, and when the ship returned to Kauai, Sheffer gave it to Kaumualii. Thus the king obtained the ship and ordered that it be brought to the mouth of the Waimea river.

Receiving the ship, the king gave Sheffer the above-mentioned province of Hanalei. This province is situated on the coast on the northern part of the island. It is mountainous all along the shore, but there is plenty of sandalwood and mahogany, as well as *miru* [?] and *tutui* [candlenut]. The Hanalei river flows through the brush-covered valley of this province into a harbor of the same name. The harbor is so large that it can hold a hundred ships, which could be anchored there in complete safety.

Having paid for the ship, the king did not fail to express his gratitude to Sheffer and Tarakanov, who arrived on the *Il'mena*. He gave each of them an allotment of land as well as some men to cultivate it. At the same time he declared that he had decided to send his eldest son to St. Petersburg to be educated, and handed over his younger son to Tarakanov to learn the Russian language.

Sheffer accepted the province of Hanalei and started to build two fortresses there, one on the right side of the river Hanalei at the mouth of the harbor and another on the same side of the river but much higher, at the harbor itself. Both fortresses were built of earth; however, both remained unfinished. The work was being done by the promyshlenniks with the aid of the inhabitants of the province, without any aid from the king. As soon as they perceived the significance of such fortresses, they started to beg Sheffer to construct similar fortresses also at the harbor of Waimea, on the first lot of land which they had ceded to the Company. They [the natives] declared that when this fortress was constructed they would move there. Sheffer prepared the plan and the king approved it. Then they started the fortress [at Waimea] which is almost finished on the sea side but not finished from other sides. During the construction of the fortress the king tried to give every possible help to our promyshlenniks, offering his own men.

While the Russians were on the island of Kauai, five American ships visited it. These ships, however, left the island immediately after their arrival because the king was repeatedly cheated by the American seamen and did not want to have anything to do with them. Whenever they tried to negotiate with him, he sent them to Sheffer, through whom they had to obtain and pay for the provisions which they needed.

This conduct of Kaumualii made everybody believe that he was entirely devoted to the Russians.

But such devotion to us alone was bitterly resented by the Americans. So they started to arouse suspicions among the inhabitants in regard to the Russians. An American, Whittemore, came to an agreement with an American, Ebbets, and together they called on Kamehameha and told him so many bad things about the Russians that he changed his opinions about them entirely. Under such circumstances they sent a message to Kaumualii urging him to expel the Russians from all the places which they occupied in his possessions. Kaumualii answered that he did not know yet whether it would lead to anything good and could not decide to accept the suggestion.

Later an American, Adams, came to Kaumualii by ship and declared to the king that he was sent by Kamehameha to lower the Russian flag and to expel the Russians from the island. Although at this time Sheffer was away in the province of Hanalei, which is situated at the northern part of the island, while the harbor Waimea where Kaumualii resides is on the southern side, he [Kaumualii] not only refused to expel the Russians, but he did not even let Adams lower the Russian flag. The latter had to leave without any success and Kaumualii immediately notified Sheffer about all this. The more devoted he [Kaumualii] was to the Russians, the greater was the bitterness of the Americans against them. The last failure made them so angry that they persuaded King Kamehameha to use force in making Kaumualii obey his orders. Four of them [Americans] offered their ships for a punitive expedition. Then Kamehameha in allegiance with the Americans sent a message to Kaumualii that unless the latter expelled the Russians, [the allies] would arrive with all their ships, seize the island by force, kill the Russians as well as Kaumualii himself, and take possession of everything.

Kaumualii, terrified by such news, told us about it and declared that for the common good he could no longer have us as his rulers. He added, however, that if we were to return with greater forces, he would be glad to accept us back. There was nothing more to do. We moved back to the ships with all our property, leaving behind us on the island our cattle and houses. The islanders did not show the least hostility on that occasion, and the king supplied us with provisions for our departure from the island.

After leaving Waimea we stopped at the harbor of Hanalei to remove from the shore cannons which were to have been placed in the fortresses. Here the governor of the province, which had been given to us, declared that he did not wish to remain on the island, but wished to accompany us. He was put on the *Il'mena,* which proceeded to Sitka, while we on the *Mirt-Kad'iak* sailed for the island of Oahu. On arrival there we asked permission to enter the harbor. The pilot who came from the island declared that the islanders were afraid to let us into the harbor, because we might start a battle with a ship of Kamehameha's, the *Albatross,* which was in the harbor. On making certain that we had a serious leak, they took away our gunpowder and arms and let the ship in to the harbor. Upon entrance they gave us provisions and permission to make the repairs.

While we were in the harbor, an American, Lewis, arrived there, who intended to depart for Canton in a short time. The Russian leaders, after a general council, decided to use this opportunity to inform the Main Office of the Company about the events which had transpired on the Sandwich Islands. Accordingly, Sheffer and the promyshlennik, Osipov, were selected to leave with the said Lewis for Canton. From Canton to Helsingor they journeyed together, but from Helsingor Sheffer went to Germany and Osipov arrived at St. Petersburg by way of Riga.

During their stay on the Sandwich Islands the Russians lived in small houses built on several lots on the land given to them by the king, Kaumualii. The islanders live in similar houses. In one place only, near the harbor of Waimea, did the Russians start to build a two-story house; but this house remained unfinished.

There is no winter on the Sandwich Islands and only three seasons, spring, summer, and autumn. There is plenty of rain, but we did not notice any storms. Fruits are borne three times a year. Except for pigs, there are not many livestock in the islands, but it might be supposed that this number will increase rapidly because the islanders do not use cattle as a food. The local livestock consists of bulls, cows, rams, sheep, wild goats, pigs, and also horses. All these animals, with the exception of bulls and horses, are found in our province. They graze there by themselves without anybody looking after them.

51. Letter, Main Office to Governor of Riga, November 23, 1818, Asking That Schäffer be Required to Return to St. Petersburg.

Copy from the original.

To His Excellency, Lieutenant-General, Adjutant-General of His Imperial Majesty, Military and Civil Governor of Riga, Cavalier and Marquis, Filip Osipovich (Paukuchcha).[?]

From the Main Office of the Russian-American Company, under the protection of His Exalted Majesty.

In 1812 Doctor of Medicine and Surgery, Collegiate Assessor Sheffer was called from Germany and signed a contract with the government. He entered the Company's service June 14, 1813, as the physician on the ship *Suvorov*, which in the same year was to sail around the world to the Russian colonies. He was supposed to remain on the ship and return to Kronstadt. His salary was to be 3,000 rubles and also 1,200 board money [*stolovye*] every year until the end of the cruise. In addition to that, there was to be a premium of 5,000 rubles.

When he arrived at the Colony he left the ship because of friction with the officers and remained there [at Sitka], and while waiting for the opportunity to return through Okhotsk, he became attached to the local hospital. In the meanwhile the ship returned without a physician.

At that time the Governor of the Colonies needed to send a man to one of the Sandwich Islands in order to rescue the looted property of the Company—the result of the shipwreck of the ship *Bering*. He chose for this purpose the above-mentioned Doctor Sheffer. The latter received instructions to recover the looted property. He did not have any other instructions. He went there on a foreign ship. Then two of the Company's ships arrived there; they were to take a load of aromatic- and sandal-wood as compensation for the looted property, if this property were too difficult to recover.

To provide an opportunity for acquiring additional wood, after compensation was made for losses [in connection with the *Bering*'s wreck], both ships were supplied with various goods in charge of special managers. In addition to these two ships, a third ship arrived there, which had started from New Albion to our colonies [in Sitka] with furs and was forced to change its course because of damage. All three ships carried property to the value of 100,000 rubles, over which Sheffer assumed control and which he handled according to his own wishes.

Instead of claiming compensation, he entered into a written convention with Kaumualii, the illiterate king of the island of Kauai, concerning a trade monopoly for the Company over the sandalwood growing on the island, the establishment of the Company's factories on this and other islands, and the rendering of military aid against another king, Kamehameha, by the Russians and by the Company's ships. In addition he also bought an armed foreign ship for the king. The Company was supposed to be paid for it in sandalwood, which has yet to be seen. The end of this adventure was that he insulted King Kaumualii and had to flee on a foreign ship to Canton, leaving the Company's men and ships at the mercy of the savages. Two of the Company's ships returned [to Sitka] without any profit, and the third remained stranded on the shore of the island.

After he [Sheffer] arrived at Canton, instead of sending a preliminary report of his actions and the use made of the Company's property to the Main Office of the Company, he sent bills to the Main Office, at first for 1,544.22 rubles, and after he reached Brazil, for an additional 3,756.52 rubles, altogether 5,300.76 rubles, which bills were paid. Then, after arriving at Helsingor he sent another bill for 1,500 rubles, which, however, the Company refused to pay, hoping that he would soon arrive at St. Petersburg and settle accounts. Instead, he appeared in Berlin, according to his own communication from there, for the purpose of being presented personally to His Majesty, the Emperor, with the report about his Commission on the Sandwich Islands. Whether this arrogant presumption was successful, we do not know. We know, however, that he obtained from the Company an additional 100 *chervontsy,* which is equivalent to 1,100 rubles, to enable him to come here [to St. Petersburg]. He left Berlin and, without sending his reports here, went to Riga, where he now lives. In his letter of October 29, he wrote to the directors of the Company that he would stay in Riga, where he would be of more use to the Company than in St. Petersburg. The Company, however, has no interests there whatsoever. . . .

The Main Office of the Company, in fulfillment of an order (from the Ministry of the Interior), draws the above to the attention of your Excellency and humbly requests that you take proper action to send to St. Petersburg this Company official now living in Riga without being of any use or profit to the Company, and without rendering accounts of his actions and of the expenditure of the Company's capital. He must report [at St. Petersburg] to the Main Office of the Company.

Director ANDREI SEVERIN

November 23, 1818

[Notation in French:]

Marquis Paukutchtcha states, in a letter from Riga dated December 1, 1818, that Scheffer promises to return to St. Petersburg to settle accounts.

52. Letter, Schäffer to Main Office, February 6, 1819, Asking Payment of Back Salary and Expenses.

Dear Sirs:

The settlement of accounts which I received from the Main Office of the Russian-American Company fell far from the just consideration which I expected as a recognition of my service [to the Company]. This settlement is based on the assumption that I have trespassed the extent of confidence placed in me and caused losses to the Company. I cannot accept it [such a settlement] without slighting my honor and therefore I am returning it. It is well known that [the life of] all commercial companies depends on the strict observance of their promises, without which the credit which gives life to a company cannot exist. I also know the regulations which guide the managers of the Russian-American Company. With all that in view, I hope to prove the fallacy of rumors spread at my expense by ill-wishers and rivals in this state institution [the Russian-American Company], and to have the remuneration due me no longer suspended. I consider it my duty to present herewith a copy of the instruction which was sent to me at the Sandwich Islands by Collegiate Councilor Baranov, which I promised to keep secret from all men who came to those remote regions in the hope of gaining profit each for himself and for his nation, but not for Russia. This secret instruction, not known, of course, to the Main Office of the Company, will be the best proof of the cautiousness with which I fulfilled the directions of Mr. Baranov. [It will reveal] the effective means I employed to achieve the aims and to gain the great objectives of the extensive designs of the Russian-American Company. From my knowledge of local circumstances, I dare say that the fate the Company depends on whether [these designs] are fulfilled or postponed.

The importance of the matter which was entrusted to me and which I carefully worked out in detail prevents me from thinking that the Main Office of the Company will break its trust and will fail to honor without satisfaction the account which I am enclosing herewith and which was made in accordance with specifications approved [by the Company]. I am also asking that my salary for this year be granted me, because I returned here against my will, engaged not in my own personal affairs, but in the affairs of the Company, and in fulfillment of the instruction given to me, which shows that I am still in the service [of the Company]. As a proof of my statement, I am enclosing this instruction also.

The justice of my request, and the clarity of my arguments, enable me to hope that my labors and the advantages which they gained for the Russian-American Company will induce the most respected directors to give me satisfaction without delay, which I need because of my present circumstances. I have the honor of entertaining this hope and remain very respectfully,

My dear Sirs, Your obedient servant,
EGOR SHEFFER

February 6, 1819

53. Statement of Accounts, Schäffer to Main Office, April 22, 1819.

St. Petersburg, April 22, 1819

1. Dr. Sheffer left Novo-Arkhangel'sk on the ship *Isabella* for the Sandwich Islands by order of Collegiate Councilor and Cavalier Baranov, and received for the initial necessary expenses 10,000 [silver rubles?] in goods and money. A part of this, according to the account already rendered, went to Kings Kamehameha and Kaumualii; another part was given to Tarakanov and Kicherov and the third part was brought back by Podushkin to Novo-Arkhangel'sk on the ship *Otkrytie*.

2. (1816) Tarakanov and Odnoriadkin received some goods from the ship *Otkrytie*. But most of them [goods], with the exception of construction timber, which was used for the construction of a fortress on Kauai, was sent back to Novo-Arkhangel'sk.

3. (1816) [Part of] the construction timber from the ship *Kad'iak* was used for the construction of Fort Elizabeth on Kauai; part of it was used for the construction of houses for the factory which belonged to the Russian-American Company. There were no other goods on the *Kad'iak* besides the lumber.

4. (1816) The brig *Il'mena,* according to the investigation of the Company and submitted testimony, lost most of its cargo, consisting of salt and wheat, as a result of leakage. Odnoriadkin must present an account as to how much other goods Tarakanov received from the *Il'mena* through Nikiforov. Nikiforov will have to give an account of how much cargo was stolen by Captain Wadsworth.

5. (1816) From the ship *Albatross* were received agricultural implements destined for California. They [the implements] were given to the workers on plantations and fortress construction. Some sealed packages and boxes and a few Chinese fireworks were received by Antipatr Baranov. The liquor designated for Mr. Kuskov was consumed by the sailors on the ship.

These and the other goods received were for the most part given to King Kaumualii and to some of the most prominent chiefs of the island in payment for sandalwood, land, subjects, and food. I cannot tell definitely how much other goods remained in the storehouse when the Russians left Kauai. Tarakanov and Odnoriadkin must know in detail. Captain Gyzelaar from Philadelphia received for the ship *Lydia* 22,000 [rubles?] in goods and cash. The ship was given to King Kaumualii, according to the contract.

I know nothing about the accounts of the ship *Rurik* and Captain Davis, because I never in all my life saw either this ship or this captain.

No record was made as to the food supply used for the upkeep of the Russians and Aleuts in the Company's service. There was no record of the provisions which were taken to the ship and sent to Sitka. In addition, many hunters received provisions from the storehouses; the record of this must be in the hands of Tarakanov and Odnoriadkin.

In regard to the repair of the *Kad'iak,* I know nothing. At present I must observe with regret that there was no excuse for sending a ship in such condition on a distant expedition. Three times the ship had to return to Sitka and the fourth time it had to seek safety on the island of Kad'iak. It was only by the will of Providence that it reached the Sandwich Islands, where it was considered as unfit by friend and enemy.

The Company would be richer by a few hundred men and a few

million rubles if it had not been for such unforgivable errors. It has happened often, however, that old and unfit vessels have been loaded and sent to sea into most dangerous waters and often in the most dangerous time of the year.

The Company itself may determine the cost of construction of the fortified place on Kauai and of the materials used. For my part, I suggest for this purpose 100,000 silver rubles.

Doctor SHEFFER

A list of expenditures made by him [Dr. Sheffer] on the Sandwich Islands for the benefit of the Russian-American Company.

1. On the island of Oahu, to Queen Kaahumanu for the land Vaikarua with eleven families, and fishing ground seven versts along the sea.

2. To the brother-in-law of King Kamehameha, chief Kuakini, otherwise called John Adams, for the land Koaiai on the Ovan', or Pearl River, with nine families.

3. On the island of Kauai, to King Kaumualii for permanent ownership of sandalwood [groves], for provisions, and for the harbor Hanalei, with 450 families, for the location for a factory along the river Waimea, as well as for a certain amount of food supplies to be delivered annually.

4. To Chief Kamahalolani for land on the right bank of the river Waimea, with twenty families.

5. To the sister of King Kaumualii, Tairikhoa, for land on the left bank of the river Waimea, with fourteen families, as well as for the uninhabited valley of Mainauri.

6. To the Taiun [chief] Obanna Platov for the land Tuiloa in Hanapepe with eleven families.

54. Minutes, Council of the Russian-American Company, May 17, 1819.

May, 1819

The Council of the Russian-American Company heard the communication of April 17 from the Department of Manufacture and Internal Trade. The Russian-American Company is asked to give its opinion of the departure for Germany of Dr. Sheffer, who was employed by the Company. [The Council also gave its attention] to the information furnished from the records of the Company which shows:

1. When Dr. Sheffer was on the Sandwich island of Kauai, he spent about 170,000 rubles in money and goods belonging to the Company for the purpose of buying lands for the Company, for gifts to Kaumualii, his wives, and relatives, for the establishment of factories and plantations, which, however, as shown by the journal of the same Sheffer, were abandoned without any profit to the Company. [That happened] when King Kaumualii refused permission for Sheffer and the Russians who were with him and who worked in these factories and plantations to live there. Besides, there are 60,000 rubles not accounted for. [It is not known] whether they were spent or not; if spent, by whom they were spent; if not spent, whether they were returned to the Company or not. To settle these questions, more information from the colonies is required.

2. Dr. Sheffer was sent to the Sandwich Islands to recover the plundered property of the Company on the island of Kauai. He was to use means advantageous to the Company. Sheffer, however, entered into a convention with King Kaumualii. He bought for the king, at the Company's expense, a war ship to be used for the conquest of other islands, which were governed by another king, Kamehameha. He even assumed the command of [the king's] army. This was probably the chief reason why, as a result of protests from the other king [Kamehameha] and the intrigues of runaway sailors from the United States who had settled on the islands, he [Sheffer] was expelled from Kauai, with the loss of all the enterprises there.

The Council also attended to the proposed reply to the communication of the above-mentioned Department. It was decided to accept the proposed reply and accordingly to send a communication together with a copy of these minutes.

GAVRIIL SARYCHEV
IVAN VEIDEMEIER, etc.

May 17, 1819

55. *Instructions, Ministry of Interior, Department of Manufacture and Internal Trade, to Main Office, July 15, 1819, Quoting Letter of June 24, 1819, from Foreign Minister Count K. V. Nesselrode, Citing Decision of the Emperor on the Hawaiian affair.*

Received July 15, 1819
No. 628

Ministry of Interior
Department of Manufacture and Interior Trade
July 15, 1819
No. 206

Containing his Majesty's resolution in regard to the Sandwich Islands.

To the Main Office of the Russian-American Company.

His High Excellency [the Minister of Interior] having received from the Main Office [of the Company] a communication dated March 21, 1819, which was addressed to the Minister of Interior, and which was accompanied by the opinion of the Council in regard to the acquisition of the Sandwich Islands proposed by the Doctor of Medicine, Collegiate Assessor, Sheffer, submitted the above documents together with the papers of Sheffer to the attention of the Acting Minister of Foreign Affairs.

Count Karl Vasil'evich [Nesselrode] now informs the Minister of Interior concerning the above papers which were submitted to His Majesty's attention. His Majesty deigned to learn, but with regret, that the friendly and commercial relations of the Company with these islands, which had started so successfully, had quickly collapsed and in a most unpleasant way.

Turning his special attention to the opinion of the Main Office, His Imperial Majesty deigned to see that in spite of this, the Company hopes, first, to reëstablish friendly relations with Chief Kaumualii; and second, to obtain and spread its own settlements on those islands by peaceful means.

After examining the Company's suggestion in this twofold respect, His Imperial Majesty ordered me to communicate to the Minister of Interior the following remarks:

As is known to the Main Office of the Company, during the seemingly very favorable circumstances [brought about] when the above-mentioned chief upon his own initiative asked to be admitted with his subject islands into the dominion of the Russian Empire, His Imperial Majesty, rejecting even then this right of possession which was voluntarily presented to him, deigned to command that the Company refuse this proposition and limit itself only to the establishment of the same friendly and commercial relations which Kaumualii has with other independent countries. This supreme will was founded on firm considerations. His Imperial Majesty, still convinced of their correctness, finds it now even less necessary to change the above-mentioned ruling, since later events themselves have proved to what degree it is well founded. Experience confirms how little one should rely on the durability of such settlements.

As to the Company's intention to work for the reëstablishment of friendly relations with those islands, His Imperial Majesty approves this and wishes it full success. He is convinced that with wise planning on the part of the Main Office and cautious selection of executors who are modest in [their conduct of] affairs, the Company will achieve with greater certainty the same advantages and profit which it had hoped for from the uncertain possession of these islands.

For this purpose His Imperial Majesty consents:

1) That the Company should use, according to its judgment, the above-mentioned gifts, which have been assigned in the exalted name [of the Emperor] to Chief Kaumualii, in accordance with the Company's earlier suggestions.

2) That after succeeding in reëstablishing relations, it [the Company] be guided absolutely only by those directions which in accordance with the Imperial will were explained in the communication by His High Excellency [the Minister of Interior] to the Main Office of the Company.

3) That for success in its enterprises and particularly in this matter, it [the Company] should behave with the greatest caution

in selecting its employees and in addition furnish them with the most exact and clear orders. By no means should it allow them to act in an arbitrary manner like its last commissioner, Sheffer, who with all his knowledge and zeal seemingly did not possess the necessary caution and therefore subjected himself and the Company to many troubles.

4) That it be encouraged by the fact that all commanders of vessels leaving from here [to go] around the world will be ordered to declare, everywhere in those distant places, that the Company enjoys the special protection of His Imperial Majesty, and that these same commanders will be required to gather the most exact information and to report on the actions of Company agents.

It pleases His Imperial Majesty that the Minister of Interior inform the Main Office of the Company of this for necessary action. In fulfillment of the will of His Imperial Majesty, and because of the illness of the Minister, the Department of Manufactures and Internal Trade has asked me to convey to the Main Office of the Russian-American Company all explanations of the Minister of Foreign Affairs, Count Karl Vasil'evich Nessel'rode, with regard to the matter.

(Original signed) *Director* MATVEI SHTER
Chief of Section PAVEL OSTROGORSKII
ZELENSKII

56. Instructions, Main Office to Hagemeister, August 12, 1819.

To the Governor of the Russian American Colonies, Captain-Lieutenant of the Navy, Leontii Andreianovich Hagemeister, or, in his absence to the acting Governor.

The ship *Borodino* is proceeding from Kronstadt to the above-mentioned colonies and will bring you a dispatch from the Main Office, dated March 15 of last year, numbered 121, which contains the expression of the exalted will of His Imperial Majesty, the

Sovereign Emperor, in regard to such relations as should be established between the Russian-American Company and the Sandwich Islands. This dispatch was sent to Okhotsk to be forwarded [to you] on the brig *Chirikov* this year. By a mistake of the local office, however, it was returned this year [to St. Petersburg], together with the other mail. Therefore it was decided to send it to you again on the above-mentioned ship *Borodino*.

Sheffer, who formerly held the rank of Commissioner on these islands, upon his arrival here submitted to the government a report, just as bold and ardent as were his deeds there on the islands. By means of this report he hoped to ensnare the government into the acceptance of the seizure of the Sandwich Islands under his leadership on the basis that might is right. You will learn about his plan from the enclosed copy of it. At the same time you will also see the opinion of the Governor of the colonies, which was requested by the government and of which the copy is also sent to you. Finally, you will find in the last set of papers the wish of the Monarch, which was delivered to the Main Office through the Ministry of the Interior, dated July 15, under the No. 206. This last resolution of the Monarch does not require any explanations on the part of the Main Office and is to be fulfilled to the letter. Zakhar Petrovich Panafidin, the commander of the ship *Borodino*, is commissioned during his present voyage to visit these islands if it is possible, and to make a detailed investigation as to why our people were expelled from there.

Taking into consideration the Monarch's resolution, the information gathered by Panafidin and such information which is already at your disposal, the Main Office commissions you to equip and to send an expedition to these islands, without any loss of time, to Chief Kaumualii, who lives on the island of Kauai. This expedition is to negotiate with him in the following manner: First it must declare to the chief that His Imperial Majesty, the Sovereign Emperor, does not deign to accept him [the chief] as a subject, although this was [the chief's] wish and request and he [the chief] has already taken an oath of allegiance. The Emperor does this because of his humane and peaceful disposition, and because he already has vast possessions occupying one eighth of the globe. The

Emperor wishes that his Russian subjects have such friendly commercial relations [with the Sandwich natives] as are enjoyed there by other Europeans. The Russian-American Company, which under special exalted protection of His Imperial Majesty, was entrusted with a commission to announce the wish of the Emperor, has sent for this purpose the ship which has now arrived at Kauai and which is under the command of a kindly and honest man. This man is to assure [Kaumualii] on behalf of our Great Sovereign that if [the chief] will again accept the Emperor's good subjects who arrived on the ship, and will consent to have friendly commercial relations with them such as were defined in several written acts submitted to the attention of the Emperor, and if he [the chief] will consent to renew these acts, then he is to receive abundant gifts. These gifts are consigned for him on behalf of His Imperial Majesty and represent a great honor. In addition [the chief] will receive assurance of the future grace of His Imperial Majesty. On behalf of the Company [the chief] must be told that he will obtain great profits if he will enter into friendly commercial relations such as he already accepted once on his own free will and which were confirmed by written documents and which were broken only because of the ill will of some envious men. The Company can furnish him [the chief] many things, and through the rise of economic productivity his subjects will profit considerably. It will be necessary for the one receiving the commission to explain all this to the owner, Kaumualii, using the most flattering expressions and kindness. The same treatment should be accorded to the members of his family and to other persons who have an influence [on Kaumualii]. By consideration of other means at his disposal he must approach [the chief] and prevail upon him to grant permission to the Russians to settle there [on the islands], especially on Niihau.

It would be better if he [the king] could be induced to sell this island to the Company; as you know, the Main Office has laid aside for this purpose 10,000 or more rubles. This [the purchase of the island] should be the main task. The acquisition of the island is of special importance to the Company since it is the nearest to the Colonies. In addition it is sparsely populated and therefore there is less danger of insolence from the inhabitants.

If you observe that Kaumualii is willing to meet the propositions of the Company—and in all probability he will accept them—and if he will do it in such a way that there will be no fear that he will again break them perfidiously, then deliver to him the gifts graciously granted by the Sovereign Emperor. Together with the gifts give him a paper in the name of the Russian-American Company written both in the Russian and English languages and add the presents from the Company. These presents were sent on the sloop *Kamchatka* and consist of glass and some porcelain, mirrors, etc. Use similar presents to win the favor and confidence of his [Kaumualii's] near relatives and other persons who have influence upon him, accordingly as whether the negotiations progress more or less favorably. Be firm, however, on the point that if Kaumualii expects to make any conquests with Russian aid, he must remember that such are contrary to the peaceful disposition of the Sovereign Emperor.

To carry out all these plans, you must have a man who is wise, of firm character, kind, and shrewd. To achieve the desired success, he must have similarly qualified subordinates. About fifty such men, in addition to the crew of the ship, ought to be sufficient for the first time. A greater number will deprive other Company enterprises of necessary men. Half of them [the group sent to islands] should be used for business activities and the other half for the maintenance of security. They must be quiet, energetic, sober men, and in addition, good shots. If settlement takes place, they should not scatter themselves in as many places as Sheffer did [with his men]. It would be best to construct in some advantageous place, near the anchorage of the ship, a building in the form of a tower. To impress the islanders and others with proper respect, it [the tower] should be supplied with a few cannons. The men should be equipped with small arms in case of a sudden attack by the savages. A strict discipline should be maintained. In case numerous islanders arrive there from other islands, the meetings with them should be held in no other place but in the fortress, and with the utmost caution. We think this here, but local circumstances may suggest the best way to achieve our objective.

You will have difficulties in finding a person qualified to

undertake this task. But the Main Office relies on your efficiency
and foresight. In addition to such a person, a reliable councilor who
could assist him in this affair should be sent. Prepare also detailed
rules and necessary instructions, telling your agents and the men
under your charge how wisely and cautiously they should behave
themselves in regard to the islanders. Because of the barbarity of the
latter they should never be completely trusted, but should be treated
in a kindly and friendly manner.

Strictly prohibit any quarrels with the islanders and all actions or
oppressions contrary to the wishes of the natives. They can use as
an example the behavior of the Company on Kad'iak and Sitka.
There we established ourselves by caution and mildness rather than
by brute force. It looks as if you will not have any shortage of
agricultural implements for gifts, trade, and use by the settlers on
these islands. There have been previous shipments of them, and
there is also one at present. It appears also that on these islands,
especially in the places where settlements are founded, it is necessary
always to have a special boat which from time to time should be
replaced by another boat. No doubt you will give complete
instructions to the commanders of the ships, as to what they should
do under all circumstances.

Not the least part of your business will be the recovery of the
cargo which was stolen and of property taken away from Sheffer.
However, you must achieve your ends in a quiet, diplomatic way. It
is better not to hurry, but to attain the results through the
friendship of Kaumualii and other influential men, as by restoration
of the trade in sandalwood concerning which Kaumualii signed a
written contract with Sheffer determining the payments to be
made.

The above directions are merely an outline; the execution of the
widely laid plans of action on the Sandwich Islands has to be carried
out in accordance with your information and the Monarch's will.
For further success in all respects, and for development of a
permanent influence on these islands, send with the expedition a
young man who will acquire a thorough knowledge of the Sandwich
language, which can later be set to writing. Thus the islanders
could be taught the rudiments of the Christian religion in the same

way that the Bible societies use in their relations with peoples speaking different languages. Serious efforts should be also made to establish family ties with the natives. This is a very certain method, used in the acquisition of Kad'iak, and which may lay a firm foundation there [on the islands]. However, you can use any other plans devised by yourself.

August 12, 1819

57. Letter, Hagemeister to Kuskov, January 28, 1818 (Extract).

. . . Matters in the Sandwich Islands have been decided—the Doctor has left. They drove him from Kauai, and it is said that he wrote himself a letter of credit to the Swedish consul in Canton, which I fear will have to be paid. The vessel *Kad'iak* has been beached at Oahu, and as if all these unpleasantnesses were not enough, Tarakanov entered into an arrangement with Davis and sent with him one creole, three women and thirty-seven Aleut men, along with the Russians Ivan Bologov and Ivan Zholin.

The *Kutuzov* arrived here on the local date of November 21, [1817], and the *Suvorov* has loaded various wares, including furs valued at 107,202 rubles 40 kop., and left safely on the thirteenth of this month. First Lieutenant Ianovskii stayed behind as Captain of the Port of Novo-Arkhangel'sk.

On the eleventh of this month I announced the directive of the Council, which I have reported to the Main Office. On the fourteenth we began to take inventory. May God help us straighten out the mess here.

I intended to go to the Sandwich Islands, in order to save the cargo left there and to receive from King Kaumualii the payment in sandalwood to which Sheffer refers in his letter to Mr. Baranov, but I fear that I must leave it to the ship *Otkrytie* under the supervision of Lieutenant Podushkin. Even if he succeeds in nothing else, he can bring our people and the materials from the *Mirt-Kad'iak*, which should be burned. . . .

58. *Instructions, Hagemeister to Podushkin, February 9, 1818.*

From Chief Manager of the Colonies of the Russian-American Company.

To the Commander of the Russian-American Company's ship, the *Otkrytie,* Lieutenant and Cavalier Iakov Anikievich Podushkin.

Having designated the ship under your command for a voyage to the Sandwich Islands, I recommend to Your Honor the following:

As soon as you are ready for the expedition, you are to proceed to the island of Hawaii, where King Kamehameha has his residence. Present him from me, as Governor of the Company's colonies, with the gifts which are stored for this purpose on the *Otkrytie.* Tell the king that I hope that he will receive you as graciously as he received me nine years ago and that I wish to maintain the same friendly relations with him now as formerly. In regard to Dr. Sheffer, you can explain that he followed the instructions given him and that peace and amity among [our] peoples are the benevolent aims of our great Sovereign, whose ways of thinking we, as his faithful subjects, have to follow. Request of him that he return to the Russian-American Company the land concessions [previously granted], even as a personal favor to me, and assure him that we shall prove to him and to his people that we can appreciate his good will and respond likewise.

According to rumors, the [Mirt-] *Kad'iak,* a vessel of the Russian-American Company, is in such condition that under no circumstances should it be used. Try to sell this vessel to the king. Charge a most moderate price. For the hull, masts, and spars, but without ropes, artillery supplies, rigging, and sails, you ought to receive in some form or another at least 10,000 piastres.

Explain to him that the framework is of the strongest wood and only needs new sheathing, but the lowest price which could be accepted for the hull of the ship is 1,000 pikuls of sandalwood. Having settled the sale of the *Kad'iak,* if the king accepts those terms, be so kind as to proceed to the island Oahu, where you will see the *Kad'iak* yourself. Tell [the king] to have the payment ready for delivery by the time you leave Kauai, and also, if the deal is concluded, ask him for an official to supervise the delivery of sandalwood from the island Oahu.

Without losing any time on Oahu, proceed to Kauai and try by gentle means to make King Kaumualii pay in sandalwood for the schooner and other property left there by Sheffer, as the king agreed [to do] in his letter to Mr. Baranov. If he has no sandalwood, try to get back the [Company's] property. Persuade the king that we do not hold the expulsion of Sheffer against him, but that we think that he had better keep the Russian flag, which would protect him even in the absence of the Russians; that Kamehameha knows of the existence of the friendship between England, whose protection he himself recognizes, and Russia, whose protection was given to Kaumualii, and [therefore] will abstain from attacking [Kaumualii]. Everybody knows the greatness and strength of our Sovereign. [Explain to the king] that it would be desirable if he returned the lands [previously granted] not to Sheffer but to the Russians. [Explain also] that you have strict orders not to molest any of his subjects on the ceded lands, or prescribe laws for the king, but that we wish to enjoy his friendship and to return it.

The chief object of your expedition is to collect from King Kaumualii the payments which he owes [us], to gather men, and to recover [our] property on Oahu and to bring everything here [to Sitka]. I hope that you will use all your efforts in settling all [these] matters successfully. Take on the ship entrusted to you Timofei Tarakanov, an employee of the Company, who has previously been on the Sandwich Islands. I am placing him under your command and asking you to supervise his behavior and actions, which, according to rumors reaching me, were detrimental to the Company's property because of his loose conduct. Try to give him every possible aid in recovering the property so as to deprive him of any excuse (however groundless) that he was interfered with [in his work].

I suggested to the Novo-Arkhangel'sk Office that it consign for the ship *Otkrytie* a small cargo of goods to be used in exchange for provisions; the latter should be doled out very economically.

After the business on Kauai is settled, go back to Oahu, and if you succeed in selling the ship *Kad'iak,* [then] load rigging, etc., as was mentioned above, on the *Otkrytie* and proceed here without loss of time.

If you recover the land possessions on Kauai and Oahu and receive complete satisfaction that their return will be granted not for a short time but permanently, then leave on the first of them [Kauai] one Russian and one creole, and on the other [Oahu] the same number of men. You will leave them your instructions, some articles suitable for barter that you will have on the ship, enough food to last for some time, the gifts for the king, etc. Ask them to observe strict economy. In addition to the taro roots and other food for themselves and for the workers, ask them also to plant something useful for export here [to Sitka], namely, the root *kurnuma* [?] (which should be dried), cotton, and similar plants. Ask them at every opportunity to buy from the inhabitants different articles which could be shipped, such as dry taro, "kukui" or "tutui" nuts, and, above all, sandalwood, taking care that it is genuine and cheaper than eight piastres a pikul. Such was the price paid recently in Canton, although the transportation [of the wood to Canton] is not cheap.

If, in spite of all your efforts to sell the *Kad'iak* in exchange for sandalwood, you find it impossible to do so, and if you receive an offer to pay you only a part of the price in sandalwood, and the other part in other articles, then you can accept such articles as dry and raw taro, "tutui" nuts, salt, and cotton, because it is absolutely impossible to bring the *Kad'iak* here. If the king offers you a price less than 1,000 pikuls, or if he refuses to buy the ship, then order your men to burn it and gather all iron and copper, watching the natives so they do not steal anything. If, however, you can not get permission to burn the ship because of its proximity to the king's boats or houses, or if you are actually prevented from doing so, then call in Tarakanov and Chernov and commission them to settle the affair. They should do everything to protect the interest of the Company and to get back the property of the Company, according to the circumstances, and presenting explanations of why they had to accept a price less than I suggested, namely less than 1,000 pikuls of sandalwood.

If you do not get back the land, try to sell the timber left on the Sandwich Islands; do not give it away free. Tarakanov does not have a full inventory of the Company's property left on the Sandwich Islands; he left it with Kycharov; ask the latter to preserve it and to deliver it to me. Try to get back the property according to this inventory.

You will have to hasten your return so that you can visit California before autumn. The business on the Sandwich Islands should be settled, if possible, because it would be very difficult to send another ship there for the same purpose as you were sent.

There is no need to bring any foreigners here, so you can refuse to take as passengers [such foreigners as were] in the Company's service. It is known that [foreigners] cannot be received here without my consent, and I shall always refuse them [admission to Sitka]. If, however, such a request is made by Mr. Elliot, who had business with the former governor of the company, then it would not be fair to refuse such a request.

From the reports given by you at the time of your first expedition to the Sandwich Islands and signed by the former chief manager, I learned that the cargo of the wrecked Company ship, the *Bering*, was supposed to include 5,000 pieces of *kitaika* [nankeens], 2,300 seal skins, and also four boxes of [———] which were to be demanded back from the king. Opposite the item *seals* [*koty*], there is a notation that they should be returned intact; opposite the item *kitaika* there is a notation: three rubles apiece. [However], neither the *kitaika* nor the *koty* belonged to the Company. Therefore no claims should be presented for them, unless Dr. Sheffer issued some receipts on leaving, which could later be presented as claims against the Company. In that case, try to get the things back.

If foreign mariners ask you for any articles which were on the ship *Kad'iak* on the basis of various business deals between themselves and Mr. Baranov, then satisfy their claims, but not unless they are in possession of notes from Mr. Baranov which definitely state what they are to receive from the Russian-American Company. If the ship owner Davis would like to receive on credit some of the Company's provisions, for the brig *Rurik,* then you can hand over to him needed articles from the ship, charging a good price for them, keeping in mind the prices here [in Sitka?] as well as [our] needs which are well known to you. Whatever items you let them have and the price charged should be stated and signed by you in the bills given to every mariner. In addition you are to receive receipts from each of them explaining that the money he owes [for these articles] will be deducted from the payment which is due him. If foreigners have taken from King Kaumualii any articles belonging to the Company and have left any receipts with him, then be kind enough to bring those receipts here for [our] accounts.

I have learned from the toen [chief] Hanalei, who together with his wife and servants, is to travel on the ship to the island of Kauai, that from his possessions in Hanalei, which are on the northern side of Kauai, 2,400 logs of sandalwood were shipped for Dr. Sheffer on board the *Il'mena*, by order of the king. According to him, this wood was left on Kauai. The testimony of the employees shows that Mr. Sheffer did not tell anybody his plans and did not mention that this wood belonged to the Company. When he started on the *Il'mena* to discover the islands, which were already known, Sheffer ordered that this wood be unloaded from the brig and taken to the shore, which was done in two barks and one small boat, and deposited in the storehouse where the property of the Company was kept. When this storehouse collapsed, other property was taken elsewhere but the wood remained in a corner of the collapsed building. Find out; perhaps the doctor had a reason for doing so [leaving the wood there], wishing to appropriate this wood for himself at the expense of the Company, because he never wrote about gathering this wood or about leaving it there. Perhaps he just forgot about it? But I consider it my duty to bring to the attention of Your Honor that, according to the toen, this wood is the property of the Company. If it belonged to King Kaumualii, it would have been transported [from Hanalei to Waimea?] in native boats and not on the *Il'mena*, but the toen had orders to prepare the wood for the *Il'mena*, and loaded it there himself.

Please treat the toen as kindly as possible, and let him have food sufficient for one and one-half months, according to the rations established since the arrival of the *Kutuzov*. Without it he claims he may perish from starvation. Give him and his wife clothing and gifts so he will forget the unjust exile from his country and the meager allowance he had before the arrival of the *Kutuzov*. I am

sending you also a Sandwich native who was educated by the
Company at great expense and baptized in Russia, who will be
useful to you as a translator. If King Kaumualii would like to take
him for himself, then you may let him go [to the king]. He [the
native] is well disposed toward us and is grateful to the Company.
Therefore he may furnish information of great value in regard to
the king . . .

I am asking you to proceed from 134° as far as 146° western
longitude from Greenwich along the 28th parallel northern
latitude. The Spaniards think that there is an island [there] called
Donna Maria Laxara.* If you find this island and if there are sea
animals and good water [there], you may send all your Aleuts
there, either on your way [to the Sandwich Islands] or on your way
back. The first will be much easier and more advantageous.
Meanwhile, if you take [on board] our [men] living on Oahu,
there will be no shortage of hands on your ship.

Lieutenant-Captain HAGEMEISTER

Fortress Novo-Arkhangel'sk
February 9, 1818

59. Further Instructions, Hagemeister to Podushkin, February 9, 1818 (Extract).

If in the absence of ready sandalwood King Kaumualii offers to
return the schooner *Lydia* to you, take it, even if it needs repairs,
provided it is in a condition to stand the journey here. There will be
enough payments in the products of the islands due for other things.
King Kaumualii may demand payment for provisions which he let
Mr. Sheffer have, and about which nothing is said in the reports of
Tarakanov and others, which he will use as counterclaims against
you. If he does, then tell him that because Dr. Sheffer used the
Company's capital, not his own, these bills will be more than settled
if the king will take into consideration the use of the ship, for which

---

* Donna Maria Laxara: a mythical island, alleged to have been discovered by an early Spanish navigator, which was still on charts in the
early nineteenth century.

he has not yet paid. Settle the accounts at the rate of two rubles for a piastre. . . .

HAGEMEISTER

60. *Instructions, Hagemeister to Podushkin, February 16, 1818.*

[February] 16 [1818]
No. 60
Letter to Fleet Lieutenant and Cavalier Iakov Anikievich Podushkin.

The enclosed copy of Doctor Sheffer's contract can serve you as a guide in demanding payment from King Kaumualii for Company property. Sheffer in his letter to Mr. Baranov supposes that the purchase of the schooner *Lydia* fulfilled his obligation to the King regarding a ship, and so you must receive two cargoes of sandalwood over and above other accounts. As you know, the vessel *Bering* was reinforced below the water line with copper sheathing, for which compensation has not been received by the Company. Try to salvage this important property, and in general, as I explained to you before, obtain all that you can; but if it proves impossible at this time to obtain all the payment proposed by Sheffer (of which you will know best), then try with all means to have the king recognize you in the presence of others and give you a letter to me in which he acknowledges himself a debtor of the Company, so that this can be presented in due course. It is unnecessary for me to tell you that patience and firmness can accomplish a great deal with the savages. It can be seen that you have the power to harm, but hold back. Although I do not on my part consider as a document a letter from a savage written in a language unknown to him and with unknown marks, such a letter should be written in the English language, because there are in those islands many people of that nation enjoying the trust of the king who could write such a letter. Moreover, if you flatter him you may remind him of the letter written to Mr. Baranov by the order of King Kaumualii. I assume the content of it is known to you. Kaumualii proclaimed that he does not want to receive settlers, but is ready to trade with all peoples. He complains of Sheffer, and promises to pay for what he received with sandalwood, the amount of which he does not indicate. With this is enclosed a copy of the letter from King Kaumualii to Mr. Baranov of May 15, 1817, and the King's treaty with Sheffer of May 21, 1816.

61. *Letter, Hagemeister to Main Office, April 6, 1818.*

REPORT

I have the honor to present the last letters written by Dr. Sheffer to the former Governor of the [Russian-American] Company, my instructions to Fleet Lieutenant and Cavalier Podushkin concerning the property of the Company on the ship, and the explanations submitted to me by the employee of the Company, Tarakanov. The Main Office will observe that Doctor Sheffer abused the confidence which the Company had placed in him, that he trespassed the limits of his instructions, and that he squandered Company property which was not entrusted to him and which he handled as if he were in charge of it. He also conceived plans not in the best interests of the Company, plans which could not have been realized by available local resources. Of the latter he had no knowledge, as can be proved by the retention of Russians and Aleuts as settlers, by his purchase of the ship *Avon,* by his demands that a few hundred Russians be sent [to him], etc. The treaties with the illiterate king are written in language which nobody can understand, and nobody knows who put the sign [cross] there. The doctor did not know the Sandwich language, and about the English language, which should have been used, he knows very little. That is clear because in the agreement concerning the purchase of the ship *Avon,* the article dealing with damages should the ship suffer a wreck is entirely different in the English translation from the original.

Of necessity, Mr. Sheffer, in negotiations with the king, used Englishmen who had lived on the island for quite a long time. As a result King Kamehameha soon learned about [Sheffer's] plans to conquer the other islands. I learned beyond any question of doubt that King Kamehameha sent a demand to King Kaumualii that he expel Dr. Sheffer. I hope that my instructions to Mr. Podushkin will not persuade the Main Office that I do not consider the occupation of the Sandwich Islands as worth while, but that I want it to be carried out in accordance with the advantages [to be derived] and the forces [available], and in such a way that it will not interfere with more important matters.

I investigated the means which were at Sheffer's disposal and found them very extensive. May the Lord help us to obtain from the king at least one cargo of sandalwood for the *Otkrytie* to cover the damages. The forest [sandalwood] of this king on the island Kauai is at a long distance [from the shore?]; besides, the larger trees have already been cut down by the Americans, who have by now ceased to use the products of Kauai. After my first voyage was the right time but no one then paid any heed. Now the Americans have used up the treasure and we must consider not what to acquire but how to avoid leaving our own goods there. . . .

Naval Lieutenant-Captain HAGEMEISTER

Novo-Arkhangel'sk,
April 6, 1818

62. Letter, Acting Chief Manager S. I. Ianovskii to Main Office, April 20, 1820, Enclosing Extracts from Journal of K. T. Khlebnikov Concerning Voyage of Brig Brutus to Hawaiian Islands.

April 30, 1820. Under No. 73.
No. 1017.
To the Main Office.

According to the agreement with Captain Nye, Mr. Khlebnikov sent the brig *Brutus* to the Sandwich Islands; Mr. Smith went as commissioner. On the return voyage, according to the contract, the American pilot Stevens would be on board.

I have the honor to enclose a copy of Captain Khlebnikov's

instructions to Mr. Smith and notes from the former's journal pertaining to the purchase of several things on the Sandwich Islands; also the answer of King Kaumualii concerning the things left behind by Sheffer.

The favors of the king are too insignificant in comparison with the cost of the expedition to the Sandwich Islands; much more might be obtained from the king by threats if one or two well-armed ships were sent there. Would the Main Office consider giving such an order? I myself cannot undertake such action, not knowing how our government would regard it.

Acting Chief Manager,
Fleet Lieutenant IANOVSKII

No. 2
Extracts from the Journal of Captain Khlebnikov concerning the reply of King Kaumualii.

. . . Upon his departure from Oahu, Mr. Smith had had instructions to find out what King Kaumualii had done with the Company's property. He arrived at Kauai and took a small boat to shore to see the king. The latter answered that though these goods had been given to him as a gift by Dr. Sheffer, he, the king, was willing either to return them or pay for them. The list of things follows: 8 pieces of rough woolen cloth, 4 pieces of blue cloth, 50 hatchets, 10 flagons of gun powder, 1 schooner, 2 cast-iron cannons, 1 large brass one, and one small one.

Kaumualii expressed his willingness to pay for all these things with his best sandalwood, 200 pikuls, with the understanding that the Company would pay him for taking care of its men with 15 barrels of gunpowder, each weighing 25 pounds. This load of wood he would be able to deliver within 3 months.

King Kaumualii asked from Mr. Smith some sort of a paper which he could later return. The latter not having anything else available, gave him his ship passport issued at Novo-Arkhangel'sk by secret journal on September 7, and officially stamped, as a receipt for the wood duly received.

Fleet Lieutenant IANOVSKII

63. Journal, Kept by Doctor Schäffer, January 1815– March 1818 (Extracts).

1815

Early in 1815, the brig *Bering,* belonging to the Russian-American Company, was lost on the Sandwich island of Kauai through the negligence of Captain J. Bennett. This captain arrived at the port of Novo-Arkhangel'sk in July, 1815, to report to Baranov, and since the hostilities between England and America had not yet ceased, Captain Bennett (an American) wanted to be put in command of another Company ship.

Mr. Baranov agreed and ordered the ship *Myrtle-Kad'iak* put in readiness. Captain Bennett declared that all Company property, and everything else on the ship *Bering,* had been stolen and plundered by the Indians [Hawaiians] and asked Mr. Baranov to send him to Kauai with several ships and enough men to fight the Indians and obtain satisfaction. Two other American captains, Smith and MacNeil, also urged that this be done.

Mr. Baranov often spoke of this with me. We felt that the Americans were too set on the matter, and decided that it would be best to arrive at a friendly settlement with the Indians if at all possible.

Meanwhile, the W. P. Hunt affair took place in the port, or, rather, beneath the very windows of Mr. Baranov in Novo-Arkhangel'sk. This W. P. Hunt (an American) was contracted by the Company to take the brig *Pedler* on a voyage to New Albion and back. He was taken by the Spaniards, which he might have avoided if he had not gone so far south, but through the Russian supercargo Nepogod'ev he was released with his ship and cargo (though of course not without loss for the Company).

Hunt returned to Novo-Arkhangel'sk with his brig, and because of the war remained here eight months, during which he received all possible aid from Mr. Baranov. On his return from New Albion

Hunt brought news (very interesting for Mr. Baranov) that Captain Pigott had sailed to New Holland with the brig *Forester*, but this was a lie. Hunt arrived here in January, 1815, remained into the summer, and carried on a secret trade with the Indians.

On April 15 I was at Baranov's when Hunt came and demanded that Mr. Baranov order me to leave, for he wanted to speak with him alone. Mr. Baranov replied that he had nothing secret from me, and that he would not listen to anything which I was forbidden to hear. Hunt then presented the commission which he had received on the Spanish coasts from Captain Pigott, about which St. Petersburg had been fully informed.

This person [Hunt] had been there for four months, he and all of his men living mainly on Company funds. Almost every day he had demanded to see Mr. Baranov, but had not said a word about having the commission. On the contrary, he deceived the old man, making him believe that Pigott had sailed to New Holland. In this way he wanted to cause Mr. Baranov great embarrassment. However, the latter discovered that the brig *Forester* was not English property, but American, for as an Englishman Pigott would not have entrusted his property to the American Hunt. . . .

Mr. Baranov was no less troubled by this, and against his will had to hold the ship *Suvorov* on the Northwest coast much longer and at a loss. The unscrupulous Hunt continued his trade with the Indians, harmful for the Russians in all respects. He even went on the trails over which the Indians brought their furs for trade with the Russians, stopping them and taking their goods for himself. Finally he even pitched a tent where not only Mr. Baranov himself but I, and also many of the Russians, could see the Indians going each day with transports of furs. The Russians even noted genuine trade between Hunt and the Indians: for example, red wool blankets and shirts were exchanged for beavers. He himself gave me a beaver for looking after his sick.

Finally the brig *Forester* arrived [June 25, 1815], not from New Holland but from California, under the English flag. Pigott now took back the commission which he had passed on to Hunt and was paid in fur by Mr. Baranov, instead of getting the monetary transfer on St. Petersburg he would have had if he and Hunt had not played the above-mentioned trick. He sailed after getting his pay.*

Meanwhile, the Indians attacked the Russians, especially women, on one of the islands opposite the Novo-Arkhangel'sk fortress. When Mr. Baranov heard of this, he sent armed men to the island during the night, and ordered the women to assemble in groups during the day and continue quietly to pick berries. If they were again troubled by the Kolosh, they were to scream as loud as they could.

-----

* Briefly, the rather complicated Pigott-*Forester* affair went as follows: The outbreak of war with Great Britain led John Jacob Astor to adopt a subterfuge in order to supply his colony of Astoria at the mouth of the Columbia River. In September, 1812, he sent Captain William J. Pigott and Richard Ebbets to London to purchase a ship, which under false colors could avoid capture by British warships. They sailed from London on the brig *Forester,* spent November and December, 1813, in the Hawaiian Islands, and reached the California coast in the spring of 1814. Hearing that Astoria had been sold to the British, Pigott sailed to Sitka, arriving in April, 1814. There he learned from W. P. Hunt that the American ownership of the *Forester* had somehow been revealed and was now common knowledge all over the Pacific.

It was now impossible to go to Canton, under British blockade, so Pigott got a written promise from Baranov to buy his cargo of trade goods, evidently within a year's time, and then went to California, probably hoping to sell his goods there at a better price.

Baranov evidently believed Pigott had gone to Australia, and would therefore not return in time to put through the transaction. On April 15, 1815, Baranov was just loading his available sealskins on the *Suvorov* when Hunt suddenly presented the written obligation Baranov had made the year before, which Pigott had earlier turned over to Hunt, and demanded the sealskins in payment. Baranov was understandably angry; the *Suvorov* had to be unloaded, and sent to the Pribylovs to get a new cargo of skins.

On June 25, 1815, the *Forester* arrived from California. Pigott now took back his commission, was paid off by Baranov in skins, and left Sitka in July. His further adventures and vicissitudes at the hands of the Russians are described in Kenneth W. Porter, "The Cruise of the *Forester.* Some new sidelights on the Astoria enterprise," *Washington Historical Quarterly,* vol. 23, (Oct., 1932), 261–285.

Schäffer's judgements on these matters and the personalities involved were highly colored by his own prejudices.

The plan was good, and its execution even better. The expected happened; the Kolosh fell upon the Russian women, who gave the signal. The armed men ran out from their cover; part of them took six boats, and the others seized the Indians and took them all to the fortress. There careful search revealed (contrary to the agreements made with the Russians) several firearms, powder, cartridges, bullets, etc.

Questioned separately as to where they had obtained these arms and the ammunition, each of the Indians replied that they had received it all from the brig, that is, from W. P. Hunt, in exchange for furs. Together with Hunt the officers of the ship *Suvorov* had also purchased furs from the Indians. When the brig *Forester* left port, a keg of powder was transferred from it to the brig *Pedler*.

When Mr. Baranov was informed of these occurrences, his suspicions very naturally rose (we know the English law, which prescribes severe punishment to those who supply powder, etc., to the enemy in wartime). Mr. Baranov therefore sent word to Hunt [July 29, 1815] ordering him to surrender this keg of powder.

Instead of obeying the commandant's order, Hunt abused Mr. Baranov in terrible fashion, and the two messengers Baranov had sent to him were mercilessly beaten. Lieutenant Lazarev, at that time a guest on the *Pedler,* aroused Hunt still more, so that the two messengers were thrown to the deck and again beaten.

On hearing of this, Mr. Baranov himself went on board the *Pedler*. Hunt, thinking that he would have to give satisfaction, left on arrival of Mr. Baranov and went on the ship *O'Cain,* shouting, "Take the brig! It belongs to you! I am your prisoner!" Mr. Baranov ordered the powder taken into the fortress, and the small arms thrown overboard in order that they should not be sold to the Kolosh and thus enable Hunt and the Indians to harm the Russians. The Main Office of the Company was informed of this.

Returning to the officers of the ship *Suvorov* and Bennett: On the following day I saw how the officers of the *Suvorov* took Hunt's part, and even Lieutenant Lazarev told Mr. Baranov: "You're a fool!" I heard him say this several times, for I was a modest witness to it. Lazarev and Bennett abused this honorable old man with the very lowest expressions. Bennett showed himself here as a true good-for-nothing, but Lazarev was so struck by the worth and right of Mr. Baranov that out of fear of being sent to Russia by way of Siberia he soon left [August 5, 1815], secretly, by night, without any documents or plan of voyage, leaving his supercargo behind. Lieutenant Shveikovskii, who was less involved in this affair than the others, wrote a letter of apology to Mr. Baranov from San Francisco, where the ship *Suvorov* made its first landfall after its flight. . . .

In September, 1815 the schooner *Columbia* arrived with Captain J. Jennings, who revealed that Captain Pigott of the *Forester,* Hunt, Ebbets, etc., were all in the service of Mr. Astor of New York, and that their ships also belonged to Astor. The day following the arrival of the *Columbia,* the schooner *Lydia* (from Philadelphia), belonging to Mr. Wilcocks, the American consul at Canton, arrived from there with the news that peace between England and America had been ratified in February, 1814.

Hunt now came and demanded his brig and property and permission to depart. After settlement of all accounts, with only the two kegs of powder withheld, Hunt pulled out of the roadstead with his brig. Bennett also demanded to be released, without account being taken of the loss of the ship. Mr. Baranov very much wanted to settle this affair, and suggested that under guise of a naturalist I set out for the Sandwich Islands to demand the lost cargo, carry on trade, and if possible to conclude contracts for both present and future.

OCTOBER. On October fifth I set out on the ship *Isabella* for the island of Hawaii. Among the passengers was also Captain Bennett, who had proclaimed previously in Novo-Arkhangel'sk his desire to pacify King Kaumualii.

NOVEMBER 7. We arrived at Kawaihae. Everyone went ashore to visit old John Young. I intended to do so too, but they left on the boat without me. It was necessary that I talk to Young, so I had to go ashore in an Indian boat.

Young came aboard and sailed with us to Kailua where King Kamehameha resides. Before the anchor was dropped, the several Americans had already gone ashore to the king and succeeded in telling him God knows what sort of tales about the Russians. They also turned old Young against me, for when I asked him to tell the king of my mission he did not do so. Even Mr. Baranov's letter to the king was returned to me unopened.

The king went through all my clothes and the cargo entrusted to me, picking out everything that he liked. I knew, of course, that the Company ship would not come for at least six months, so I had to allow his plundering, because he promised to have three houses of straw built for me according to their custom, and to dispense provisions, which were given to me punctually until the arrival of Hunt.

The ship *Isabella* stood here at anchor for several hours and then moved several miles away. They told the Indians a thousand stories about the Russians, so that various rumors reached the king and spread over the whole island. Captain Bennett, however, from fear that I would hold him here, never came ashore, and sailed on the *Isabella* to Canton. The day after the *Isabella* sailed, I was informed of all his intrigues and malicious slanders against the Russians.

I found a man other than Young who would take me to the king and had him relate more reliably the circumstances of my mission and quests. The king promised me that I would receive the lost cargo of the ship *Bering* from King Kaumualii on Kauai, and appeared well disposed regarding other matters. I assured him that if he would be friendly to the Russians and begin to trade with them, he could expect not only friendship but even more benefits than from other peoples. He gave me permission to tour the islands and promised to furnish me one of his two ships and a crew. I bestowed on him with various ceremonies the silver medal which Mr. Baranov had sent him. He received it on his knees and kissed it, as I had done beforehand. I also gave him a patent. He showed the greatest respect for both of these things and asked whether the Russian sovereign had written this patent himself. I told him it was not written by His Majesty but at his order. This information pleased him greatly, and he exclaimed that of course the Russians had more friendship for him than the English; for Captain Vancouver had already promised a long time ago that the king of England would send him a letter, but up to that time he had received nothing. The king himself went for a walk with me, told me to select a place for my houses, and came there himself the next day and spent six hours supervising their construction.

After the usual ceremonies and farewell visits to the queen and the First Chief of the island, I set out. The mountain Mauna-Kea and its environs was my objective, so that I might occupy myself not only with natural history, but examine the most populated, the best cultivated, and the most fruitful part of the island. The southern and southwest parts of it are altogether barren.

DECEMBER 12. I returned to Kailua, summoned because of the illness of Queen Kaahumanu. The schooner *Columbia* arrived this day, and on the fourteenth the brig *Pedler*. On the fifteenth Captain Bailey bought a cargo of sandalwood from the king at eight and one-half Spanish piastres per pikul.

On the sixteenth the schooner *Columbia* set out for Canton. Captain Jennings conducted himself nobly; the king asked him about everything he had heard of the Russians from the Americans, and Jennings told him just the opposite of what the others had said and also hinted to me about those who were unfriendly to the Russians. With this same Captain Jennings I sent a transport of live plants for His excellency Count N. P. Rumiantsev in St. Petersburg. They were brought safely to Macao and thence forwarded by Anders Ljungstedt. . . .

On the eighteenth the queen recovered. On the nineteenth Captain Ebbets the elder arrived, and Hunt, who sailed yesterday and returned with Ebbets. Again abuse and slander were spread about the Russians. Ebbets the elder is a friend of the king, which has led the king to place complete trust in them.

[DECEMBER] 21. During the night Ebbets set sail, and when they had already raised anchor, sent word asking me to come aboard. The night was dark, but I knew that the anchor was raised, and therefore declined his invitation, for it seemed to me suspicious. Queen Kaiva-Pollumoia told me of the conversation Ebbets and Hunt had had with the king, the minister Philip Pitt, and other chiefs. From what she said I became convinced that Captain Jennings is an honest man and a friend of the Russians, for he told the king the same things he had told me. . . .

After Ebbets and Hunt had left, the king became more fearful, constantly changing his place of residence. Whenever he saw me he asked, "Will the Russians come to fight? Will they take the island?" No reply would satisfy him. When I began to speak of matters pertaining to trade I could get nothing out of him, although I showed him my orders. Even my rations began to be cut down.

JANUARY 1. I moved into the new houses which the king had ordered built for me. I gave presents to the king and queen, and also to several of the first chiefs. The queen's brother, Kuakini, or John Adams, as he is called, gave me the land of Koaini on Oahu Island, with a deed.

The king had a cold and fever, and to my surprise he accepted medicine from me; he got well in a short time. On recovery he ordered a temple built in honor of physicians, and gave me the local name of Papaa. (Note: Papaa was a former doctor of the king.)* The rumors spread by Hunt and Ebbets would soon have been disproved had they not been supported in part through old Young, and in part through secret agents of Hunt and Ebbets.

[January] 18. I visited the king in a camp five miles from here, where he taught military discipline to about a thousand men, two-thirds of whom had wooden arms. I dined and supped with the king in his tent, but I slept in the tent of Queen Kaiva-Pallama. On the next day I went to Kawaihae, ate roast dog with old John Young, and on the following morning climbed the mountain Mauna Kea for a second time.

On the way to Kawaihae I met the brig *Forester* coming from Kamchatka. Young Ebbets, who was clerk, passed himself off as captain of the brig. He told me that the cargo had been sold in Kamchatka, and that Captain Pigott had gone overland to Petersburg to obtain his payment. As I explained before, this brig belonged to Mr. Astor in New York. During the war it was

---

* Papa: an uncle of the Hawaiian historian John Ii. He is mentioned in the latter's *Fragments of Hawaiian History,* 33, 46, 115.

supplied with English papers in England by Messrs. Wilson and Porter, and for several years it carried on an extremely advantageous trade on the Northwest coast and in California under the English flag. After the brig left London their deception was discovered. All warships were ordered to pursue them, but the brig sailed very fast and disappeared from view. Because the brig actually belonged to France, it could return neither to America nor to England. Through old Young it was therefore sold to King Kamehameha for sandalwood.

[JANUARY] 24. I arrived at the island [!—valley] of Waimea, where I established my headquarters and inspected every locality. The valley of Waimea is one of the most pleasing, with abundant foodstuffs and fresh water, and nearby is the best sort of hunting with four to five thousand wild oxen. Their meat is superb. In general the most fruitful places on the island of Hawaii are Waimea, Vanniu [?], and Hilo, which is on the eastern side of the island.

After touring these places I returned to Waimea, but hardly had I arrived than a messenger came from Mr. Marshal telling me to be on my guard, because the king had been advised to do away with me. Philip Pitt was a leading advocate of this, though the king did not agree. I wrote the king the following letter:

Your Majesty:

I hope, my good king, that you are in good health, and enjoying tranquility; at least this is my heartfelt wish, as with all good people; also I would like to assure your most gracious queen of my esteem, and similar wishes. I have finished my survey of the large timber and the island[!] of Waimea, and wish now to go to Mauna-Kea. I hope that Your Majesty will permit this little journey. You will receive news of this important objective soon; not one foreigner has yet visited this mountain. It would be of great importance if I could explore it at Your Majesty's order, etc.

To this I received no reply whatsoever. I climbed the mountain to such a height that I was able to examine the greater part of its vegetation. Wild *muzy* [?] cover most of it, and there is also much good building timber of all sorts, and enough sandalwood to keep the Chinese idols satisfied for a long time.

Mr. Marshal, the ship's officer, who went along on the trip to hunt, told me that the sandalwood in the Marquesas Islands is the best, and that the Chinese pay four Spanish piastres more for it than for any other. It is easier to trade with the inhabitants of the Marquesas Islands than with others. Several years ago one could obtain everything for old iron, walrus tusks, etc., but since the last peace the Americans have acquainted them with firearms and powder, which by reason of their constant internecine warfare they prefer to all other goods. A ship setting out on an expedition to the Marquesas Islands must supply itself with sufficient strong boats which can be armed. The inhabitants are even now cannibals. Seamen who have got into trouble on English and American ships and have fled to these islands, have caused much mischief among the natives, which without these people they would not know and do. The lowest of them is a certain Englishman who goes by the false name of Wilson; one like him known as Vaker [Walker?] lives on Kauai. Both were on an English ship but they killed all the officers and left with the ship. Nothing is known of the ship to this day.

[JANUARY] 28.   I learned that N. Winship had arrived at Kailua on the ship *Albatross,* and at once sent a man there to look for him. The king was not at home, for he had moved several miles into the mountains to look after his spring planting. Winship had to visit the king in his dacha, where he was very coldly received because several years previously he cheated the king out of a whole cargo of sandalwood. The first thing Winship did was to try and slander the Russians and to spread the same sort of rumors as his predecessors.

MARCH 11.   They informed me that I could not receive any more provisions of any kind, so I had to return to Kailua, arriving on the eighteenth. The king and especially the queen appeared in a good mood.

[MARCH] 20.   Queen Kaahumanu gave me the land of Veikarua in Kallau, on the island of Oahu, along with ten sheep and forty goats.

[MARCH] 23. The ship *Beverly,* with Captain Edes, arrived to buy sandalwood, but did not obtain any although they offered nine piastres per pikul.

[MARCH] 24. The [anniversary of the] accession of our Sovereign Alexander I to the throne. I received word of the restoration of peace and the imprisonment of Napoleon on St. Helena. All this called for a great holiday, which I celebrated with honest Captain Edes at Chief Cox's, near the place where the unforgettable Captain Cook was killed. At noon Captain Edes ordered the flag raised and a twenty-one-gun salute fired. I invited the king and all his chiefs to attend. The prince and chiefs came, but not the king, although I had told him before that if he did not appear I would take it as a sign of unfriendliness toward Emperor Alexander.

[MARCH] 25. I asked permission of the king to go to Oahu on the ship *Beverly,* and arranged with him about land for the Company, but because of old Young's influence nothing came of it. He also refused to let me build a stone warehouse on the island of Oahu for the Russian factory, as previously agreed, but offered me his own warehouse, which he could always supervise.

[MARCH] 26. I left the island of Hawaii for many reasons: provisions were supplied me irregularly or not at all; from time to time the king was roused against me; and I was called a Russian spy. Hunt and Ebbets had their agents on the island who not only spread evil tales about the Russians but even began to make attempts on my life. Not only are there more provisions on Oahu, but the people are better disposed toward foreigners. They make it clear that they feel themselves slaves of such a tyrant. . . .

[MARCH] 28. We arrived at the island of Oahu. On the twenty-ninth Captain Edes sailed for Canton without cargo.

[MARCH] 31. I took possession of the land of Vaikarua, which I bought from Queen Kaahumanu, and found enough fields suitable for growing taro, and so many lakes filled with fish that several hundred families could live there. Several versts north of Vaikarua is a small island near which a ship can anchor safely.

APRIL 2. I returned to the island [!] of Honolulu.

[APRIL] 4. I set out for the Pearl River and took possession of the land of Taiai [Kawaihae?]. . . .

[APRIL] 7. At high tide I returned to the harbor in an Indian boat.

[APRIL] 14. The brig *Panther* arrived, under Captain Lewis. He was sick, and I cured him.

[APRIL] 23. Captain Hill arrived on the ship *Ophelia*. I heard that he was at Kauai and he told me that Captain Ebbets had demanded of King Kaumualii the furs from the ship *Bering,* representing himself as entitled to do this by Mr. Baranov, and had received them.

[APRIL] 28. Through the brig *Forester,* arriving from the island of Hawaii, I received word that the Company vessel *Otkrytie* had arrived there, and that the *Forester* had been given to the king for a cargo of sandalwood.

MAY 3. The vessel *Otkrytie,* under command of Fleet Lieutenant and Cavalier Podushkin, stood at anchor outside the harbor of the island of Oahu.

[MAY] 5. We guided the vessel to a safe anchorage inside the harbor. Certain repairs were made on the vessel, because in accordance with orders I had to set out on it for Kauai. Supercargo Pavel Verkhovinskii was assigned as manager of the factory and Company lands at this place, and I prepared for him the following instructions:

By order of his—Alexander A-ch Baranov,—commander of Russian-American possessions, I appoint supercargo Pavel Verkhovinskii as manager of the Russian-American Company factory on the Sandwich Islands, and in accordance with the desire of the Chief Manager of the Russian-American Company his duties will be:

1) to live in the settlement of Honolulu on the island of Oahu;

2) to check and accept goods acquired from the ship *Otkrytie* according to the register; to store these goods in a

house held in readiness by the local commandant, Mr. Holmes; and to carry on trade for barter and cash;

3) to manage two plantations, 1) Koaiaina on the Pearl River and 2) Vaikarua on the southeast side of the island of Oahu in the gubernia of Kolau. He must see that the inhabitants of the plantation (Aine) look after it, pay annual tribute to King Kamehameha, try to raise cattle, fish, et cetera, and deliver fresh or dried taro to Honolulu. For a third of the year he can employ the subject people for the benefit of the Company in planting arable land with tobacco, cotton, grapes, sugar cane, nuts, maize, lemons, and whatever else Mr. Pavel Verkhovinskii thinks worthwhile. At the same time he is to treat the inhabitants tactfully and kindly. Force is not to be applied under any circumstances. It will be better to excuse a thousand faults than to punish a troublesome person once; it will be better to send him away without any punishment.

4) Here at the port of Honolulu I have planted a garden, with local products, medicinal herbs, and other plants, which I particularly commend to Mr. Verkhovinskii.

5) There will be assigned to him as many Russians and Aleuts as may be needed, and for factory assistant I recommend to him Ivan Larionov, who knows planting, the language, and a great deal about the local trade.

6) Such necessary provisions as may not be obtained here will be provided from the cargo of the ship *Otkrytie*, until such time as another ship from Novo-Arkhangel'sk reaches these shores.

7) Political conversations of all kinds are forbidden. Until I return or he receives other instructions from the Chief Manager of the Russian-American territories, he will be the manager of the plantations here.

8) When he has received his share of the cargo he must give the remaining cargo, and an account. I will be responsible for what remains on the ship.

9) When there is important work to be done for the Company he can hire people.

10) I recommend that he live in friendship with the

taiuns and all *hetmans* of this island, and finally I commend him to conduct himself carefully and honestly, not shamefully but honorably, toward his sovereign, his nation, his Company and himself—

> Signed: *Commissioner of the Expedition of the R. A. Co. in the Sandwich Islands,* EGOR SHEFFER.

As Verkhovinskii did not accept this position, it was entrusted to the promyshlennik Petr Kichirev, well-known for his diligence and sobriety.

[MAY] 11 [?]. The company brig *Il'mena* arrived. It had left Port Rumiantsev, on the shores of New Albion, with cargo for Novo-Arkhangel'sk. Captain W. Wadsworth (an American) proclaimed falsely that a big leak had forced him to come here, but I soon found that his own interests had caused him to do so. I intended to sail from the island of Oahu on the ship *Otkrytie,* and therefore wrote the Captain of the brig *Il'mena* as follows:

> In the name of the Chief Director of the Russian-American Company, Collegiate Councilor and Cavalier Baranov, I ask Captain W. Wadsworth, commander of the Company brig *Il'mena,* to repair the leak in the seams as well and as fast as possible, along with other repairs. If this is done before the return of the Company ship *Otkrytie* to this harbor it is my definite wish that you remain here in the harbor with the brig until 15/27 June at my responsibility.
>
> EGOR SHEFFER

[MAY] 10 [?]. We sailed for the island of Kauai as planned.

Without breaking the rules of forestry, one can cut 12,000 pikuls of sandalwood on all of the Sandwich Islands; but if careful methods are employed, that is, dividing the forests into strips, trying to plant new ones, and correctly cutting the logs which are best for the Chinese trade, more than twice as much can be acquired annually.

There is a great deal of dissatisfaction among all inhabitants of Hawaii, Maui, Lanai, Molokai, and Oahu over their present situation and government. The people are so poor, however, so weakened, and so terrified by the present ruler of these islands that they have no idea of founding a new state, but wish all the more for some European power to take them under its more favorable protection. Many of the leading inhabitants told me that I should ask the great Russian monarch *Iriru Kinipui* * to take over these islands, only leaving them their taro fields. More than two-thirds of the plantations on all the islands belong to the king, who has taken them by force. From others he takes annually whatever he thinks necessary. If the owner of the land cannot pay the taxes levied by the king, he loses it and it reverts to the king. Often the king places a *tabu-kol* on the land, and the owner has no recourse but to quit his land. . . .

The king often levies taxes which are completely impossible to fulfill. Thus he demanded recently from every one of his subjects a certain number of copper nails for ship building. . . . The Indians said, "The King has lost his mind demanding such things, which our land does not produce. He could demand of us taro, bread plants, dogs, pigs, chickens, fish, and fruits; we could satisfy him with these things, but not with copper nails." I lived on the island of Oahu for only a short time but I learned enough about the state of affairs there.

The harbor of Honolulu, on the island of Oahu, lies at 21° 21′ 40″ North latitude and 157.51 West longitude; [ ] according to the compass is 8¾. The tide at full moon is seven feet. At the present time the tide is 2′ 20″ after the full moon.

The mountains abound in fine sandalwood. A chain of mountains divides the island in two parts. There are many fruitful, well-watered valleys in both parts. However the west side is more pleasant, for on the east side the east wind blows almost the year round. The hills furnish firewood and various kinds of construction timber. Foremost among the latter is genuine sandalwood. There is also the false type, which the Indians call "nagi," a type of ebony, and mahogany [?]. Particularly notable are the oil trees (the particular species *Pikh jugulaus* [?] and the rare [——] tree.†

North of the harbor of Honolulu flows a river which supplies this side with fresh water by which one can establish any type of

---

* In modern transcription *Alii Lukini nui,* "great Russian chief."

† Unfortunately, Schäffer's botanical observations are too scanty for much to be made of them.

manufacturing; it falls into the harbor where ships get fresh water. Seven miles from the north the river Eva (the Pearl River) flows into the sea. It furnishes a remarkable number of fine quality pearls. The pearl harvest takes place twice a year.

On the east side of the island are many rivers, which descend in various directions to the sea. They flood the land along their courses and make it very fertile.

The island of Oahu is the most fertile and populous of the Sandwich Islands (although Kauai can be compared with it). Generally speaking, on all these islands scarcely a tenth of the land is worked. The inhabitants number not more than 10,000 persons. The people refrain from working the land partly because of natural laziness, partly because not one of them can be master of his own property. If one of the inhabitants works his land, or fattens a pig, evil people of King Kamehameha take it from him under various false pretenses. This even happens to the foreigners, most of them fugitive criminals from New Holland who purchased land from the king for money and valuables.

Oahu, just like Maui, Lanai, etc., rightfully belongs to King Kaumualii on Kauai. His father Kaeo ruled all these islands. The well-known commander Kalanikupule killed Kaeo. Kaumualii fled to the island of Kauai, where he now rules. Kalanikupule was conquered and killed by Kamehameha in 1801, and Kamehameha conquered all of these islands. From that time the most extreme tyranny and poverty has existed on all of these islands, for he does not allow any of his subjects to sell even one pig to foreigners. Only the king trades, and every foreign ship must first come to him on the island of Hawaii and allow itself to be plundered by him before receiving permission to enter the harbor of Oahu. Oahu could be a paradise if these islands were under the mild rule of this blessed land of the right hand of the Almighty. It could be made a fortunate land which each man could consider it the greatest fortune to inhabit! If only the people were not burdened by such heavy shackles of tyrants! If the Sandwich Islands could have a monarch like Russia's great Alexander, truly the majority of our brothers could live in a golden age. Here bread grows in trees and on the ground; each can prepare what foods he wishes: pineapples, grapes, bananas, cocoanuts, sugar cane, oranges, lemons, etc . . . , grow here in abundance; wild and domestic livestock abound, domestic cattle can pasture on lush meadows the year round, and the sea teems with tasty fish. Everyone can choose the climate which suits him best; the islands are free of all epidemic ills—even smallpox is unknown here. On all the islands you will meet nothing harmful, not even a poisonous serpent. All human needs and all types of delight can flourish on the Sandwich Islands! With what beautiful garb are their fields covered! What a prospect for maritime manufactures and trade! But these islands are now in a state which recalls the verses of Alois Blumauer about George Forster's description of the island of Otahiti.* Only under a mild rule, under the scepter of a monarch by whom human rights are defended, where property is inviolable, and where a man can sincerely be a man—under such a government the Sandwich Islands would be Elysian fields!

[MAY] 11/23. We anchored at Kailua on the island of Hawaii. I and our Captain Podushkin visited the king, but could get nowhere with him. In order to avoid us, or, as he usually tries to do, to hold us here as long as they wish, he disappeared into Taboo. I was so displeased at losing several days here that I went into Taboo myself in order to have another serious talk with the king. He was not angry at me for this, but told me again that if we would wait just two days longer, he would send a man to Kauai with us to demand our property, although Hunt had told him that the Russians had left the ship *Bering* at Kauai on purpose, just to have a reason to conquer the islanders. . . . As for trading matters we could get nowhere at all with him. He refused to let us build a store on the island of Oahu, but he assured me that I could use half of his own store there at any time.

During our stay on the island no one visited us except Chief Cox and the three queens. The king himself refused our invitation.

Chief Cox gave Captain Podushkin a letter to King Kaumualii on the island of Kauai in which he wrote that he would soon visit him on the brig *Forester,* which now belongs to Kamehameha.

---

* George Forster was a German writer who sailed with Cook. His overly idyllic picture of Tahiti was satirized by the poet Alois Blumauer (1755–1798).

Not long before our departure old Young came on board. Ratafia* fairly opened his heart and mouth, and he assured us that only Hunt and Captains Ebbets and Winship were enemies of the Russians.

[MAY] 13/25.   We left Hawaii and only 16/28 dropped anchor at the island of Kauai. On the same evening I notified the king of our arrival. The messenger was very well received and a loud "Hurrah!" was heard several times on the shore. That night the ship was borne a fair distance from the anchorage, so that we had to maneuver until noon the next day before we again reached the same place. Meanwhile several Indians had come aboard to spy. . . .

After dinner I went to visit the king and was satisfied with his reception. I can only note that he seemed confused and that here too, as with Kamehameha, the Americans acted against us. When I gradually revealed my friendly intentions, he acquired an open look, his features became more relaxed, and his voice more distinct. In the end he promised everything that I wished. Then he ordered a pipe of tobacco to be brought, from which he and I should smoke.

[MAY] 19.   The king agreed today to all my demands and proposals, and said that I should prepare the papers. In a few days he will visit our ship and will drink to the health of Emperor Alexander, with whom he wishes to maintain friendly relations. I spoke a great deal with him of the latter. I also spoke with our Captain Podushkin, and asked how far he thought I should go in this, and obtained his agreement to the negotiations which I began with the king.

MAY 19 [20?] JUNE 1.   According to my conditions with the king we prepared all documents in detail, a contract between him and the Russian-American Company by which he should give the Company the cargo of the ship *Bering* or pay for it in money, confirm a monopoly trade in sandalwood on Kauai, and permit the establishment of a Russian factory on Kauai. King Kaumualii also cedes to the Russian-American Company a province on Kauai for a plantation, freeing it from all taxes in perpetuity. He must fur-

---

* Ratafia: a Hawaiian alcoholic beverage.

nish the first cargo of sandalwood within six months, and the second cargo twelve months after that. He must not trade with the Americans, except to render aid to distressed vessels, and must assist me in collecting rare specimens. I prepared an act of submission and a request of King Kaumualii to our Most Enlightened Emperor Alexander. All these papers were translated into Russian by Mr. Podushkin and written out.

[MAY] 20 [21?] [JUNE]2/. The king arrived on the *Otkrytie* with his court, wives, and children. We set aside this day as the holiday of Saint Constantine and Saint Helen, and offered our prayers to the King of Kings for the health of his Imperial Majesty, of Grand Duke Constantine Pavlovich and of all the high imperial family. Both the officers and all the crew were in holiday dress. Thus we received the king and all his chiefs and others, bringing them into the captain's cabin, where they sat.

Through our interpreter I once more asked the king whether he had changed his mind in anything or stood firmly on his wishes and promises. He replied in English that he kept his word. I read the convention, ordered it translated for him, and again asked if it was all right and he had no objection to it. Finally I ordered explained to him that he could still refuse and we would continue to be friends, but that he could not refuse after he had signed the paper.

"All this is correct," he said; "I want to do it." At this point we gave him the paper to sign, and put on him the staff officers' uniform of the fleet of His Imperial Russian Majesty. When he had donned the uniform I took the king into the general cabin which was prepared for prayer service, ordered the prayers for the holiday to be read, and afterward the solemn verses *Tebe Boga Khválim!* to be sung.

After the service I placed the Holy Cross on the Bible, and told the king to place his right hand on it and swear a second time to give his sacred word as a loyal subject of Russia and to kiss it. I then led him on deck and ordered Mr. Podushkin to read the act before all the crew. As a sign of citizenship the king accepted the Russian flag. . . .

Here we began to drink the health of His Imperial Majesty,

etc.—after this to the health of Mr. Baranov and all Russians, and
to King Kaumualii and the entire island of Kauai.

After dinner I went ashore with the king and asked the
interpreter to proclaim the Act of Subordination publicly in the
Indian language. The king himself hoisted the Russian flag and
gave a thirteen-gun salute, to which the *Otkrytie* replied with
twenty-one guns. Everyone on shore cried *"Maishai! Maishai!"*
[*Meitei! Meitei!*], meaning "Very good!"

[MAY] 22/3.   This day the king gave us dinner on shore and was
very hospitable to the whole crew. The king told me that Captain
Ebbets had actually demanded from him in my name the furs from
the *Bering,* which he received. He also took a large anchor from the
Bering.

[MAY] 25/6.   I selected a place in the Waimea valley for building houses for the factory and for setting out gardens. The king
gave us a stone building for a store. I placed the promyshlennik
Aleksei Odnoriadkin in charge, over several Russians and six
Aleuts. But as for me, I wanted to sail on the *Otkrytie* to the island
of Oahu, there to settle affairs and await the Company ship
Myrtle-Kad'iak, on which I would sail back to Kauai, where I
would load it with sandalwood.

JUNE 11.   We raised anchor and suffered a storm for thirty-
four hours, seeing now Oahu, now Kauai.

On the thirteenth at 1:00 P.M., the storm increased, and within
eight minutes we lost the main and mizzen masts. I myself was on
deck when this misfortune occurred. Captain Podushkin told me
that nothing remained for him but to take a course to Kamchatka,
Unalaska, or Novo-Arkhangel'sk. As we happened to be not far
from the island of Niihau, I asked Captain Podushkin to keep as
close to the shore as possible and to land me there; I promised all
possible help from the Indians, subjects of King Kaumualii. From
Niihau it would be quite possible for me to go to Kauai by baidarka.

We made false masts with which we could approach fairly close
to Niihau. The king's pilot and several Indians arrived in boats and
towed the ship to a safe place where it could be repaired and sup-

plied with other false masts. When I saw the ship was out of danger, and the courage of the officers and seamen revived, I gave Mr. Podushkin copies of several important papers for Mr. Baranov, and supplied the ship with as much provisions as could be taken from the island of Niihau. Captain Podushkin assured me that he would go directly to Novo-Arkhangel'sk. On arrival I sent several Indians to Kauai to inform the king of our misfortunes. At once several persons arrived to help us and the king wrote me and Mr. Podushkin, telling us that we could treat the island of Niihau like our own property.

[JUNE] 21. The ship was in such condition today that nothing else could be done for it here. It was repaired as well as possible, and supplied with provisions for a sufficient time. Entrusting it to Divine Providence and Captain Podushkin, I myself set out after dinner for Kauai in a baidarka.

I remained alive thanks only to the skill of the Aleut. A violent storm, which struck with all its horror in the channel between Niihau and Lehua, threatened our lives. In the dead of night, after a sharp struggle with death, we reached the northern shores of Niihau. I spent the night in an uninhabited place, and the next day, not without danger, however, reached Kauai. The king, accompanied by our Russians, met me and ordered the Russian flag raised and a seven-gun salute given. The Russians told me that the king had wept when he learned of our misfortune.

[JUNE] 24. Taboo. The Russian flags flew over Kauai just as on Russian holidays. The king assigned three houses on the shore as dwellings for our Russians. I lived and slept at the king's until the factory was built. The king told me today that the islands of Maui, Oahu, Lanai, and Molokai belonged to him, and if Russia would help him get them back, he would give her half of the island of Oahu and all of the sandalwood forever, and also whatever provinces I might want to select on all the other islands. The king wanted to have two hundred armed Russians constantly on Kauai. He told me also of several other things which he wanted to have, and asked me to make presents to several chiefs designated by him so that they would be more attracted to the side of the Russians, giving me to understand that he wished this very much, and all to be at his expense. From this it was clear that the king wants to establish a general friendship between the Russians and his subjects.

[JUNE] 30.   This morning the king went into Taboo. He ordered the Russian flag raised as usual and said I need only ask for anything I want on the island; all that belongs to him belongs also to the Russians. I moved to the house built for me and began to plant.

JULY 8.   The king visited me with all of his court and raised the Russian flag. I drank to the health of the king and had a seven-gun salute given when he left.

[JULY] 9.   Taboo. The Russian flag waved over the house of the king.

[JULY] 16.   Early in the morning a ship was seen on the south side of the island. The king ordered the Russian flag raised, and I did the same in front of the factory. It was a brig. It approached the shore but then changed course to the west. After dinner an Indian brought a note on which was written: "Captain Clark sails for Canton." He ordered the king to be told orally not to tell me that he had passed by.

[JULY] 20.   The king paid me a visit, and again on the twenty-second, when we celebrated the name day of Her Imperial Majesty the Mother of the Emperor and of Her Imperial Majesty his sister. I ordered the large cutter from the ship *Bering* prepared. I wanted to send it to the island of Oahu, in order to find out how the Russians there were getting along and to receive word from them. Six weeks had already passed since the brig *Il'mena* should have left the island of Oahu, I assumed that it would at least come to Kauai and learn of the ship *Otkrytie,* but I had seen neither the *Il'mena* nor the expected ship *Myrtle-Kad'iak.* . . .

AUGUST 10.   The ship *Atala,* under Captain Lannert, arrived from Boston. He bought provisions from the king; the king sent him to me and asked me to deal with him; whatever I decided to do with him would be satisfactory. . . . Captain Lannert told me that he had come from New Holland, that there were no fresh provisions of any sort on his ship, and little of anything else, and asked me very humbly to give him supplies. He said there was nothing at all to be had on the island of Hawaii because many ships there ahead of him had taken everything. I asked the king to let him have several pigs, yams, and taro, and to obtain whatever he wished from him. I asked Mr. Lannert and his clerk Mr. Prince into the factory, where they lived until they got all the provisions. Mr. Lannert told me that he was sailing to Novo-Arkhangel'sk, so I wrote to Mr. Baranov and sent fruits there.

[AUGUST] 12. The ship *Atala* sailed. Mr. Lannert wrote me from the island of Niihau, thanking me for the friendly reception and at the same time letting me know that I should not take him for a deceiver, informing me that not he but one of the Winships is the commander of the ship, and that he only supervises it.

[AUGUST] 15. The schooner *Lydia,* under Captain Gyzelaar, came from the island of Oahu with letters for me from our Russians, and others from Captain Ebbets for King Kaumualii. Ebbets proposed that the king buy the schooner. The king came to me, saying that this was just the sort of ship he wanted, but he did not want to interfere in trade, and if it was possible for me to do so, I should buy it for him at any price. I had no choice but to agree; for in my first contract I had promised the king such a ship. I could not expect to obtain such a ship for him from Novo-Arkhangel'sk in the appointed time, and wishing to keep my word, so that the king would not have any reason or cause to break his, I went to the schooner with a carpenter, looked it over, and began to bargain.

For the first few days we could not agree on the price. When I told the king of this, he told me that I should give as much sandalwood for the ship as I wanted, so I closed the deal. In order to satisfy Mr. Gyzelaar I had to go to the island of Oahu, pay him off, and receive from him formally the schooner's papers. This took place on the twenty-fourth in the presence of all there, including the younger and elder Captains Ebbets, N. Winship, Captain Betts, Captain Gyzelaar, Doctor Frost, John Young, our Russian Captains Young and Wadsworth, and others.

After the ceremonies I invited all these men to the factory for dinner. The supercargo of the *Myrtle-Kad'iak,* D. Toropogritskii, who was our host, placed two soldiers in the court of the factory, so as to hold back the crowds of Indians. I myself did not know of this until almost all of the guests had come except John Young. When Young arrived he at once began to quarrel with the guards, and wanted to take the guns out of their hands by force. . . . He entered the gathering in a fury and told me that if I did not take the guards away he would bring his own. I replied coolly (not knowing yet what all this meant) that he could do this. I conferred with Toropogritskii and heard from him that Mr. Baranov had ordered him to post these two guards in all harbors where he would be. Not removing the guards, I told the guests that the guards were inside the factory and were solely an honor guard, that Mr. Young was making a great mistake attacking such people who carried the emblem of the Russian Emperor, and that he should thank God that they did not impale him on their bayonets. I heard very distinctly this Young being egged on still more by young Ebbets, and they were the first to leave the gathering. . . .

Meanwhile we sat around the table, and when the first course was eaten, the other Americans also got up from the table and left us on the pretext that they feared unpleasantness. I did not trouble myself, for I saw very clearly the deliberate plan and continued with complete calm to dine with one Russian. After dinner, in order to get satisfaction because of the personal offense, I donned the uniform of the Moscow gubernia and remained in the factory all day. I asked our captains to leave for their boats after dinner and to be on their guard.

In the evening Ebbets the elder, Winship, and old Young came. The latter was so drunk that he fell in the doorway. He proclaimed himself to be the governor of the island of Oahu and said that I must establish friendship with him. Ebbets and Winship wanted to be mediators. . . . I sent all three of them away with the contempt that the honor of the Russian Emperor demanded, and that these vile people deserved.

I knew them all very well. John Young, a deserter from an English ship, having the vilest character and a low soul, had made himself more than an Indian on the island of Hawaii. He not only adopted all the manners and customs of the Indians, but even surpassed them in cruelty. Through his diabolic counsels King Kamehameha became a usurper and a tyrant. Of course he acquired his friendship and trust, for the latter made him governor of the island of Hawaii. There are no cruelties perpetrated by him as governor about which he is ashamed to tell! With the construction of a great temple in Kawaihae, John Young sacrificed to the pagan idols six hundred people and two thousand pigs, all of which he ordered to be killed and burned! He has served twenty-five years, and when I was there, according to his own son Jim, was still a secret supplier of bait for fishing to the king, to whom he was extremely attached. It is well known that there is nothing which will attract and catch fish so easily as human flesh, and so whenever the king thinks of fishing, Young has a boy put to death and cut into pieces, which are supplied to King Kamehameha in tied bladders.

Now he is a secret agent of the Americans. . . . On the fourth of July this human monster, in a gathering of many American captains, including Clark, Ebbets, and Winship, gave a toast to the damned Russians. There was still no guard at the Russian factory at that time. Captain Clark grabbed our mariner Madison by the throat and told him: "You will be damned if you do not stand up and drink with us and will not leave the Russian service." * When Clark left Oahu, our supercargo Mr. Toropogritskii asked him by letter to leave one thousand sealskins on the island of Kauai for me, but he did not do this.

AUGUST 25.   A certain Adams, who serves Kamehameha as captain of the brig *Forester,* came to the factory today and reviled me in various ways. Finally he said that he would come to Kauai soon,

---

* Exactly what took place here is not clear. *Niles Weekly Register,* Baltimore, April 5, 1817, p. 96, gives no hint of the fracas described by Schäffer in this report: "The fourth of July, last year [1816], was duly observed at the Woashos [Oahu], one of the Sandwich islands, by the Americans there, and others. At meredian, a grand salute was fired from the American ship *Enterprize,* which was repeated by a brig from Boston, by a Russian ship and brig [the *Il'mena* and *Kad'iak*] and by an English brig. After which the Americans gave a dinner to the gentlemen belonging to the place, and those from the ships in the harbor. In the evening there was a display of fireworks."

haul down the Russian flag, trample it under foot and ——— on it. This Adams is a deserter from an English ship, served on American ships during the war between England and America, and entered the service of Kamehameha because it was impossible for him to return to his homeland. I went to Mr. Holmes, who usually decided the affairs of foreigners, and demanded satisfaction for all the insults to which Russians were subjected. He replied that he can order nothing when John Young is on the island of Oahu.

The malice of these American hotheads comes in part from a grudge over the defeat dealt their idol Bonaparte by the Russian heroes.

After establishing as much order on Oahu as possible, I left on the evening of the twenty-seventh and the next day was in the harbor of Hanalei, on the north side of the island of Kauai. I found the province and the harbor extremely suitable for the Company and decided upon transferral of the ship *Lydia* to the king to demand from him at once this province for the Company. With Captain Whittemore, with whom I went to Hanalei, I concluded preliminary arrangements for purchase of his beautiful ship, very suitable for loading cargo, and sent it to Novo-Arkhangel'sk for conclusion of this deal. This ship, a war vessel with twenty-two guns, would be extremely practical and good against all political eventualities, but also because of speed could serve for a quick turnover of the Company's capital and double its income. To my regret I learned that Mr. Baranov did not agree to this purchase, and I remained on Kauai without help, without people, and without a ship, which I needed to further the enterprise or to which I could entrust a cargo. I had nothing left but to hope for the arrival of the ship from St. Petersburg. The Company ship *Myrtle-Kad'iak* was in a much worse condition than the ship *Otkrytie*. Only the brig *Il'mena* remained usable, but she was very small for a cargo of sandalwood, and being without news from Novo-Arkhangel'sk, I did not want to send her from the island. I wanted to use the vessel *Myrtle* as a fire watch in the harbor of Hanalei, where it could serve as a fort and a store. . . .

When I returned to Waimea from Hanalei I found the king on our brig *Il'mena*. He shed joyful tears when he saw me. I went with him on the schooner *Lydia*. The captain gave him a flag, Russian of course. He ordered it raised and a seven-gun salute fired. The schooner was formally given the king by a convention. Captains Whittemore, Smith, and Gyzelaar were witnesses and signed it. I reminded the king of his promises and demanded the promised province for the Company, telling him that I liked the harbor of Hanalei best, and he assured me of it.

SEPTEMBER 6. The ship *Avon* sailed with Captain Whittemore to Novo-Arkhangel'sk, and with it Baranov's son, with whom I sent all the original acts and agreements I had made with the king. Then I turned to defense of Russian property and of the whole island. I spoke with the king and he proclaimed that the whole island is under my command, and everything on it is Russian property.

[SEPTEMBER] 12. I measured out the plan for a fortress in Waimea, and several hundred people were assigned to work.

Captain Gyzelaar took the schooner *Lydia* to the island of Oahu and returned on the twenty-second of this month. The vessel not only brought war news from the island of Oahu, but news that all Russian factories there had been destroyed by the Indians, all of which, as the supervisor Kicherev informed me, was done at the instigation of John Young and other Americans.

[SEPTEMBER] 24. The American ship *O'Cain* arrived bearing N. Winship, McNeil, Smith, Ebbets the younger, Gyzelaar, and Doctor Frost. Winship, Smith, and Gyzelaar came ashore, intending to haul down the Russian flag which the king had raised. However, the king was firm and ordered a guard of ten men, with fixed bayonets and ten cartridges, placed beneath it, so that the Russian flag would not be dishonored by the American seamen.

[SEPTEMBER] 25. Unable to achieve their aims by open means yesterday, when the Americans again saw the Russian flag waving today, on the day of Taboo, they wrote the king a letter in which they tried in every way to achieve their aim, but in vain. The letter was written by Ebbets the younger. I ordered him told that he should come ashore and I would answer his letter then.

[SEPTEMBER] 30. I went to the harbor of Hanalei, which the king had given the Company, and to which he had asked me to attach my name, and to give Russian names to several of the persons living there.

I discovered a spy from the island of Oahu and informed the king.

OCTOBER 1. I arrived at Schäffer Valley (Schäfferthal) at Hanalei. There I found waiting a commission appointed by the king. They informed me that they had been ordered to look after all of my needs and to sell the province to me, which was completed in the presence of all the elders of this province.

[OCTOBER] 2, 3, 4, and 5. I established the borders of the province and looked over the harbor, rivers, countryside, etc., etc. I ordered a fortress placed on three hillocks, designated the spot for it, and set about preparing for its construction.

[OCTOBER] 6. A solemn ceremony of transfer of the province was held, attended by all the inhabitants, including men, women, and children. While we toasted the health of a) His Imperial Majesty the Sovereign Emperor Alexander; b) the Russian-American Company; c) King Kaumualii; and d) the nobles of the island of Kauai, the Russian flags were waving, twenty-one guns were fired, and the people were given a substantial amount of wine, rum, and various small gifts.

I renamed the harbor, the valley, rivers, and several people. The main fort received the name of Alexander; to the main chief, Kallavatti, I gave the old name of the valley of Hanalei; to the chief Taera I found it fitting to give the name of Vorontsov; and to the Main Commissioner, the chief Obana Tupigea, who transferred the land to me, I gave the name Platov. I appointed the chief Hanalei captain of the valley and Petr Kicherev the manager. The landowners in the province were named in the bill of sale.

[OCTOBER] 8. I returned to Waimea. On my arrival the king ordered the Russian flag raised and a seven-gun salute, and visited me in the factory before I had time to visit him. He signed the transfer of the province and the harbor to the Company and I replied (honeurs). When the king began giving land to the Russians, the high chiefs of the island also began proclaiming their devotion by giving land for the gifts received from me previously.

[OCTOBER] 10. I received for the Company from Chief Kama-halolani a village on the right bank of the river Waimea, with twenty families.

[OCTOBER] 11. In the presence of our Captain Young and Mr. Tarakanov I received from the king's sister Tairinoa a village on the left bank of the river Waimea with eleven families.

Today after dinner the king and I looked over the fortress construction. He even put his own wives to work dragging stones for the construction. . . . The King asked me whether a declaration of war against old Kamehameha should be sent to the island of Oahu. I dissuaded him from this, saying that I would not go nor would I send anyone there to demand or to take satisfaction for the offense borne by Russia on the island of Oahu until I was sufficiently fortified.

[OCTOBER] 14. I again undertook the trip to Hanalei (Schäffer Valley), going by foot along the southern part of the island to explore it personally. I spent two days in Hanapepe, where I received for the Company from the chief Obana Platov a village with eleven families. It lies in the province of Hanapepe on the right bank of the river Don and is called Tuiloa Platov.

[OCTOBER] 16. I rested in Tippu. It is a landing place for large boats and even small ships.

[OCTOBER] 17. In Hannamaure [Hannamauli?], there is a good bay for ships of about a hundred tons.

[OCTOBER] 18. In Gannaure [Hanalei?], an incomparable valley.

[OCTOBER] 19. I reached Hanalei (Schäffer Valley), crossing forty valleys, watered by large and small rivers, rich in fish, covered with perpetual captivating greenery, and these streams irrigate the fruitful fields and their shores. Since I made the journey afoot, through the mountains and valleys, over logs and stones, I could make a very detailed investigation of the condition of the island. Nothing could escape my eye. Unfortunately I noted that the inhabitants of Kauai are much ruder than the inhabitants of the southern islands. They are divided into various parties. Upon my arrival in Hanalei the well-to-do among the inhabitants brought me thirty pigs as *obrok*.*

I planted a small garden around the house.

[OCTOBER] 27. Chief Platov arrived with an order from the king to support me in everything, so that I could more quickly occupy my places. Platov assisted me with his own people.

NOVEMBER 1. The garden was dug and fenced, and today I planted maize, sugarcane, bananas, bread fruit, trees, papaya . . . , etc. Platov himself worked all morning transplanting cabbage. Women and children are busy gathering oil nuts (*Ölnüsse*). In the Russian provinces one can collect a large shipload of them each year.

The worst people among the Russian subjects are the elders Taupia, Puari, Kabita, Tuapalauri, and Papiaula.

[NOVEMBER] 15. Until now I have worked energetically on Forts Alexander and Barclay. Platov has supplied us and our ships with pigs for a long time, and works daily with his Indians on construction of the fortifications. Everything that I sowed and planted in the garden grows successfully.

[NOVEMBER] 16. I left the harbor and went to Mirori, near the northern cape of the island, where I spent the night.

[NOVEMBER] 17. At sunrise I left Mirori, sent the boat to Waimea and went with Ivan Larionov and one Indian to the highest mountain of this island in order to look over the island from its highest point. . . . I found nothing but yellow and red iron soil. The condition of forestry on this mountain was my main object, but the weather for the greater part of the day did not conform with my wishes; from mid-day to evening it rained and made my journey afoot, about twenty-five miles, through partial woods and shrubs, and even on open places through moist grass from six to seven feet high, very unpleasant. I noted a great deal of sandalwood in the forest, a great many thick stumps of [   ] wood, and so forth. I could not get enough of the view from the mountains. I arrived late

* *Obrok:* A Russian term for quitrent, a fixed sum paid by a serf in lieu of personal service.

in Waimea, extremely tired. The boat which I had dispatched this morning returned three hours later to call for me!

[NOVEMBER] 18. This morning at sunrise, when the king left Taboo, he ordered the Russian flag raised and gave a seven-gun salute from the shore and the same from his schooner and visited me in the factory. I answered him with honors (*honeurs*) and together we visited Fort Elizabeth, the construction of which is well along. . . . I heard of unpleasant behavior of Vorrol Madson, in our service. . . .

[NOVEMBER] 20. The king assured me today that 24,000 pieces of sandalwood lie ready, and since Fort Elizabeth is finished he wanted to order cutting for us continued. However all sandalwood, as well as everything else produced on this island belongs to the Russian-American Company, so it does not matter what the islanders do. I am obliged to supply annually an amount of things which he wants and which I have. I was content with this and tried to attract to me more closely the minister Kamahalolani, who up to now I did not dare trust, although he tried to show his serviceability and readiness.

[NOVEMBER] 21. Minister Kamahalolani visited me with all his princes. I showed him as much attention as the king himself.

[NOVEMBER] 23. I visited three villages in the valley here and found them in good order.

[NOVEMBER] 27 to 29. There was such a heavy rain that the river Waimea rose six feet about its usual height.

[NOVEMBER] 30. I set out for Hanapepe, inspected the estate of Platov on the river Don, and found it extremely rich in taro fields. I ordered the dry land planted into cotton, tobacco, maize, and also transplanted here sufficient orange, lemon, and olive trees. I delivered there a number of brood sows and assigned two old Aleuts as watchmen.

DECEMBER 2. I sighted a sailing ship from afar. Hearing that it was two-masted, I hurried to Waimea, for I always expected the arrival of the brig *Forester,* which would require my presence. But it was the schooner *Traveller* with Mr. Wilcocks, the American consul in Canton [!] aboard. Mr. Wilcocks was informed on the island of Oahu of my presence on Kauai, came immediately to the factory, and he and his friend Gaal moved into my apartment. He was not well and asked me for medicaments.

[DECEMBER] 3. We celebrated on Kauai the name day of Alexander Andreevich Baranov. I had reason enough for this; not solely to pay a flattering compliment to this estimable man, but because carrying out his orders many thousands of versts away, not only on this day, but perpetually, is the duty of every honest and well-disposed Russian who knows him personally or his detailed history!!! Not only has he deserved the wonder and esteem of every Russian but even of many nations; even the Indians hold him in highest esteem, even though some envious American shipmasters rouse them against him.

Russia has had few such patriots, people so selfless, patient, and tireless as Alexander Baranov. He alone maintains in its entirety the possessions and trade of the Russian-American Company, in the distant and unenlightened islands of the Northwest archipelago of America, and he continues that still, despite his advanced age, sacrificing himself for his fatherland, living for many years on products of nature, just enough to keep going. For five years he ate only what was brought from the sea—fish, and the flesh of foul-smelling whales, caught at risk of life and struggle with the savages. There was neither salt nor bread nor other necessaries of life, nor even a few drops of enlivening drink to strengthen him and to ease his sorrowful life. Even his subordinates often had to ease their hunger with pieces of animal skin (*Lasrtak* [?]). Besides enduring very unfavorable weather, they had also to struggle with the barbarians, but Alexander Baranov knew how to bear all these difficulties; his personal sacrifice, his manliness, his patience during extreme danger, and contempt for his own wounds received from barbarian enemies instilled such bravery in his small group that he was always victorious. Captain Lisianskii imputes rash bravery to him as a fault. Of course he can manage twenty or thirty seamen in accordance with Russian military law, and he knows how to command a ship; but could he keep order among an ignorant mob, and Indians from Kad'iak, Unalaska, the Fox Ridges, and other uninhabited [*sic*] places which were then under command of Alexander Baranov? This is an entirely different story, something which would be difficult for anyone but Alexander Baranov to do. I drink to the health of Mr. A. Baranov and hope that every honest person who knows him will agree with me.

Here is an excellent example: Mr. Langsdorf, in his *Journey Around the World,* wrote a great deal concerning the Russian-American Company, particularly of the abuses on the Northwest coast of America. However, at the time that Mr. Langsdorf was on the Northwest coast not one Russian ship had yet sailed around the world to the entirely unenlightened islands of the Northwest archipelago of America, occupied by a small number of Russians. They were not yet in a position to entertain and supply their European guests with all necessary provisions; however, when I asked Mr. Langsdorf during my last visit to Brazil about several of these points, he praised Mr. Baranov highly and even admitted frankly that Mr. Baranov shared everything with him and General Rezanov throughout their stay in Novo-Arkhangel'sk.

Of course I found everything otherwise. Ships now arrive directly from St. Petersburg from time to time, and in case of need Mr. Baranov can make deals with the English and Americans, and through settlement of New Albion the Russian holdings on the Northwest coasts of America and the Aleutian Islands have ceased entirely to be in need of all necessary goods. I found not only the necessary provisions in Novo-Arkhangel'sk, but even a sufficient supply of other things. Novo-Arkhangel'sk, the settlement of Ross, and particularly the island of Kad'iak have had very great successes in cattle raising. Patience is still needed for strengthening the political conditions of this village, and then anybody can live there as happy and content as anywhere.

Today there is no one with the Company on the Northwest coasts of America who can complain of hunger and who cannot live well the whole year, as long as he does not drink up his annual salary in rum. Complaints of such persons can be heard, but it is not necessary to believe them. I can testify that the promyshlenniki exchange their supplies of potatoes and turnips for certain kinds of vodka on the American ships, and thereby put themselves in debt to the Company. Others, however, sold their surplus for several hundred Spanish piastres and yet lacked nothing during the entire year.

Mr. Wilcocks gave me very pleasant news that the Russian brig *Rurik,* under the command of Mr. Kotzebue, was at Oahu, that this brig was sent on a voyage of discovery, that they have already made many [discoveries], and that it will come to Kauai to visit me.

At my request the king sent Mr. Wilcocks ten pigs, taro, and potatoes, demanding nothing in return. Mr. Wilcocks sent the king a gift with which he was completely satisfied. Mr. Wilcocks was so pleased with his reception that he could not express his thanks enough. He gave me the very important news that he had three letters from Governor MacQuarie in New Holland for transmittal to King Kamehameha, and gave me copies to read. Two of the letters, both written in 1812, were from London, one from Lord Liverpool and the other from Lord Bathurst, as follows:

One states that King Kamehameha's letter was received in London, but because of the King's illness it was not presented to him. However the Prince Regent was informed of its contents and Kamehameha is assured that all commanders of the British fleet have been ordered to respect King Kamehameha's small vessels found in those waters.

Another is as follows: Kamehameha's letter was transmitted through the captain of the English military sloop *Cherub,* which Kamehameha supplied with provisions. They thank him for his kindness, and they say that as they know that Kamehameha wishes to have a small vessel, the Governor of the port of New Wales has been ordered to build one for him.

In the third, Governor MacQuarie sent a uniform as a gift to the king and informed him that a vessel of about forty tons which he had ordered built for him would be finished in four months. He recommended that the king give Mr. Wilcocks a friendly reception.*

---

* In 1816, the letters to Kamehameha were shown to Kotzebue as evidence of British interest and friendship. Kotzebue, *Voyage of Discovery,* vol. 1, 334. For modern mention of the letters, see Harold W.

[DECEMBER] 6.   Mr. Wilcocks left us and sailed for the Spanish coast. During his stay here I ordered cotton to be picked, and he assured me that this quality can be sold in Canton at any time for twenty-two to twenty-five Spanish piastres per pikul.

Cotton should be Russia's main objective in the Sandwich Islands, and yields in a short time more return for a small expenditure and effort than all the fur trade on the Northwest coasts. But the main thing is to bring in as soon as possible some inhabitants of Hindustan, the island of Malaga [?], Africa, China, etc. for their knowledge of how to grow and process it, so as to teach the Russians, Aleuts, and the natives.

[DECEMBER] 9.   Today I noticed three hundred women among the workers at Fort Elizabeth. Today in the American paper *Independence Chronicle* of November 4, 1813, I read of the working of sugar cane, an extract from a letter written by a man from Khapelo [?] in Georgia to a friend of his in Beaufort, North Carolina, regarding its cultivation, and the processing of different kinds in the West Indies . . . , etc., etc., etc.

The Sandwich Islands lie 10 ° farther south, the sugar cane is more profitable, of special height and quality, and the labor is much cheaper. We submit also that the above noted price was received in wartime, and that a pure profit of only half as much would still be a large sum.

Bradley, *The American Frontier in Hawaii. The Pioneers, 1789–1843,* Stanford, 1942, 49–52.

The vessel mentioned, the *Prince Regent,* a 70-ton schooner mounting six brass guns, built at Port Jackson, New South Wales, reached Honolulu on April 22, 1822, convoyed by the cutter *Mermaid* (Lieut. Kent), and on May 1 was presented to Kamehameha II as a gift from the King of England. During the summer "Billy Pitt" (Kalaimoku) ran her aground among the breakers at Koolau, Oahu. She was reportedly recovered, but afterward sank in Honolulu harbor with all her armament aboard. See Gilbert F. Machison, *Narrative of a visit to Brazil, Chile, Peru and the Sandwich Islands, during the years 1821 and 1822* . . . , London, 1825, pp. 424, 462; Thomas G. Thrum, "Hawaiian Maritime History, a Brief Sketch of Noted Vessels and Commanders in the Development of the Coasting Service of the Hawaiian Islands," *Hawaiian Almanac,* 1890, pp. 66–79; and Bernice Judd, *Voyages to Hawaii before 1860,* Honolulu, 1929.

[DECEMBER] 11 & 12. A hurricane blew so strongly that it leveled many houses and trees, and the river Waimea rose seven feet above its normal level.

[DECEMBER] 17. I planted four hundred grape vines in the garden of the factory at Waimea.

[DECEMBER] 22. King Kaumualii gave Timofei Tarakanov a village with thirteen families, on the left bank of the river Don, in the province of Hanapepe.

[DECEMBER] 23. Taboo. The wives of all the chiefs visited me today. The queen's sister Taininoa, who previously gave the Company land, today transferred also the valley of Mainauri, while Queen Monolau, whom I cured of illness, presented me with land in the Georg (Kainakhil') Valley in Hanapepe province. I gave her a piece of silk material.

[DECEMBER] 24. I celebrated the name day of our exalted Sovereign Alexander I. King Kaumualii fired fifty-one cannon salutes, to which I replied.

[DECEMBER] 26. The king ceded the uninhabited island of Lehua to the Company. I sent several goats and sheep there to stock it.

[DECEMBER] 27. Our brig *Il'mena* arrived. After dinner the captain of the brig, W. Wadsworth, came to see me. I gave him the reception a drunken seaman deserves. The assistant commissioner, the clerk Nikiforov (one of the most honest Russians in the Company's service) told me of many bad deeds of Wadsworth. I told him that he should write everything in his journal and should tell Mr. Baranov all about it when he arrived in Novo-Arkhangel'sk.

[DECEMBER] 29. Nikiforov came to Tarakanov and told him the bad story of Wadsworth; Tarakanov came at once with Nikiforov to tell me of this. In Europe they would consider this man a traitor.

I went immediately to the king and asked him what stories Wadsworth had told him about the Russians, telling him that I

knew all about it, but wished also to hear of this from him. The
king related to me word for word what I had heard from Nikiforov
and I no longer had any doubt. Arriving at the factory, I found
Wadsworth drunk there, ordered him arrested and put under guard
immediately, and on the following day had him taken to the ship
Myrtle-Kad'iak. I ordered Captain Young to give Wadsworth food
from the officers' table after awhile, to keep a watch on him, not to
let him off the ship, and not to let him talk with anyone. This
morning Wadsworth gave in exchange to the Indian woman
Namakhanno the last kettle from the brig; even the cabin curtains
went by the same road. There and then I chased five of his women
off the ship. Now I was forced to appoint the pilot Voroll Madson
as captain of the ship *Myrtle-Kad'iak,* although this was not very
agreeable to me; for he too is an American. But where could I get
anyone else?

I heard that Captain Ebbets the elder arrived on the island of
Oahu not long ago, that he had bought the armed ship *Albatross*
from N. Winship, and had presented it to King Kamehameha. He
traded him several guns, cannon balls, powder, etc., for a load of
sandalwood and made a contract with him to furnish in several
months a sufficient number of cannon and ammunition. At the same
time he did not forget to fix anew in the head of King Kamehameha
strange rumors about the Russians and even of Russian war ships,
in order more truly and advantageously to conclude trade with him,
in which John Young helped in every possible way.

[DECEMBER] 31.   I ordered Tarakanov to sail to the island of
Oahu with the brig *Il'mena,* to take a letter to Mr. Captain
Kotzebue and have necessary conversations with him, for it seemed
suspicious to me that he had not arrived on Kauai where he already
wanted to arrive two weeks ago. I gave Voroll Madson necessary
instructions, but he sailed without Tarakanov; he was even bold
enough to open Tarakanov's chest on the way and in general to do
everything which he had no right to do.

After the brig *Il'mena* had sailed, I set out for Hanapepe. Queen
Monalau sent me forthwith a man for transfer of the lands in the
Georg Valley (Kainakhil') which she had promised me. On my
arrival at the factory I ordered a deed prepared, which the queen

signed, as I have done with all lands given to the Company. The most important things were written twice. The king meanwhile had received a great deal of goods and wanted still more. I at once ordered the release from the store of anything that he wanted. I assured him of the supply of various cargo for his needs each year, for a certain sum: he was to give all sandalwood to the Company for all time. I insisted on this convention all the more because I have already fulfilled all the promises made in my first agreements with him. The king and also Minister Kamahalolani were satisfied with everything.

1817

JANUARY 1. The contract was presented to King Kaumualii and signed by him and Minister Kamahalolani. In consequence, all sandalwood must belong to the Russian-American Company, which can obtain from 50,000 to 60,000 Spanish piastres return from it annually.

The Russians under me had a holiday, so for want of anything else to do I measured some lands and calculated the growth of cotton on Kauai. Upon my arrival on this island I planted in the garden of the Russian-American Company factory ten square sazhens of land in cotton. That was at the end of December, 1816 [?], and in the first picking of this January I obtained 272 poods of fine and best quality cotton fiber cleaned of seeds. The second picking will be in June of this year, when just as much or even more is to be expected, and so one can assume an annual yield of ten pounds of clean fiber per square sazhen. The main work lies in the transplanting, for the land must be well cleaned beforehand. For the picking and cleaning of the cotton fiber itself, one can use women and children. More and faster cultivation can be done by machine. A Rhineland *desiatine* of 600 square feet should bear annually 1,000 pounds of the cleanest cotton fiber, at the lowest price 16 cents a pound in Canton; consequently, annual return will range up to 160 Spanish piastres per Rhineland desiatine. Cotton can be grown on hills and fields unsuited for other crops. It likes best soil containing iron, which is found everywhere here. In the provinces and other small holdings belonging to the Russian-American Company 200,000 Spanish piastres worth of cotton fiber can be obtained annually, from no more than about 1,200 to 1,300 Rhineland desiatines of poor soil. At the very lowest estimate, enough cotton could be grown on all the Sandwich Islands, not counting those fields suited to something better or which are already worked, to yield five million Spanish piastres annually.

Taro and maize are two important products of the Sandwich Islands. They are particularly important for the Russian settlements on the Northwest coast of America and even for Okhotsk and Kamchatka, for these are unrivaled as foodstuffs, and extremely suitable for transport and for prolonged storage. I sowed maize and obtained 180 poods from a Rhineland desiatine. Even if we figure only two harvests from the same field, that will be a great sum. I am convinced that from Kauai alone the Company can obtain more than 200,000 to 300,000 Spanish piastres worth of maize and taro.

A fourth item, of which very little has been grown in these islands until now, is tobacco, which brings an excellent price in the Russian holdings on the Northwest coast and in the Aleutian Islands. Tobacco which is well cultivated is equal to that of Virginia, is of far better quality than Russian snuff tobacco, and is not subjected to delay and spoilage by long round-the-world transportation. I can guarantee to supply tobacco from the Sandwich Islands not only to the Northwest coast of America but even to Kamchatka, Okhotsk, Japan, etc. Although not comparable to the others, this item can bring an annual return of 100,000 Spanish piastres. I must mention, of course, if one counts on a low selling price, of sales in Russia itself at three assignations per pood. . . .

Salt, which is plentiful in the Sandwich Islands, would be the same. What a boon for the Russian holdings on the Northwest coast of America, and Okhotsk and Kamchatka! If we take only half of the most moderate price for which this substance so necessary to the health and growth of man is sold in these places, it could easily yield an annual profit of 100,000 Spanish piastres, not counting the profit which the Company could receive annually through salt herrings, salmon, and other fish.

The sandalwood on Kauai, which is the sole property of the Russian-American Company, was previously the main item of trade of the Indians. If Russia should happen to occupy all of these islands, which is certainly necessary, this item would be exclusively in the hands of Russia; the Chinese would be forced to let us trade freely in Canton, from which we are [now] excluded by the intrigues and machinations of the English and Americans, etc. . . . If the trade were exclusively ours, then the present price of seventeen Spanish piastres per pikul would of course rise; we would already have a return of 200,000 Spanish piastres.

The sugar cane in these islands is of a height and quality which I have never seen anywhere else. Processing the sugar and rum would bring no small return.

Oil nuts are in great medical demand. In 1813 Mr. Tal' in St. Petersburg charged one of my patients eleven rubles for eighteen ounces, and I am in a position to supply not only Russia but all Europe with this oil from the Sandwich Islands. The oil nut (*kukui*) brings no small return. Grapes grow twice in a year; I have planted enough of one kind which if carefully prepared ought to make wine which should surpass Madeira. I need not mention the fruits of the bread plants, pineapples, coconuts, oranges, lemons, bananas, melons, etc. These items will bring no small price and if correctly handled can upset in one blow the trade of the English and Americans in China, etc.; of this I am convinced.

Even in case of war we can manage without another country, and Russia will not suffer any shortage; of this I will say more another time. There are not only the profits obtainable from products grown in the Sandwich Islands through nature, art, and effort, through forestry, tilling the soil, from rivers rich with pearls, stock breeding, trade, shipping, and factories; but also the political possibilities of these possessions are innumerable! Through these holdings Russia can obtain in a short time the most skillful and experienced seafarers. The Chinese will have to permit the Russian flag to wave in Canton. The English and Americans will have their trade cut and limited in Europe as well as in China, for Russia stands for free trade by sea with the whole of Spanish America, Japan, the Philippine Islands, and all of the islands of the Southern Ocean, with the islands of Timor, Domingo, Sumatra, Akhen, etc. Russia is in a position to disrupt the trade of the English in the East Indies, and can be as strong on the sea as she is invincible on the dry land.

(Note [in original]: These aphorisms are taken from Mr. Schäffer's own journal written by him in Russian.) May God will it so! E—— Sch——!!!

The Sandwich Islands must be made a Russian West India and likewise a second Gibraltar. Russia must have these islands at any cost!! Not only are these necessary for her trade in the East Indies, but even on the Northwest coast of America and the entire Pacific Ocean. The Americans arouse the Kolosh just as they try to sway the inhabitants of the Sandwich Islands toward them. They support the savages, and the small number of Russians found on the various Aleutian islands of the Northwest coast of America will be wiped out in one day—No, may it please God! If I myself do not inform the St. Petersburg Cabinet of my views and experience, and the sacrifice of my health for it, I have ordered delivery of these papers through a true adherent of Russia, my second fatherland.

Has Russia the right to occupy the Sandwich Islands? There is no question of this. King Kaumualii is a subject of Russia, and King Kamehameha has proclaimed himself his enemy, and no nation in the world has up to this time more right on these islands than Russia. From the letters sent Kamehameha from England in 1812, signed by Lord Liverpool and Lord Bathurst, it is clear that England does not take the islands of Hawaii or King Kaumualii under her protection. Kamehameha gave the island of Hawaii to England in his act with Captain Vancouver, but up to this time she has not done anything about it. The other islands in any case already belong to Kaumualii, and consequently to Russia. . . .

JANUARY 12. Indian Taboo. Captain Brown arrived with the brig *Cossack* from the Northwest coast of America, but without putting down anchor sent the king my letters and offended the Russians in the presence of the Indians.

[JANUARY] 13. The Russian New Year's Day.

I have been occupied most of this month with sowing the Company's lands.

[JANUARY] 20, 21. Very disturbed weather, with heavy rain. For seamen it will be extremely serious, for if at Kauai and Waimea the wind blows steadily from the south or the west or southwest, a heavy storm will soon follow. It is then necessary to put out to sea in order to avoid being thrown on shore.

FEBRUARY 6.   Our brig *Il'mena* arrived from the island of Oahu. Captain Kotzebue had already left that island before arrival of the brig. Mr. Elliot, who is in service of the Company, arrived on the island of Oahu and declined my invitation to come and see me on Kauai. He allowed himself to be taken by the Spanish and when he arrived in San Francisco after liberation he hid himself from the manager Mr. Kuskov. From all his undertakings one can conclude that he is a deceiver. . . .

During this journey our brig was driven by the storm from the northwest and they saw an island which they thought to be a new discovery. I informed myself thoroughly of all of the proceedings, and the Captain asserted that there ought to be plenty of wood and water on the island. . . . I thought the news very important, especially since the Captain declared that one could sail there in three days.

In order to convince myself fully I went there myself. We arrived exactly on the third day, but unfortunately found nothing but rocks. Moreover, I found that these had been charted a long time ago.

We sailed to Hanalei, arriving at the end of March.

APRIL 1.   I visited the fortifications, and found Forts Alexander and Barclay both nearly finished.

[APRIL] 4.   I inspected the ship *Myrtle-Kad'iak*. Most of our people declared that at this time of year the ship could reach Novo-Arkhangel'sk without cargo. Others said it could not. . . . Captain Young, more than the others, voted to sail, so I ordered him to get the ship ready for the voyage.

[APRIL] 6.   The Russian Easter. I allowed three days for celebration.

[APRIL] 9.   I arrived at Waimea in the morning. While I was away the brig *Forester* was there. It sailed from Waimea to Canton with a cargo of sandalwood in account of Kamehameha. Master Adams tried to destroy the Russian flag on Kauai, but has failed so far. He sent a boat to the island of Oahu with news of the result of his mission.

As political news I learned that the Northwest Company of Canada has applied to the English government for permission to occupy the Sandwich Islands and also Queen Charlotte Island on the Northwest coast of America. Queen Charlotte Island is the most important on all the Northwest coast. It is the main collecting point for trade. One can get superb beavers there, and the island has a good climate and soil.

I visited the king and several chiefs. I found everyone very friendly, but for the first time the king did not raise the Russian flag and did not salute.

King Kaumualii and his minister Kamahalolani took much more from the store during my absence than I had given them. I spoke to them about this, and the king repeated and increased his promises, and on the twenty-third, in the presence of Timofei Tarakanov and Aleksei Odnoriadkin, adopted a new convention which as No. 9 was sent to Novo-Arkhangel'sk.

The brig *Columbia* sailed to the North. Captain Jennings told me of the arrival on Oahu of Captain Ebbets the elder, from China, and also that on Oahu there is talk of disagreements between Russia and the United States, and that the Russian minister has left America. He also said that King Kaumualii had concluded a contract with him for exchange of his brig for sandalwood, but that the time had passed and the contract was void. I was very astonished at this, because when I had asked the king if he had made any prior commitments he assured me that he had not. I approached the king with the suggestion that he keep his word, and also hinted to him of the agreement with Captain Jennings, and he replied that he had forgotten all about it. I again asked him to load our ships as soon as possible so that they could be sent to Novo-Arkhangel'sk, which he promised to do. Knowing the king's usual negligence, I turned at the same time to the minister, who also promised everything. In order to hasten the departure of our ships and to make the minister more favorably disposed, I borrowed an English pocket watch from Tarakanov and presented it to Kamahalolani. Then I went to Hanapepe, in order to finish the work begun there in the spring, and on the seventh returned to Waimea to send our ships. I also wanted to learn what was taking place on the island of Oahu, because Chief Platov had told me in Hanapepe that five boats had arrived from Oahu, carrying war news.

MAY 8.   Early in the morning I called on the king, who was in a gathering of ministers at the river, surrounded by a thousand men. I demanded that he send our ships as soon as possible and they promised. I gave them my hand as usual, they replied by pressing it, and I returned along the road leading to the factory. I had hardly gone a hundred paces when I was seized by the king's man Tupiia Pill and six American seamen. Several Indians told me that I would not see the king any more, that I was to be escorted to our ship immediately, and that all other Russians should leave Kauai. I replied that I would not leave the island until I received orders from Russia, and that I would not be forced into it merely because I was alone and unarmed. But without any ceremony they put me in a miserable boat and sent me to the ship *Myrtle-Kad'iak,* not even allowing me to return to my dwelling to take my few belongings.

When I arrived on the deck of the ship, I heard cannon shots on shore and saw a piratical flag raised: the flag had white and blue panels with four spheres: *

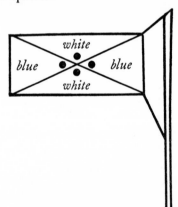

---

* I have been unable to find anything on the origin or significance of this flag. It is not mentioned in W. D. Alexander, "The Maker of the Hawaiian Flag," Hawaiian Historical Society, *Annual Reports,* 5 (1898), or by Mrs. Charles Lucas, "Captain Alexander Adams and the Hawaiian Flag," *ibid.* (1921), pp. 99–101.

I immediately sent our storekeeper Tarakanov, who was on the ship, ashore to see what they would do with him. At first they refused to let him ashore, but on his request to the king, that it was to get Company property, for which he was responsible, and that he wanted to take his wife and children, they let him pass. They permitted eight persons to remain on shore; all other Russians and Aleuts had to return to the ship. The king assured Tarakanov that he would give the Company both sandalwood and also the promised provisions.

[MAY] 9.   The same flag was raised on shore. All trade with us is forbidden.

[MAY] 10.   Today the pirate flag was raised again. The Englishman Fox-Bennick was tortured on the shore and then sent to our ship, told to go to Russia into slavery; that the Russians and English are all slaves; only the Americans are a free people, and without them the Russians and English would die of hunger.

From the beginning of this speech it was very easy to conclude, and although it seemed unbelievable, I myself began to believe the rumor, that war had been declared between Russia and the United States. This news was thought up by the Americans themselves on the islands of Oahu and Hawaii and then communicated to King Tomari, with the threat that since Russia and America were now at war, if he did not chase the Russians from the islands there were now eight ships ready at Oahu to come to Kauai and kill not only every Russian but even all the Indians. The Indian Nani on the island of Oahu told me that already long ago there was talk on this island that if the Russians were chased out of Kauai, Kamehameha would attack and that he wanted to get this island for himself. He doubted whether Kaumualii would remain alive.

[MAY] 13.   The traitor Wadsworth pretended to be crazy, tortured by his conscience. After lunch he jumped overboard. An Indian boat picked him up and went ashore with him as fast as possible.

Captain Young, who has proved himself devoted to the Company, went ashore with Madson to see the king and demand the return of Wadsworth, who owes the Company several thousand dollars, but in vain. Wadsworth told Young that he would rather be killed than sent to Novo-Arkhangel'sk, for the Russians there would of course kill him. Tupikhea Pil' told Captain Young that one of them [Madson or Young] would have to remain if they took Wadsworth. Madson told me the same thing. Several of our seamen were also held on the shore and were questioned extensively. Madson told me nonsense about himself, but I paid no heed, for I did not want to give him reason to leave us, which was his intention, as I wanted very much to send him to Novo-Arkhangel'sk.

[MAY] 21. We noted a large three-masted vessel which stood in this bay on the twenty-second. It was the American Whittemore. I could not get a satisfactory answer from Captain Whittemore. He spoke ambiguously about everything. He confirmed the expulsion of the Russian minister from America; he said also that the Russian consul in America was in shackles, but he thinks however that the affair is coming to an end. I told him that all the sandalwood on Kauai belongs to the Company.

Since we could obtain nothing from the king, nor of our property, we sailed to Hanalei—to Schäffer Valley—where we arrived on June 8, to pick up our cannon and other things. I gave orders to embark at once and sent Tarakanov to Waimea with a letter for the king, as follows:

[See English text, No. 32]

Tarakanov returned from his mission and reported that at least the letter was read in the presence of the king. The king gave an ambiguous answer, saying: "Yes, this is true! This is also true, that all the sandalwood belongs to the Russians. I can now do nothing. Farewell, Tarakanov. Give my greetings to the doctor.". . .

Our Captain Young told me that Captains Ebbets, Whittemore, Davis, and others had prepared a letter at Oahu in the name of King Kamehameha, and had sent it to King Kaumualii in order to cause a revolution with the intention of seizing several loads of sandalwood.

[JUNE] 17. They have ordered us to leave Hanalei or await hostile action! I took possession of the whole island of Kauai in the name of His Majesty, the Great Emperor of Russia Alexander Pavlovich, ordered the Russian flag raised on Fort Alexander, fired three cannon shots, and declared myself chief of Hanalei Valley. I then sent people to the Russian farmyard to collect our pigs, sheep, goats, etc., but the Indians had already stole them all, and began to shoot at the Russians, wounding one Aleut. Upon hearing of this I immediately ordered our men to retreat, but when I saw the Indians rushing there from all sides I had a volley fired from the six-pounders and ordered the Russians to retire, not losing a single man. Before our arrival two Aleuts were killed in abominable fashion.

I held a conference with all our Russians and Captain Young. Everyone now saw clearly that it was impossible to undertake a trip to Novo-Arkhangel'sk in the ship *Kad'iak,* which took in forty-eight feet of water every twenty-four hours.

I gave command of the brig *Il'mena* to Captain Young, for I could entrust it to no one else, sending him to Novo-Arkhangel'sk with the documents. Madson went along as a passenger.

I took command of the *Myrtle-Kad'iak* and on the fifth day out of Hanalei dropped anchor outside the harbor of Honolulu on Oahu, on sandy bottom thirteen sazhens deep. On the foremast I ordered a white flag raised, and on the mizzenmast the Russian flag upside down, in order to show that we were in distress. A cannon was fired so that we might get a pilot to bring our ship into the inner harbor as quickly as possible. Our Captain Young had written a letter to the commandant, Kalanimoku, explaining our situation and asking necessary aid. Pilot Harbottle came aboard and said that we must first hire a tow boat, promising to come to us again the next morning. I sent Captain Young's letter ashore with him.

[JUNE] 24. I sent Kicharev ashore, and prepared everything required for putting the ship safely in the harbor as soon as possible. But even here the monster Young put up an obstacle. I then sent Tarakanov, who met several boats paddling out from shore, bearing several Americans, Englishmen, and natives, who were supposed to inspect our vessel. They found our report correct and the ship to be in such bad condition that they all agreed that we could not have reached another harbor. I was told that I could go ashore and make agreements with the chiefs. I had to submit to this and went with Tarakanov. A boat awaited us near shore, but when we approached they ordered us instead to go on an American ship, to Captain Wills [Wildes?], and so we went there.

The sailor Beckley and twelve chiefs arrived from shore and declared that if I went at once to Hawaii as a prisoner, and we gave up all guns and ammunition from the ship, the vessel and the people aboard would not be harmed. It seemed a little early to me to be a caught fish, so I refused the trip to Hawaii.

Much was said, but nothing was concluded. It was suggested that we wait for Minister Philip Peel [Pitt?], and I demanded that they send our Captain Young's letter to the island of Hawaii, so that the king would be sufficiently informed.

[JUNE] 25. The pilot Harbottle visited us and said with impartiality that the Americans for some time have tried to hinder the Russians here and on Kauai, and that old Ebbets is the ringleader. He also mentioned N. Winship and W. P. Hunt. Old Young ordered Kicharev to tell me and several of our people that if any one of us went on shore he would be shot immediately. Old Young also asked Kicharev and Poliakov whether our crew would agree if they wanted to send me to America as a prisoner. Tarakanov replied that if they wanted to send any one of us they would have to send all the others there too. Ebbets the elder told King Kamehameha that a Russian expedition would soon come from Europe to take over the islands. It may be that he spoke prophetically. Old Young himself told Tarakanov that Ebbets, Winship, and Hunt are responsible for the way we have been treated.

An Irishman came aboard and confirmed the intrigues of the Americans. He said, moreover, that they were gathering strength to cause an uprising in the Sandwich Islands against the English and to persuade them to accept the American flag, for both the English and the Russians are slaves anyway.

During the past five months the Island of Oahu has supplied twelve foreign ships with provisions and has sent eight shiploads of prepared taro and salt fish to Hawaii.

JULY 1. This morning we brought the ship into the harbor. The Indians tried to make our entry very costly, almost running our ship on a coral reef. I saw what they were up to in time and ordered the anchor dropped. Our Aleuts then towed the ship to the assigned place. I had to pay the Indians 52 Spanish piastres, 2 wool blankets, 1 table knife, 48 mirrors, and 42 small and 2 large axes.

This morning when we raised our large anchor only the iron part came up; the wooden anchor remained in the sea, probably destroyed by worms. A fresh wind from the shore would have carried us to sea, and our difficult path of life would soon have ended.

[JULY] 4. This morning the ship *Panther,* with Captain Lewis, arrived from Hawaii. As soon as Captain Lewis dropped anchor he paid me a visit.

He also informed me of other evil undertakings against the Russians which the elder Ebbets and old Young had forced into the mind of King Kamehameha.

The Americans celebrated their Fourth of July. All ships were decorated with flags; at twelve noon I ordered the Russian flag raised also, upside down. The sailor Beckley was sent to me by the American captain Wills to order me to turn my flag around. I replied that I could not display my flag otherwise until my ship was out of danger.

This caused a great commotion on the American ships; however, Captain Lewis, who declared the Russian position just, settled the dispute, which in the meantime cost several broken goblets and glasses.

Captain Lewis arrived in these islands last year unwell. I treated him, and eight days after his arrival he left the harbor of the island of Oahu, well and happy. His feeling of gratitude now forced him to be my friend. We talked of our situation and he counseled that if I wanted to evade all dangers I must leave the islands. He invited me to share his cabin if I wanted to go with him to Canton. I put this matter before my Russians and they asked me to go not to Novo-Arkhangel'sk but as soon as possible to St. Petersburg in order to try to get strong and sufficient help. Both the chief management of the Company and the Russian government should be informed of all the brigandage taking place on these islands and on the Northwest coast, the Company not being strong enough to demand satisfaction for the plunder suffered and the insult to the honor of the Russian State. . . .

I established a commission on our ship, made Tarakanov chief, told each how to conduct himself, and prepared myself for the voyage. Tarakanov gave me two good traveling companions: the Aleut *taiun* Grigor'ii Iskakov, and the promyshlennik Filip Osipov.

[JULY] 7. We left Oahu and arrived the next day in Waimea Bay, the island of Kauai. Captain Lewis wanted to buy taro and yams. So that he could not be hindered in this, I had to remain in my cabin under house arrest in order not to be seen by the Indians. Many of the first pirates came aboard, including W. Wadsworth, who puffed himself up about all the mischief he had committed against the Russians. I heard every word of it, and what happened on the shore I heard partly from Captain Lewis, and partly from Mr. Marshal, the ship's officer. Captain Lewis bargained for taro, but Chief Kamahalolani wanted under no condition to let any go except for cannon balls. Lewis, an honest man, sent the chief twenty-three piastres and ordered him told that if he did not want to sell him taro for good money he would let him have more cannon balls than he would find pleasant. The pirates sent the taro. Captain Lewis told me that the Indians had decided to fight any Russians who came near the island. We sailed west from Kauai and I was freed from arrest.

Nothing noteworthy occurred during our voyage, except that I received from Mr. Marshal some valuable information about subjects very interesting for me. This man is a German, a nephew of Mr. Astor, who took him from Germany as a boy and taught him seamanship.

He was shipwrecked near the Sandwich Islands three years ago, and made a living by teaching the English language to Prince Liholiho, son of King Kamehameha, staying on in Hawaii for several years in this capacity. He was my daily companion throughout my stay in Hawaii. He left Hawaii last year to serve on the brig *Panther*. Being acquainted with the people who sailed on ships under his uncle Mr. Astor, and having a thorough knowledge of their nature and character, he told me openly of all the rascality committed by Ebbets and Hunt, who although servants of his uncle, had acted against the Russians in these islands. Besides this, he assured me that King Kamehameha and King Kaumualii were in secret agreement and had adopted a joint plan to plunder the Russians.

When Kamehameha heard that the Russian flag was flying on Kauai, he wanted to set out with all his army to conquer it, hiring several American ships for transport, but old Ebbets and Winship kept the king from open war and made up the plan [which was used], for they of course feared going openly with their ships against Russia.

Captain Brintnell, with the ship *Zephyr,* was eight months in the service of the king, who promised him a full cargo of sandalwood for his service, but when Kamehameha heard that the Russians had left Kauai, he dismissed Captain Brintnell and his ship without paying him a single piece of sandalwood.

Mr. Marshal and Captain Lewis also confirmed the murder of two of our Aleuts on Kauai. They heard it from the Indians themselves. Even though Mr. Marshal is himself a settler in America, he told me very frankly of his experiences on voyages from the United States to the Northwest coast of America, of their usual nature, of the form and type of trade with the Kolosh, and of their [the Americans'] dishonesty in their fatherland, all of which confirmed my own previous experiences. Craft, flattery, and deception characterize every American seafarer wanting to acquire command of a ship assigned for trade on the Northwest coast. Such command is never entrusted to the honest and just, Mr. Marshal emphasized, for a ship sent out under an honest man always shows a loss. Without villainy it is impossible to expect profits from such expeditions. Their sole aim is plunder and deception. Usually they sail directly from Boston or New York around Cape Horn to the Sandwich Islands, where they obtain fresh provisions, water, and fuel. They usually promise the sailors high pay, but treat them so badly that many leave their earned pay and flee. In their place they hire Indians, to whom they give old clothes. From the Sandwich Islands they sail to Norfolk Sound (Alikhu) under the pretext of trading with the Russians, not only to find out where and how trade is taking place, but even to trade secretly in the harbor itself with the Kolosh, whom they stir up against the Russians and supply with arms and ammunition. They supply themselves here with water and firewood, and sometimes during the season catch a good part of their provisions in herring and salmon. They send many Indians to other places to acquaint the others of the ship's arrival, so that they then await [the ship] with their furs instead of taking them to Russian holdings and selling to the Russians. Near the Russian holdings they pay three and four times more for beaver, just to make the trade impossible, or at least dangerous, for the Russians.

To make up for losses which they have suffered in one place and to make their trip pay, they lure parties of Kolosh on board their ships, take their furs from them, and force them to jump overboard; or they seize the Indian chief, who must then ransom himself with a large quantity of beavers. Not infrequently they even kill Indians and take their furs, but more usually they lure on board ship several Indians, overpower them, and take them as unwilling hostages to distant places for furs. This is common knowledge, which according to Mr. Wilcocks, the American consul, is also known to the American government. He also assured me that several of their young men were hanged in America. Many sailors tell how they stole from churches on the California coast.

After such glorious deeds they return to the Sandwich Islands to replenish their supplies of provisions. Here they land their Sandwich Islanders and again take on good sailors who are destitute and willing to serve without pay for the return to their fatherland. They force others, to whom much salary is owed, to leave the ship.*

If the voyage is unsuccessful for them, they try here through intrigues and quarrels, one against another, to obtain a cargo of sandalwood to take to Canton.

---

* This report of the conduct of American skippers in Hawaii is confirmed by John C. Jones, Jr., U. S. Consul at Honolulu, in a report to Washington from Oahu, December 31, 1821: "A practice has for many years existed with the Commanders of Ships touching at the Sandwich Islands, either for supplies or trade, to turn on shore all Seamen, against whom they could alledge any trivial misconduct, and employ in their lieu Natives of these Islands, by this means lessening their portage Bills, & depriving their Country of valuable subjects." U. S. National Archives, Consular Letters, Honolulu. Vol. 1, 1820–1843.

The crafty and sly actions of these people against the Russian-American Company on the Northwest coast of America were well known to me during my stay in Novo-Arkhangel'sk, but I learned still more in the course of my journey.

In all enterprises which Mr. Baranov entered into with these dishonest persons he was deceived every time. He could of course not act otherwise during such time when he was completely cut off from Europe. Lacking news from St. Petersburg for several years, lacking every kind of aid from Europe, lacking necessary provisions, he was forced to put himself in the hands of certain rascals who flattered him with pure friendship while ready to take everything he had. Although many save their lives and property through him, others enriched themselves through his aid, but such were their evil plans that they not only planned to plunder and rob this serviceable old man, and the whole Russian-American Company on the Northwest coast of America, but, if possible, to destroy it, and this plan is still being followed!

There is proof enough of this; not only is it known to me and to Mr. Baranov by experience, but to other honest men, particularly in Macao. The first attempts of Winship and Davis failed. The expeditions of the ship *Eclipse* under the command of Captain O'Cain met with great losses and supplied proof of the most evil intentions of this rapacious person. The Russian supercargoes, Bakadarov and Toropogritskii, gave me several examples of this robber! but in Macao I learned still more of him. If Sir Anders Ljungstedt had not protected the interests of the Russians, the whole rich cargo of the Company, worth several hundred thousand rubles, would have been lost. Sir Anders learned that O'Cain wanted to go to Batavia, there to subject the Russians to danger and even death, so as then to do as he pleased with the cargo. Ljungstedt forced him to sell his cargo in Canton and thus saved the greater part of it for the Company, although O'Cain tried many deceptions which Ljungstedt could not entirely resist because he was not the formal representative of the Company. (Among other things he was able to obtain five Spanish piastres more for the beaver.) Captain O'Cain put up great resistance, but Ljungstedt's noble and unselfish attempt destroyed the main part of O'Cain's plan and saved a large amount of Company property.

The commissions and enterprises of W. P. Hunt on the brig *Pedler* are still fresh in the memory, so that there is no need to go over the circumstances of these losses for the Company.

The expedition of the ship *Orina* [*Isabella*] under Captain Davis ended in similar dishonest fashion. Instead of loading the ship with sandalwood at the Sandwich Islands and setting out for China as agreed, he took another ship to Canton with sandalwood and sent the ship *Orina* to Manila under the pretext of repairs. Mr. Kuglinov, nephew of Mr. Baranov, was supercargo, and had orders from him to transfer the load and commission to Mr. Ljungstedt in Canton. Thereby the Americans could undertake no further deceptions with this ship, but for this reason they did not send it to Canton at all.

This expedition of the unworthy fellow J. Bennett, who according to many of his countrymen as well as every Indian and sailor on Kauai, purposely lost the ship *Bering,* was new proof that they all had agreed to ruin the Company. But when they noted later on that they were up against someone stronger, they worked out the diabolical plan through which they perpetrated a revolution on the Sandwich Islands against Russia.

AUGUST 26.   This morning we passed Petro Blanco and took a pilot who would guide us through the many islands to Macao. He asked payment of sixty Spanish piastres in advance. Thus far nothing remarkable had occurred during our entire voyage. We passed the island of Agrigan at 19° 1′ 00″ North latitude. It appears on many charts at 146° 10′ 00″ East longitude, but through observations of the moon and stars on the brig *Panther* it was found to have a longitude of 145° 4′ 00″. The island was settled by several Americans and Indians from the Sandwich Islands. The first settlers found bread fruits, coconuts, yams, and other things, and sowed taro and other fruits which they had brought with them from the Sandwich Islands. . . .*

The Reaumur thermometer indicated 23° warmth here. . . .

---

* Further mention of this small colony was made a year or two later by Captain Samuel Hill (*Packet*): ". . . touched at Agrigan, one of the Marian Islands, at that time Inhabited by some White men, & Natives of

SEPTEMBER 2.   Because of a dead calm we had to stand at anchor from August 26 to September 2. On the second a fresh southeast wind came up and we lay at anchor before noon several miles from Macao on a soft silt bottom four sazhens deep.

Today I went in the boat of the commissioner on the brig *Panther* to Macao with my Russians, for I learned that Sir Anders Ljungstedt was there. I stopped in an English inn, but Sir Anders at once asked me to transfer with my people to his place, and on this same day took me to the Portuguese minister and commandant, who received me pleasantly.

The next day I moved to Sir Anders' house, and I could not have had more friendly treatment from my own brother. During the first days he acquainted me with the best Portuguese families and took several days off to show me around. With Mr. Minister Arriaga I spoke of several matters touching on Russia and the Company and found him very well disposed toward everything. Here I heard that news Ebbets had brought to the Sandwich Islands and spread among the Indians was well grounded, namely that the English ambassador had been sent to Peking to negotiate about several islands of Lintin and Hainan, and of a monopoly of trade with the Chinese, but that he had not obtained an audience and had been denied entry by the Chinese.

While in Macao I made the important discovery that it would not be difficult for any Russian ship to enter Canton and trade on an equal basis with all other nations. I was sure that the experience of the two Russian ships *Nadezhda* and *Neva* was due to intrigues of the English. The worst news of the Chinese and their threats reported to Captain Krusenstern originated with the first supercargo of the English factory and with Thomas Peel, who directed the commission of the Russian ships, and who reported to the factory each day and received orders from it. Even the order of the

---

the Sandwich Islands, who had been brought thither by some of the American Trading Ships from the N.W. Coast, I believe chiefly by Captains T. Brown & Lemuel Porter, both of Boston, & I think Capt. W. Sturgis had also some share in it. These poor people have since been all taken away by the Spaniards from Manilla, & I understand from various Sources they have kept them as Slaves." "Autobiography," Samuel Hill MS, New York Public Library, p. 19.

Emperor from Peking was of altogether another content than was reported to the Russians. They wanted to frighten the Russians away once and for all in order to keep them from trading here.

I made various surveys on the island of Macao, but found most interesting here the gardens of Senator Manuel Pereira, Antonio de Silva Joakhima, Jos dos Sindos, Mr. Billia of the Dutch factory, and the small garden of our friend Ljungstedt. I do not want to dwell upon Macao, the Portuguese, the Chinese and everything interesting, but I want to express deep gratitude for the hospitality which I received from my Swedish friends Sir Anders Ljungstedt, G. Leffler, Gulian, and all of the Portuguese.

To make a fundamental description of a country, its inhabitants, government, and way of life, manners and customs, etc., etc., demands not only a knowledge of the language of that country but more time than I had. I informed myself about as much as I could, then discovered that my friend Ljungstedt had already finished a composition containing observations he had made in the course of twenty years. I take it as a privilege to draw this to the attention of everyone who might be interested. It will probably appear in St. Petersburg in 1820, in French, over his signature.*

OCTOBER.   I was informed that the vessel *Lydia,* under command of W. Wadsworth, would soon arrive with a cargo of sandalwood from Kauai, together with the ship *Avon.* I asked Sir Anders Ljungstedt to sequester upon arrival not only the sandalwood, which belonged to the Russian-American Company, but the schooner *Lydia.* The Portuguese Minister, Mr. Miguel Arriaga, also promised to do so after I showed him the justice of my request and the Russian-American Company's rights to the Island of Kauai.

At the same time I gave Sir Anders Ljungstedt legal power to take on himself in Macao the affairs of the Russian-American Company in the Sandwich Islands and to do anything concerning them. On October 3, 1817, I prepared for Sir Anders the following letter, witnessed by the notary public and signed by Mr. Minister Arriaga:

---

* This work by Ljungstedt, mentioned by Schäffer, was never published. For another, perhaps a variant of the same manuscript, see Bibliography.

Under the Highest, etc., from Egor Schäffer to His Excellency Mr. Anders Ivanovich Ljungstedt in Macao:

The kind attention which your Excellency has always deigned to show to the Russians, the fact that the Chief Manager of the Russian-American Company in our Northwest America, His . . . , Collegiate Councilor and Cavalier Baranov, has entrusted his commission to you; the considerable benefit which has accrued to the Russian-American Company through Your Excellency, and the acquaintance which I myself have had the honor to make, permits me to ask Your Excellency to take the Commission of the Russian-American Company, and to send all accounts to the Chief Manager, A. A. Baranov in the Port of Novo-Arkhangel'sk, pending other instructions from St. Petersburg. Particularly do I have the honor to commend to you the Company interests which, as you know from various documents, the said Company has in the Sandwich Islands, and namely on Kauai, with King Kaumualii, on which island all sandalwood belongs to the Russian-American Company.

I wish you———— E. Sh.

I was informed in Macao that not long ago the English ambassador in China, the well-known Lord Amherst, wanted to set up an English agency in Peking itself, toward which end he took with him a resident secretary and Doctor Pearson. He demanded for England the islands of Lintin and Hainan, which have a secure harbor for a thousand ships, and which command the route into the Tigris, to forbid all other nations trade with the Chinese, with the thought of delivering her into the hands of Englishmen only. This was known to many Europeans. Informed by the latter, the Chinese told their sovereign about the intentions of the English, and Mr. Lord was not even allowed to catch sight of the imperial visage. To his dismay nothing was accepted from him. They brought him with bandaged eyes to the border, where he was told to remove himself as soon as possible.*

---

* William Pitt, Earl Amherst (1773–1857), British envoy to China in 1816, was expelled without seeing the Emperor because of refusal to perform the kow-tow.

The Chinese began at once to build forts on the island of Lintin and others at the mouth of the Yellow River (Hoang-ho); they are looking suspiciously on the fact that for six years English ships have cruised near their shores, spying out everything. The Chinese also turned their attention to the proximity of the English in the East Indies, for they are already so close that they can go from Batavia to Peking in twelve days.

The Chinese, incidentally, are inclined toward friendship with the Russians, and I think that now is the time for Russia to conclude an advantageous treaty with China. One must approach them with extreme care, and not sacrifice the general interests of the whole state to obstinacy against the ceremonial of another land.

The Russians should have an agency in Canton, and if possible also in Peking. Sir Anders Ljungstedt should head the first establishment. He has lived in Canton and Macao for nineteen years; he is a true and devoted friend of Russia, where he lived for ten years; he speaks and writes Russian and almost all European languages; and he is extremely perceptive, and of exemplary honesty. The Russian-American Company must know, of course, that he has performed important services for it without any compensation. Russia is obligated not only to thank him but also to distinguish him.

NOVEMBER.   Mr. Gravford, Captain of the English ship sent for discovery, told me that he had with him a Russian seaman given him by Captain Adams from the brig *Forester*. I remembered at once that this was the man in the Company service whom Adams kidnapped from Kauai. I asked Captain Gravford to hand over this man and after several days received word that this man Ivan Krivoshein had died.

[NOVEMBER] 25.   The French frigate *Cybèle* under command of Count Kergariou arrived from Manila to give compliments to the Chinese in the name of the French nation. . . .

The Portuguese ship *Luconia,* under command of the Portuguese fleet Captain Mr. Leao, was ready for a voyage to Rio de Janeiro, and I found it a favorable chance to continue my journey. My friends honored me with a farewell dinner, and friend Ljungstedt afterward invited everyone to his house in order to pay me other indications of esteem according to the custom of the inhabitants of Macao.

[DECEMBER] 4 and 5. I left Macao.

MARCH 8, 1818. I visited my friend Langsdorf (in Rio de Janeiro), finding him as busy and active as when I left him four years ago.

Here I found a Russian vessel, the brig *Natalia Petrovna,* from Riga. I considered it best to use the first chance to set out for Russia. On the tenth of April I came aboard, and on the eleventh, at a very early hour, we left the harbor of Rio de Janeiro. . . .

NOTES AND BIBLIOGRAPHY

UNITS OF MEASURE AND VALUE

sazhen (Russian)—7 feet.

verst (Russian)—0.66 mile.

desiatine (Russian)—2.70 acres.

pood (Russian)—36.11 pounds avoirdupois.

pikul—a Chinese measure of weight equalling 133⅓ pounds.

ruble (Russian)—U. S. $0.50.

kopeck (Russian)—U. S. ½ cent, or ¹⁄₁₀₀ ruble.

piastre—a Spanish peso or dollar of the early nineteenth
century, equivalent to about U. S. $1.00 of the time.

Notes

NOTES TO PREFACE

[1] One of the earliest descriptions appears in K. T. Khlebnikov, *Zhizneopisanie Aleksandra Andreevicha Baranova, glavnago pravitelia rossiiskikh kolonii v Amerike* (Biography of Alexander Andreevich Baranov, Chief Manager of the Russian Colonies in America), St. Petersburg, 1835, pp. 155–169. The main source was long the summary account in P. A. Tikhmenev, *Istoricheskoe obozrenie obrazovaniia Rossiisko-Amerikanskoi Kompanii i deistvii eia do nastoiashchago vremeni* (Historical Survey of the Origin of the Russian-American Company and its Activities up to the Present Day), St. Petersburg, 1861–1863, 2 vols. This account was drawn upon by H. H. Bancroft, *History of Alaska, 1730–1885,* San Francisco, 1886, and by W. D. Alexander, "The Proceedings of the Russians on Kauai, 1814–1816," Hawaiian Historical Society *Papers,* no. 6, Honolulu, 1894, 20 pp. Tikhmenev's and Alexander's accounts were used by N. Vishniakov, "Rossiia, Kaliforniia i Sandvichevy ostrova (Istoricheskii ocherk)," *Russkaia Starina,* 1905, v. 124, pp. 249–289. F. A. Golder, "proposals for Russian Occupation of the Hawaiian Islands," in A. P. Taylor and R. S. Kuykendall, eds., *The Hawaiian Islands,* Honolulu, 1930, pp. 39–49, contributed new facts derived from earlier work in the Russian archives.

The only publication of primary material has been in S. B. Okun', "Tsarskaia Rossiia i Gavaiskie ostrova" (Tsarist Russia and the Hawaiian Islands), *Krasnyi Arkhiv,* no. 5 (78), 1936, 161–186, comprising eight documents. These form the core of Anatole G. Mazour's "Egor Scheffer: Dreamer of a Russian Empire in the Pacific," *Pacific Historical Review,* 6 (March, 1937), 15–20, and of Klaus Mehnert's *The Russians in Hawaii, 1804–1819,* Honolulu, 1938, 86 pp., which includes translations of some of the documents, in whole or in part. Okun' also discusses the subject, although with a number of erroneous interpretations, in a chapter of his book *The Russian-American Company* (translated from the Russian by Carl Ginsburg), Cambridge, Mass., 1951.

[2] Alphonse Pinart, born February 25, 1852, at Marquise, Pas-de-Calais, France, displayed unusual linguistic talent from an early age. He spent the period 1869–1872 in California, Alaska, and other parts of North America studying Indian languages and cultures. During 1874 and 1875 he gathered materials in St. Petersburg for H. H. Bancroft. Subsequently he traveled in North and Central America and Oceania, and engaged in anthropological and linguistic research, written up in many professional journals. The last decade of his life is obscure. He died in 1911. The Bancroft Library possesses many unpublished notes and other materials concerning Pinart. See his *Journey to Arizona in 1876*, translated from French by George R. Whitney, with biography and bibliography by Henry R. Wagner, Los Angeles, 1962, 47 pp. He also figures in Henry Reichlen and Robert F. Heizer, "La mission de Leon de Cessac en Californie, 1877–1879," *Objets et Mondes. La revue de le Musée de l'Homme, Musée National d'Histoire Naturelle*, 3 (Spring, 1963), 17–34.

[3] F. A. Golder, *Guide to Materials for American History in Russian Archives*, Washington, D. C., 1917, 2 vols., v. 1, p. 145.

[4] H. H. Bancroft, *Works*, vol. 39, *Literary Industries*, p. 622.

[5] Golder, *op. cit.*, p. 139.

[6] S. B. Okun', "Tsarskaia Rossiia i Gavaiskie ostrova," *Krasnyi Arkhiv*, no. 5 (78), 161–186.

[7] *Ibid.*, pp. 165–166.

[8] *Ibid.*, pp. 173–177.

NOTES TO INTRODUCTION

[1] See Document No. 45 here, and *Puteshestvie vokrug sveta v 1803–1806 na korable "Neve" pod nachal' stvom flota kapitan-leitenanta, nyne kapitana 2 ranga i kaval'era Iuriia Lisianskogo* (A Voyage Around the World in 1803–1806 on the Ship *Neva* under Fleet Lieutenant-Captain, now Captain of 2nd Rank and Cavalier Iurii Lisianskii), St. Petersburg, 1812, as quoted by Mehnert in *The Russians in Hawaii, 1804–1819*, Honolulu, 1938.

[2] Langsdorff, Georg Heinrich, freiherr von, *Voyages and travels in various parts of the world, during the years 1803 . . . 1807*, London, 1813–1814, p. 165, as quoted by Mehnert, *op. cit.*

[3] F. A. Golder, "Proposals for Russian Occupation of the Hawaiian Islands," in *Hawaii. Early relations with England-Russia-France. Official papers read at the Captain Cook Sesquicentennial Celebration, Honolulu, August 17, 1928*, p. 40. See also H. H. Bancroft, *History of Alaska*, p. 471, note; and P. A. Tikhmenev, *Istoricheskoe Obozrenie . . . Rossiisko-Amerikanskoi Kompanii. . . .*

[4] Golder, *op. cit.*, p. 40.

[5] Campbell, Archibald. *A Voyage Around the World, from 1806 to*

1812, in Which Japan, Kamchatka, the Aleutian Islands and the Sandwich Islands Were Visited, p. 81.

[6] *Ibid.,* p. 86. See also Mehnert, *op. cit.,* p. 19.

[7] Bancroft, *op. cit.,* p. 491 note.

[8] See also Tikhmenev, *op. cit.,* I, pp. 165–166, apparently based on the same letters.

[9] F. W. Howay, "The Last Days of the *Atahualpa,* alias *Behring,*" Hawaiian Historical Society, *Forty First Annual Report,* 1933, pp. 70–80.

[10] *Ibid.,* p. 79. Cf. Schäffer, in Journal (No. 63), who states they left the island in May, 1815.

[11] Most of this biographical data on Schäffer has been supplied by Professor Enrico Schaeffer of São Paulo, a collateral descendant. Professor Schaeffer is the author of "De velhas cronicas de familias: O Cavalheiro Georg Anton de Schaeffer," *Revista Genealogica Latina,* São Paulo, 1959, and "Aus alten Familien-Chroniken: Georg Anton Ritter von Schaeffer, Seelenverkaeufer und Freund der brasilian. Kaiserin," *Revista Sueda-merika,* Buenos Aires, 1960. The brief biographical account in Bancroft, *op. cit.,* p. 507 n. contains several gross inaccuracies. The balloon episode is mentioned in Eugene Tarle, *Napoleon's Invasion of Russia, 1812,* London, 1942, pp. 157–158.

[12] Described in "Solid Men of Boston in the Northwest," an account of the careers of the Winship brothers, written by an unknown contemporary. Typescript, Massachusetts Historical Society, Boston; original in Bancroft Library, Berkeley, California. See also Samuel Eliot Morrison, "Boston Traders in Hawaiian Islands, 1789–1823," *Washington Historical Quarterly,* 12 (1921), 171–173; and his *Maritime History of Massachusetts, 1783–1860,* Boston, 1961 edition, p. 204.

[13] Charles H. Barnard, *A Narrative of Sufferings . . . ,* p. 219, as quoted by Mehnert, *op. cit.,* p. 26. (Barnard's account is also reprinted in *The Ship, the Sea, and the Sailor.* See p. 96 for this reference to Schäffer.)

[14] K. T. Khlebnikov, *Zhizneopisanie Aleksandra Andreevicha Baranova,* p. 163, states that the *Otkrytie* left Sitka March 3, and arrived at Oahu April 21, 1816. Podushkin, commander of the vessel, states (No. 16) that he arrived at Oahu on April 21 and dropped anchor in Honolulu harbor on April 23. Schäffer, in his Journal (No. 63), agrees with the latter date when he states that the *Otkrytie* arrived on May 3 (New Style). Khlebnikov states that the *Il'mena* arrived on April 30, which would be May 11 New Style.

[15] For accounts of Tarakanov's earlier exploits, see Clarence Andrews, "The Wreck of the St. Nicholas," *Washington Historical Quarterly,* January, 1922, and Hector Chevigny, *Lord of Alaska.*

[16] See Bancroft, *op. cit.,* p. 493, and Otto von Kotzebue, *A Voyage of Discovery . . . ,* I, pp. 287, 292–294 ff.

[17] Adele Ogden, *The California Sea Otter Trade,* Chapter IV, and "Russian Sea-Otter and Seal Hunting on the California Coast, 1801–1841,"

California Historical Society, *Quarterly,* XII (September, 1933), 217–239. The foregoing corrects the account in Bancroft, *op. cit.,* pp. 493–494 on several points.

[18] Ogden, *op. cit.*

[19] See No. 7.

[20] See note 14 above.

[21] Khlebnikov, *op. cit.,* p. 163.

[22] John M. Lydgate, "Ka-umu-alii, the Last King of Kauai," Hawaiian Historical Society, *Twenty-fourth Annual Report for the year 1915,* Honolulu, 1916, p. 30.

[23] N. B. Emerson, "The Honolulu Fort," Hawaiian Historical Society, *Eighth Annual Report* (1900), 11–25.

[24] James J. Jarvis, *History of the Hawaiian or Sandwich Islands,* London, 1843, p. 184.

[25] S. B. Okun', "Tsarskaia Rossiia i Gavaiskie Ostrova." *Krasnyi Arkhiv,* No. 5 (78), 1936, p. 168; Tikhmenev, *op. cit.,* I, p. 188.

[26] Kotzebue, *op. cit.,* I, p. 294.

[27] *Ibid.,* p. 323.

[28] *Ibid.,* p. 327.

[29] *Ibid.,* p. 333.

[30] *Ibid.,* vol. 2, p. 241.

[31] Alexander Adams, "Extracts from an Ancient Log. (Occurrences on Board the Brig *Forester,* of London, from Concepcion Towards the Sandwich Islands)," *Hawaiian Almanac and Annual. 1905,* (Honolulu, 1906), 66–74.

[32] *Ibid.*

[33] Peter Corney, *Voyages in the Northern Pacific,* p. 73.

[34] Pinart documents, f 58 r. Not included here.

[35] Okun', *op. cit.,* pp. 167–168.

[36] *Ibid.,* p. 166.

[37] *Ibid.,* p. 168.

[38] *Ibid.,* pp. 166–170. The vicissitudes that could beset Company correspondence were shown in the fate of a dispatch of a few days later, March 21, 1818. Sent to Okhotsk for forwarding to Sitka, it was returned to St. Petersburg by error, and then sent out again, finally reaching its destination in 1821 (No. 56).

[39] *Ibid.,* p. 164.

[40] *Ibid.*

[41] Memorial in French, in Pinart folio, 84–86. Russian translation, with appended comments, in Okun', *op. cit.,* pp. 173–177.

[42] See Russian-American Company, *Journals of Correspondence,* Main Office to Sitka, vol. 1.

[43] In French, Pinart folio, 87. In Russian, Okun', *op. cit.,* pp. 181–182.

[44] Russian-American Company, *Journals of Correspondence,* Main Office to Sitka, vol. 1.

[45] Okun', *op. cit.,* pp. 182–185.

[46] The dates of the *Otkrytie's* 1818 voyage to Hawaii are unknown. However, James Hunnewell, "Voyage in the Brig *Bordeaux Packet,* Boston to Honolulu, 1817, and Residence in Honolulu, 1817–1818," Hawaiian Historical Society, *Papers,* No. 8 (1895), 17, describes her visit to Oahu thus: "Apr. 10. Arrived, Russian ship *Cretie,* from Owyhee. . . May 5. Sailed, 'the Russian ship.' " The condition of Kaumualii by that time is indicated by the American shipmaster Samuel Hill *(Packet)* in his log on November 7, 1818: "Tamooeree [Kaumualii], who is now absolutely no more than 40 years of age, has every appearance of a man of 70 years old, & appears to be rapidly declining—he has led a very intemperate life by Indulging to an Excess in Smoking Tobacco, taking the Ava, and Keeping a Number of Females." Samuel Hill, "Journal and Logbook, *Ophelia* and *Packet,* 1815–1822," MS, New York Public Library.

[47] Frank A. Golder, *op. cit.,* pp. 39–49.

[48] Oskar Canstatt, *Kritisches Repertorium der Deutsch-Brasilianischen Literatur,* Berlin, 1902, pp. 31–32.

Bibliography

Adams, Alexander. "Extracts from an Ancient Log. Selections from the Logbook of Captain Alexander Adams in Connection with the Early History of Hawaii. Occurrences on Board the Brig *Forester,* of London, from Conception Towards the Sandwich Islands," *Hawaiian Almanac and Annual* (1906), 66–74. Selections from Adams's logbook, Jan. 16, 1816–Dec. 26, 1818.

Alexander, W. D. "The Proceedings of the Russians on Kauai in 1814–1819," Hawaiian Historical Society, *Papers,* No. 6, 1894. 20 pp. Summary of facts provided by Rev. Samuel Whitney, in account published in *Hawaiian Spectator,* 1 (1839), 49–51, Archibald Campbell, Tikhmenev, Kotzebue, and H. H. Bancroft, with plans of Russian fort and harbor, Waimea, Kauai.

Bancroft, Hubert H. *History of Alaska,* 1730–1885, San Francisco, 1886, 775 pp.; reprinted, New York, 1959.

———. *History of the Northwest Coast.* San Francisco, 1884. 2 vols.

———. *History of California.* San Francisco, 1885. 7 vols. Volume 2 deals with the Russian period.

Barnard, Charles H. *A Narrative of the Sufferings and Adventures of Capt. Charles H. Barnard, in a Recent Voyage Around the World, Including an Account of his Residence for Two Years on an Uninhabited Island.* New York, 1836. 266 pp. Reprinted in *The Sea, the Ship, and the Sailor,* Salem, Mass., 1925.

Bradley, Harold W. *The American Frontier in Hawaii. The Pioneers, 1789–1843.* Stanford, 1942.

———. "The Hawaiian Islands and the Pacific Fur Trade, 1785–1813," Pacific Northwest Quarterly, 30:3 (July, 1939), 275–299.

Campbell, Archibald. *A Voyage Around the World, from 1806 to 1812 in Which Japan, Kamchatka, the Aleutian Islands and the Sandwich Islands Were Visited.* Roxbury, 1825.

Chamisso, Adelbert von. *Reise um die Welt mit der Romanzoffischen Entdeckungs-Expedition in den Jahren 1815–1818 auf der Brigg* Rurik,

Kapitän Otto von Kotzebue. Published in vols. 3 and 4 of his *Sämtliche Werke in vier Bänden,* 4 vols. in 2, Leipzig, n.d. Parallels Kotzebue's account, with additional material.

Chevigny, Hector. *Lord of Alaska: Baranov and the Russian Adventure.* New York, 1937 (reprinted, Portland, Ore., 1951). 320 pp.

————. *Lost Empire. The Life and Adventures of Nikolai Petrovich Rezanov.* New York, 1937. (Reprinted, Portland, Ore., 1958). 356 pp.

Corney, Peter. *Voyages in the Northern Pacific. Narrative of Several Trading Voyages from 1813 to 1818, Between the Northwest Coast of America, the Hawaiian Islands and China, with a Description of the Russian Establishments on the Northwest Coast.* Honolulu, 1896. 134 pp. Reprinted from original serial account in *London Literary Gazette,* 1821.

Golder, Frank A. *Guide to Materials for American History in Russian Archives.* Vol. 1, Washington, 1917; vol. 2, 1937.

————. "Russia and Russian Alaska," in *The Hawaiian Islands* (Albert Pierce Taylor, ed.), Honolulu, 1930, 93 pp.

Howay, Frederick W. "A List of Trading Vessels in the Maritime Fur Trade," Royal Society of Canada, *Transactions,* 1930, Part 2, pp. 111–134 (1785–1794); 1931, Part 2, pp. 117–149 (1795–1804); 1932, Part 2, pp. 43–86 (1805–1814); 1933, Part 2, pp. 119–147 (1815–1819); 1934, Part 2, pp. 11–49 (1820–1825).

Hunnewell, James. "Honolulu in 1817 and 1818. Voyage in the Brig *Bordeaux Packet,* Boston to Honolulu 1817, and Residence in Honolulu, 1817–1818," Hawaiian Historical Society, *Papers,* 1895. Reprinted, and published separately, 1909. 23 pp.

Judd, Bernice. *Voyages to Hawaii Before 1860.* . . . Honolulu, 1929, 108 pp.

Khlebnikov, Kiril Timofeevich. *Zhizneopisanie Aleksandra Andreevicha Baranova, glavnago pravitel'ia Rossiiskikh kolonii v Amerike.* (Biography of Alexandr Andreevich Baranov, Chief Manager of the Russian Colonies in America). St. Petersburg, 1835. 209 pp.

Kotzebue, Otto von. *Entdeckungsreise in die Sud-See und nach der Berings-Strasse zur Erforschung einer Nordöstlichen Durchfahrt, unternommen in der Jahren 1815, 1816, 1817 und 1818, auf Kosten Sr. Erlaucht des . . . Grafen Rumanzoff auf dem Schiffe Rurick unter dem Befehle des Leutenants der Russische-Kaiserlichen Marine Otto von Kotzebue . . . ,* Weimar, 1821. Translation published as *A Voyage of Discovery . . . ,* London, 1821, 3 vols.

Langsdorff, Georg Heinrich. *Bemerkungen auf einer Reise um die Welt in den Jahren 1803 bis 1807 . . . .* Frankfurt-am-Mayn, 1812, 2 vols. Translation published as *Voyages and Travels in Various Parts of the World . . . ,* London, 1813, 362 pp.

Ljungstedt, Anders. *An Historical Sketch of the Portuguese Settlements in China: and of the Roman Catholic Church and Mission in China.*

(With a supplementary chapter describing the city of Canton, republished from the *Chinese Repository*), Boston, 1836, 323 pp.

Mahr, August C. *The Visit of the Rurik to San Francisco in 1816*. Stanford, 1932. 194 pp. (Stanford University Publications, University Series, History, Economics, and Political Science, Vol. II:2). Contains extracts from Chamisso, Choris, and Kotzebue accounts, and Spanish documents.

Mazour, Anatole G. "Doctor Yegor Scheffer: Dreamer of a Russian Empire in the Pacific," *Pacific Historical Review*, (March, 1937), 15–20.

Mehnert, Klaus. *The Russians in Hawaii, 1804–1819*. Honolulu, 1939, 86 pp. University of Hawaii Occasional Papers No. 38, University of Hawaii Bulletin, 18 (April, 1939).

Morgan, Theodore. *Hawaii, a Century of Economic Change: 1778–1876*. Cambridge, Mass., 1848. 260 pp.

Morison, Samuel Eliot. "Boston Traders in Hawaiian Islands, 1789–1823," *Washington Historical Quarterly*, 12 (1921), 166–201.

———. *Maritime History of Massachusetts, 1783–1860*. Boston, 1921, 400 pp. (A new, revised edition, Cambridge, Mass., 1961, 421 pp.)

Ogden, Adele. *The California Sea Otter Trade, 1784–1848*. Berkeley, 1941. 251 pp.

———. "Russian Sea-Otter and Seal Hunting on the California Coast, 1801–1841," California Historical Society *Quarterly*, 12 (Sept. 1933), 217–239.

Okun', S. B. "Tsarskaia Rossiia i Gavaiskie ostrova" (Tsarist Russia and the Hawaiian Islands), *Krasnyi Arkhiv*, No. 5 (78) (1936), 161–186. Contains 8 documents.

———. *The Russian-American Company*. Cambridge, Mass., 1951. 296 pp. Translated from the Russian by Carl Ginsburg; preface by Robert J. Kerner.

Porter, Kenneth W. *John Jacob Astor, Business Man*. Cambridge, Mass., 1931. 2 vols.

———. "John Jacob Astor and the Sandalwood Trade of the Hawaiian Islands, 1816–1828," *Journal of Economic and Business History*, 2 (1929–1930), 495–519.

———. "Cruise of Astor's Brig *Pedler*, 1813–1816," *Oregon Historical Quarterly*, 31 (Sept., 1930), 223–230.

———. "More About the Brig *Pedler*, 1813–16," *Oregon Historical Quarterly*, 33 (Dec., 1932), 311–312.

———. "The Cruise of the *Forester*. Some New Sidelights on the Astoria Enterprise," *Washington Historical Quarterly*, 23 (October, 1932), 261–285.

Russian-American Company, Sitka. *Journals of Correspondence*, MS, 1802–1867 (with a gap from 1802 to 1817). 92 vols. National Archives, Washington, D. C. Referred to as *Sitka Archives* by some earlier writers. Copies of incoming and outgoing correspondence, bound in separate volumes. The several documents from this series which are presented here may be found in the initial volumes of each category.

Russkie moreplavateli (Russian Seafarers). Moscow, 1953. 672 pp. Edited by V. S. Lupach. Biographies, with indices of Russian names on marine maps of the world, and names of persons, places, and ships.

Schäffer, Georg Anton. *Brasilien als unabhängiges Reich, in historischer, nercantilischer und politischer Beziehung Geschildert vom Ritter von Schäffer, Dr., Major der K. Brasilischen Ehrengarde* . . . Altona, 1824, 464 pp. A Dutch edition, Amsterdam, 1825, 2 vols. Concerns his stay in Brazil, 1821–1823.

"Solid Men of Boston." MS, probably written in the 1850's, concerning the adventures of the Winship brothers on the Northwest coast and in the Pacific sandalwood trade. Original, Bancroft Library, University of California, Berkeley; a typescript, Massachusetts Historical Society, Boston.

Tikhmenev, P. A. *Istoricheskoe obozrenie obrazovaniia Rossiisko-Amerikanskoi Kompanii i deistvii eia do nastoiashchago vremeni* (Historical Survey of the Origin of the Russian-American Company and its Activities up to the Present Day), St. Petersburg, 1861–1863, 2 vols.

Vishniakov, N. "Rossiia, Kaliforniia i Sandvichevy ostrova (Istoricheskii ocherk)" (Russia, California and the Sandwich Islands [Historical Sketch]), *Russkaia starina,* 124 (1905), 249–289.

INDEX OF NAMES AND SHIP MOVEMENTS

Adams, Alexander. Navigator on brig *Forester;* was given command after sale of vessel to Kamehameha, April 16, 1816: 13, 19, 91, 129, 181, 198, 214.

"Adams, John." *See* Kuakini.

Albatross. Ship, 165 tons; built at Weymouth, Mass. in 1803. July, 1809, left Boston under Capt. Nathan Winship; Feb. 23–Apr. 13, 1810, Hawaiian Islands; June 17, Columbia River; Nov., Drake's Bay, Calif.; Sept. 28, 1811, under mate, William Smith, Kaigahnee; Nov. 1, Hawaiian Islands; Feb. 26, 1812, Whampoa; 1813, left China with news of outbreak of war with Great Britain; July, Hawaiian Islands; Aug. 20, Columbia River; Nov. 15–24, Marquesas Islands; Dec. 20, Hawaiian Islands; —— June 26, 1814, Calif.; July 9, Hawaiian Islands; July, 1815, Sitka; Jan. 14, 1816, Capt. Smith and five others seized by Spanish off Santa Barbara, but remaining personnel made off, sailed to Cerros Island; Mar., Honolulu; Oct. 16, vessel sold to Kamehameha; Nov. 1818, reported beached at Honolulu: 5, 47, 77, 130, 136, 193.

Alert (Porter). Ship. Oct. 5, 1816, left Boston; July 4, 1817, Hawaiian Islands; ——, NW coast; Oct. 7–25, Honolulu; Dec. 28, left Canton. *See* Porter, Lemuel.

Alexander I. Emperor of Russia, 1801–1825: 11, 26, 29, 139–143 *passim*.

Anson, George, Baron (1697–1762). British navigator: 114.

Arbuzov, Lt. On *Neva* at Kauai, 1805: 115.

Astor, John Jacob (1763–1848). American capitalist: 159 n., 161, 164, 206.

Atala (Nathan Winship). Ship, 260 tons. Sept. 1815, left Boston; July 12, 1816, Honolulu; Aug. 10–12, Kauai; Nov., left Sitka; traded on NW and Calif. coasts; Aug., 1817, coast of Peru; Oct. 19–Dec. 9, Hawaiian Islands; May 1, 1818, at Canton: 178, 179.

Avon (MS: *Eban;* Whittemore). Ship. 1815, left Boston; Sept. 6, 1816; left Hawaiian Islands; Nov., Sitka; early 1817, Calif. coast; May, Hawaiian Islands; Dec. 1, sailed for Valparaiso; Apr., 1818, sold at Coquimbo after death of master: 13, 16, 20, 76, 98, 107, 124, 154, 183, 212.

Bailey, Samuel G. (*Millwood*): 61, 163.

Bakadarov. Russian supercargo on *Eclipse* (O'Cain): 209.

234 INDEX

Hawaiian Islands; Nov., 1818, reported beached at Honolulu: 13, 19, 91, 158, 159 n., 160, 161, 164, 168, 173, 181, 187, 198.

Fort Alexander, Hanalei, Kauai, 15, 92, 186, 198, 202.

Fort Barclay, Hanalei, Kauai, 15, 186, 198.

Fort Elizabeth, Waimea, Kauai, 13, 135, 183, 187, 191.

Fox-Bennick (or Bonnick), Charles. Englishman on Kauai, 1816–1817, assistant to Schäffer: 78, 100–101, 104, 201.

Frost, Daniel W. (Dr.). American surgeon. Dec. 26, 1815, arrived Valparaiso, Chile, on ship *Indus,* of Salem (Capt. Nathan Page), imprisoned for want of a passport; 1816, in Hawaiian Islands; Sept. 30, sailed on *O'Cain* for Canton: 13, 14, 179, 183.

Gaal (Gaul?), William. Companion of James Smith Wilcocks (*Traveller*), on voyage from China: 188.

Gamalea. Tract on river Mattaveri, Waimea province, Kauai: 80.

Georg (Kainakhil') (Kuunakaiole?) Valley, Hanapepe province, Kauai: 15, 192, 193.

Golovnin, Vasilii Mikhailovich (1776–1831). Russian naval officer. 1807, commanded sloop *Diana* on voyage from Kronshtadt to Kamchatka; 1814, returned to St. Petersburg via Siberia; 1817–1819, commanded sloop *Kamchatka* on round-the-world voyage: 25, 27, 110, 113.

Gravford (?), Capt. of a British discovery ship. Nov., 1817, at Macao: 214.

Guramaia. Tract of land, Kauai: 15, 79.

Gyzelaar, Henry. New York shipmaster. 1814, commanded schooner *Lydia* of Philadelphia on Pacific voyage; Jan., 1816, vessel seized at Santa Barbara, Calif., by Spanish authorities, but Gyzelaar secured release; Mar. 11, sailed to Hawaii; Sept. 4, 1816, vessel sold to Schäffer at Kauai, for transfer to King Kaumualii; Oct. 30, Gyzelaar sailed for Canton on *O'Cain,* continued to Boston on *William and John;* Sept. 1, 1817–Mar. 1821, commanded brig *Clarion* from Boston to Hawaii, Sitka, Calif., Hawaii, Canton, and back: 12, 13, 14, 77, 136, 179, 183.

Hagemeister, Leontii Andreianovich (1780–1834). Russian naval officer. 1806–1810, commanded sloop *Neva* on voyage to Russian America, returning by way of Siberia; 1816–1819, commanded ship *Kutuzov,* and 1828–1830, sloop *Krotkii,* on round-the-world voyages: 3, 4, 27, 29, 30, 37–40, 141, 146, 147, 152, 153, 154.

Hanalei. Chief. *See* Kallavatti.

Hanalei. Valley, river, and harbor, Kauai (MS: Ganarea): 14, 77, 87, 91, 92, 130, 137, 182, 183, 184, 185, 198.

Hanapepe. Town and province, Kauai: 15, 185, 187, 192.

Hannamaure (Hanamauli?). Port, Kauai: 185.

Harbottle, John. Englishman long resident at Honolulu, employed as pilot: 203, 204.

Hawaii (MS: Oveaga), 115, 170.

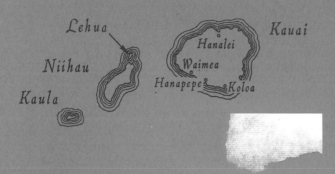

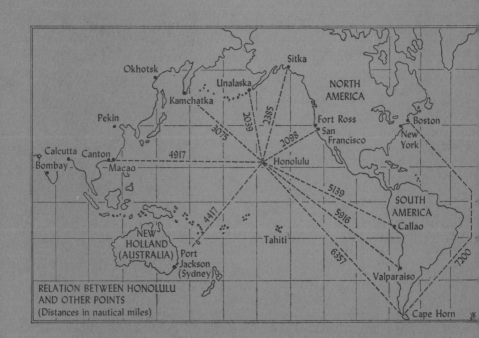

RELATION BETWEEN HONOLULU
AND OTHER POINTS
(Distances in nautical miles)